Complete South-East Coast

© 1974 Ward Lock Limited

ISBN 0 7063 1528 6

Photographs by Peter Baker, Tony Kersting and T. H. Williams.

Plans based upon the Ordnance Survey map with the sanction of the Controller of Her Majesty's Stationery Office.

Text phototypeset by Technical Filmsetters (Europe) Ltd., Manchester.

Printed and bound by Editorial Fher S. A., Bilbao, Spain.

RED GUIDE

Complete
South-East Coast

The coast resorts from
Whitstable to Selsey and
excursions inland.

Edited by Reginald J. W. Hammond F.R.G.S.

WARD LOCK LIMITED

116 Baker Street, London W1M 2BB

Plans

Contents

CONTENTS

Illustrations

THE RED GUIDES

Edited by Reginald J. W. Hammond

Barmouth and District

Bournemouth, New Forest

Channel Islands

Cornwall : North

Cornwall : South

Cornwall : West

Cotswolds

Dorset Coast

Isle of Man

Isle of Wight

Lake District

Llandudno, Colwyn Bay

London

Norfolk and the Broads

Peak District

St. Ives and W. Cornwall

Tenby and South Wales

Wales N. (Northn. Section)

Wales N. (Southn. Section)

Yorkshire Dales

Northern Ireland

SCOTLAND

Aberdeen, Deeside, etc.

Edinburgh and District

Highlands

Northern Scotland

Western Scotland

RED TOURIST GUIDES

Complete England

Complete Scotland

Complete Ireland

Complete Wales

Lake District (Baddeley)

Complete Devon

Complete West Country

Complete South-East Coast

Complete Yorkshire

Complete Scottish Lowlands

Britain

Portugal (Sarah Bradford)

Japan (William Duncan)

WARD LOCK LIMITED

Introduction

This Guide describes the coast of Kent and Sussex from Whitstable round to Bognor Regis, Chichester and the Selsey Peninsula. From each of the main resorts on this long coastline numerous walks and drives are suggested to include a host of inland places of interest that may be visited within the compass of a day or half-day excursion. Along this coast are a number of England's largest and most famous holiday resorts. Some are sizeable towns, attracting thousands of visitors, but also having a considerable residential population. The whole area is one of the sunniest and healthiest regions of Britain. It is also second to none for the facilities it affords for an open-air holiday, by the sea or inland, with open country of no little beauty close at hand. This great playground offers something to almost every type of holidaymaker. Golf, bowls, tennis, fishing, first-class bathing, boating and sailing, and every indoor entertainment and pursuit imaginable is there for the taking. Brighton, the largest of all British resorts, is world famous. Hastings, Eastbourne and Worthing run close to it for the amenities they can offer. Littlehampton, Bognor Regis, and the Thanet resorts of Margate, Broadstairs and Ramsgate are renowned for their safe sandy beaches. Dover, famous Channel port, Folkestone and Newhaven with busy harbours, each offer pleasant holiday attractions. Charming little Deal has the tang of the sea and finds much favour with fishermen. For those preferring the rural life, there are, just a little way back from the coast, innumerable villages of great charm. The whole countryside carries the history of England and the churches, castles, lighthouses, mills and farms have all-absorbing tales to tell. At each end of our region lie cathedral cities – to the west, Chichester, unique in Britain with its free-standing bell tower and, in the east, famous Canterbury which itself is both important and interesting for so much besides its cathedral and the murder of Becket.

Near Cissbury Ring, Sussex

Whitstable

Angling. – Good sea-angling, and sport on marshes beyond Seasalter. *Whitstable Angling Society.*

Banks. – *Lloyds, National Westminster, Midland* and *Barclays,* High Street, Whitstable, and Tankerton Road, Tankerton.

Bathing. – Most visitors bathe from Tankerton Marine Parade with beach huts on the Slopes, but safe bathing may be enjoyed along the entire coast-line. The beach is shingle at first with mud and sand further out.

Boating lakes at West Beach, near Seasalter Golf Links.

Bowling-Green in Castle grounds.

Cinema. – Oxford Street.

Early Closing. – Wednesday.

Golf-Links. – *Seasalter,* 9 holes, and *Chestfield Golf Club,* 18 holes, a mile eastward from Tankerton.

Hotels. – *Tankerton,* Marine Parade; *Royal,* Marine Parade; *Wheatsheaf Inn,* Swalecliffe; *Marine,* Marine Parade; *Duke of Cumberland,* High Street; *Nazdar Guest House,* Queen's Road, Tankerton; *Anchorage Guest House,* Marine Parade; *Iona Guest House,* Tankerton Road; *Crestley Guest House,* Wave Crest.

Population. – 23,780.

Post Office. – High Street. Sub-offices, 45 Canterbury Road, Seasalter, Swalecliffe, Tankerton Circus.

Sailing. – The *Whitstable Yacht Club* has its headquarters on sea wall. Other clubs are *Tankerton Bay Sailing Club* and *Seasalter Yacht Club.* Annual Regatta.

Stations. – *Whitstable and Tankerton* (main line), about ½-mile from sea, near Tankerton. *Chestfield Halt* serves Chestfield Golf Club, Chestfield Village and Swalecliffe.

Tennis. – Public hard courts at Tankerton and West Beach.

The focus of Whitstable's importance has moved curiously during the changing centuries. At first there was a cluster of cottages – the present village of **Church Street** – round the old parish Church of All Saints, using the port of Whitstable. Then the oyster trade increased, shipbuilding, and later coaling, were active, and Whitstable became an important centre of trade and industry, while **Seasalter** carries in its name the remembrance of its salt-pans. Then with modern demands for holiday-making and country homes, with the possibilities of cheap and rapid transport, Tankerton, and to some extent Swalecliffe, were laid out on a definite plan. **Tankerton** became the predominant partner as a resort, with its charming gardens and open sunny terraces, though the Urban District boundaries, enlarged in 1934 to include all four, as well as the residential old village of Chestfield, are still those of Whitstable, the little crowded town with its narrow streets remaining the business centre. Although the sea-front at Whitstable is rather shut in by the harbour and fishermen's stores, from the Shrubbery and the well-wooded grounds of the **Castle** – a picturesque castellated structure – there is a fine, open coast-line, the parade along the cliff-top being upwards of a mile in length, with extensive views, and a delightful undercliff with many beach huts. The air is pure and invigorating, the bathing good and safe, especially along the Tankerton beach, while yachting and fishing are additional attractions. Slightly to the west lies the Isle of Sheppey, and pleasant hours may be spent sailing on the Swale and the adjacent Medway.

The older quarters of Whitstable have many picturesque corners, especially the part sacred to the oyster fisheries, which in many respects resembles the Old Town of Hastings. Though shipbuilding on a large scale has been discontinued, Whitstable-built yachts are still famous.

Whitstable Oysters. The oyster industry of Whitstable has an unbroken record of 2,000 years behind it. Roman legions enjoyed the delicacy as some considerable compensation for exile. In more modern times the industry flourished and has been able to provide a good deal of employment. The private beds, or layings, start about two miles from the shore, so there is no danger of sewage contamination, and extend to nearly seven miles out. The total area of the private beds is nearly 5,000 acres, and is about equally divided between the Whitstable Oyster Fishery Co. and the Seasalter and Ham Oyster Fishery Co., Ltd., the former company's bed being nearest to the shore. The Whitstable Oyster Fishery Company are the successors of the former Company of Free Fishers and Dredgers of Whitstable, and are entitled to describe their best Natives as "Royal Whitstable Natives".

A small fleet of yawls – picturesque sailing-smacks, now fitted with motor engines – is employed in dredging and carrying. Each yawl generally has a crew of four men and works five or six dredges, while the motor-boats work up to sixteen dredges. The dredge is wrought-iron, triangular in form, and weighs from 15 to 25 lb.

Whitstable still has a considerable coasting trade which has recently been increasing. Ships from Scandinavia and the Low Countries call here regularly.

A little east of the Harbour a long causeway, known as the **Street,** stretches out to sea, and is almost entirely uncovered at low tide. Near the north end many Roman tiles and other remains have been found.

All Saints' Church in Church Street, half a mile from the town, has traces of Saxon work in the font and fabric, but the greater part is a fifteenth-century reconstruction. The tower originally served as a watch-tower and place of defence and the mussel gatherers supported a special light called the Muskyll Taper. There is a fifteenth-century brass in the nave.

At the western end of the main street, which then becomes the Canterbury Road, there is an old **Toll House,** and nearby is **Barn House,** a beautiful fifteenth-century manor.

The **Castle,** originally called Tankerton Tower, is a castellated mansion of which the octagonal tower is probably fifteenth century. The Castle was acquired by the town, the house being used for the Council Chamber and municipal offices, while the beautifully kept grounds were opened as a public park. Just below the imposing red-brick Gatehouse are some *Almshouses,* administered by the Wynn-Ellis Trust.

Between Tankerton and the sea a fine **Marine Parade,** reached by the steep Tower Hill from Whitstable and bordered by attractive houses, runs for more than a mile. There are shelters and seats on the pleasant grass plateau. Instead of cliffs there are sunny grass slopes with lines of gay beach huts, and at the foot a promenade.

Near the middle of the Parade a road to the right leads to **Tankerton Circus,** with shops, banks and post office, hotels and tennis-courts.

Tankerton is one of the best centres for walkers along this coast, with delightful contrasts between the open breezy cliffs and the sylvan beauty inland.

Mention must be made of the "new old" village of **Chestfield,** which lies beyond the low plain on which stand the modern houses of **Swalecliffe.** After leaving the roundabout at Swalecliffe, sophisticated with its urban shops and houses, the kerbed road leads round into Chestfield Village, with pretty dwellings in old half-timbered style and a park-like golf-course, its clubhouse 600 years old. Close to the club-house is a fine fourteenth-century barn, furnished in a style appropriate to its age, and now open for most of the year as a restaurant. The whole estate was the old Manor of Chestfield, and while there are ample modern amenities, including a station close by, all the attributes of a mediaeval manor are retained.

The road leads through **Blean Woods** to Tylerhill and Canterbury (bus service) while a branch to the left goes to Herne. The woods, enclosed in places and dotted with modern houses, are lovely at all times, but perhaps most beautiful in autumn, with all shades of yellow and gold in the leaves of lime, chestnut, oak and ash.

At Gypsy Corner on the Chestfield–Canterbury road begins a $2\frac{1}{4}$-mile "Forest Walk" signposted by the Forestry Commission. The walk follows a metalled road through the 580-acre Clowes Wood lying to the south-east of Whitstable.

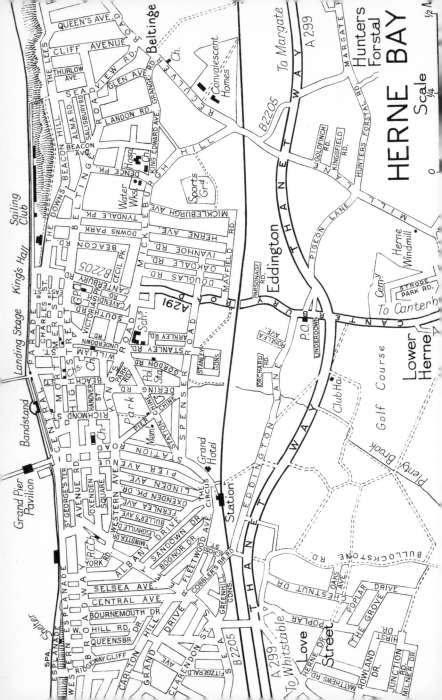

Herne Bay

Banks. – *National Westminster*, High Street; *Trustee Savings*, High Street; *Barclays*, Mortimer Street; *Midland* and *Lloyds*, High Street.

Bathing. – Excellent and safe bathing. Shore is shingle. At low tide there are numerous pools and a large expanse of very shallow water over sand. Bathing chalets may be hired for the season or short periods.

Boating. – Rowing-boats, motor-boats, and sailing-boats are available, and some interesting excursions are arranged. *Herne Bay Sailing Club*, East Cliff. *Herne Bay Rowing Club*, West Cliff. Children's boating lake in War Memorial Park and at Hampton.

Bowls. – Two excellent greens in War Memorial Park. The local Bowling Club welcomes visitors.

Buses. – Excellent services in town and district.

Caravans. – There are several well-organized caravan sites.

Car Parking-Places. – Various sections along the sea-front, William Street Car Park and Hampton Car Park.

Cinema. – Avenue Road.

Cricket. – Cricket pitches are available in the War Memorial Park, Cherry Orchard, and Burton Downs Playing Fields. One of the attractions of Herne Bay is that it is within easy distance of Canterbury, so that many devotees stay here during the Cricket Week (first in August) in preference to the city.

Distances. – Birchington, 12; Canterbury, 9; Chislet, 5; Faversham, 13; Herne Village, 2; London, 60; Minster, 11; Margate, 16; Ramsgate, 16; Reculver (cliff), 3½; Reculver (road), 5; Sturry, 6; St. Nicholas, 9; Upstreet, 6; Whitstable (coast), 4; (road), 5.

Early Closing. – Thursday.

Entertainments. – In King's Hall, Pier Pavilion, and Central Bandstand. Summer concert party, and productions in winter by local dramatic clubs and choral societies.

Fishing. – Sea-fishing in autumn is good. Plaice, dabs and flounders, all the year round. June to September, bass, mullet, and dog-fish (tope); June to November, pouting, whiting and eels; September to February, codling. The local societies are the *Herne Bay Angling Association* and the *Heron Angling Society*.

Golf. – *Herne Bay Golf Club* course (18 holes) at Eddington.

Hotels. – *Beauvalle*, Central Parade; *St. George*, Western Esplanade; *Queen's*, Canterbury Road; *Pier*, Station Road; *Dolphin*, Central Parade; *Hailey* (Private), The Downs; *The Carlton*, Central Parade; *Laleham* (Private), Central Parade; *Hertford House*, Sea Front; *The Oaks*, Victoria Park; *Railway*, High Street; *Cliff Dene Guest House*, East Street; *Woodstock Guest House*, Canterbury Road; *Northdown Guest House*, Cecil Park; *Woodford House*, Canterbury Road.

Library. – High Street.

Population. – 24,000.

Post Office. – Head Office, Cavendish Road, Branch offices, William Street; corner of High Street and Station Road; Eddington; Reculver Road, Beltinge; Sea Street; The Broadway; Broomfield; Herne.

Recreation Grounds. – The Downs, East Cliff, Cherry Orchard Playing Field, Herne, War Memorial Park and Burton Downs Playing Fields.

Putting. – Lane End Green, and at Hampton.

Station. – About half-mile from Pier.

Tennis. – Public courts (hard) in the Memorial Park.

Herne Bay, being appreciably nearer London than the Thanet resorts, has grown in favour for residential purposes. The locality enjoys a delightful and bracing climate.

The town itself is symmetrically laid out, the principal roads running parallel to the sea, with short connecting streets at right angles. There is a total sea-front of about seven miles with rising ground at the eastern end. The broad, level promenades, the Downs, the extensive beach, and boating pool at Hampton, are delightful for children; while the well-wooded and slightly hilly country behind is equally charming for walking and motoring.

HERNE BAY

There is an excellent golf-course and there are ample facilities for tennis, cricket and boating. The boating, indeed, is a leading feature of the place, the rarely ruffled bay affording excellent facilities. Regattas and a carnival are held in August. The bathing and fishing are also good. Herne Bay is an excellent centre from which to visit Canterbury, Sandwich, Fordwich, Reculver, Richborough and the other living histories of the past – some within walking distance, and all easily reached by car or bus.

The Pier. This enterprise has had a somewhat chequered history. The first pier, erected in 1832, was designed by Telford and was 3,500 feet in length. It was replaced in 1873, when a less ambitious structure, only 320 feet in length, was opened. An extension was opened in 1899, and electric trams ran from end to end. In 1908 the District Council bought the Pier, and built an additional Pavilion, and in 1928 fire destroyed the original Pier Theatre and the heterogeneous collection of shops and stalls which for many years characterized the pier entrance. The way to the Pier now lies through pleasant gardens. The Grand Pier Pavilion, a short distance from the shore, is used during summer for variety shows; in winter for roller-skating, badminton and wrestling.

Eastward from the Pier

The shingly shore, with its many groynes, is bordered first by a paved walk; then by a succession of lawns and flower-beds, the Tower Gardens, with shelters at either end; and finally by a broad roadway overlooked by boarding-houses and hotels. A semicircular projection has been built on the seaward side of the promenade, forming the **Central Bandstand,** where throughout the summer, concerts, party nights and competitions are held. On Sundays special musical entertainment is provided.

The **Clock Tower** is Classical in style, and rises in four stages to a height of 85 feet. Two guns at the base formerly stood on the old pier.

William Street, on the right, named after William IV, and **Mortimer Street** and **High Street,** crossing it at right angles, are the principal business thoroughfares. Near the point of intersection is the Fire Station. In William Street is **Christ Church,** the parish church, erected in 1837, and several times enlarged.

Near the far end of William Street is the **Memorial Park,** consisting of sixteen acres of recreation ground crossed by paths having at their intersection a red granite obelisk commemorating Herne Bay men who fell in two World Wars. The park includes an ornamental yacht-pond and boating lake, tennis-courts, bowling-greens and cricket ground.

East of the Tower, the sea-front gradually becomes narrower than the other portion. Mention must be made of the old *Ship Inn*, with its outer staircase, and stirring memories of smuggling days.

The grassy slope farther to the east is known as **The Downs,** a very pleasant and popular part. In places here the cliffs reach a considerable height. The beach is reached from the top of the Downs by a series of steps known locally as the "Hundred Steps."

In a central position is the **King's Hall,** adapted as a Memorial of King Edward VII. The hall is used for dances, conferences and exhibitions, as well as for dramatic and operatic performances.

Buses connect Beltinge with the railway at Herne Bay. An enjoyable walk may be had along the cliffs to Reculver.

Westward from the Pier

The beach is bordered by Western Esplanade, where are shops, cafés and amusement arcades.

Western Esplanade leads past the western Bathing Station and the modern quarter of Herne Bay upward to **Hampton Mill,** on which stand pleasant houses and the *Hotel St. George*. From the cliff there is a delightful view of the town, with the Reculver towers in the distance. Seaward the Isle of Sheppey is well seen.

The hill drops abruptly on the farther side to **Hampton,** where there are sunny terraces. From the pier it is possible to walk along the sea-wall to Swalecliffe, and thence to Tankerton and Whitstable.

Beyond Hampton is the bungalow estate of **Studd Hill,** and a motor road through Swalecliffe to Tankerton, the urban district boundary between Herne Bay and Whitstable lying about half a mile west of Hampton.

Herne

The village, now within the urban district, from which the popular seaside resort takes its name, lies about one mile to the south of the pier on the main road to Canterbury.

Those on foot may take either the Eddington Lane, leading from the station to the Golf Course (18 holes) or the Canterbury Road, starting at the East Cliff. The routes meet close to the course, and Herne is three-quarters of a mile south. Apart from the interest of its Church and park, Herne is worth a visit as a typical English village, with modern houses standing cheek by jowl with quaint and picturesque cottages of the sixteenth and seventeenth centuries.

Herne **Church,** dedicated to St. Martin, and originally a chapel-of-ease to Reculver Abbey, is finely situated with a chestnut avenue leading from the beautiful lychgate (1955) to the porch. The massive Decorated flint and stone tower, called by Ruskin one of the few perfect things in the world, is in good proportion to the church. The aisles and chancels are embattled. The early fifteenth-century font bears, among other arms, those of Henry IV. Another notable feature is the handsome carved screen in the Lady Chapel. Between this Chapel and the chancel is a "squint." There are several tombs and old brasses of great interest, especially one extolling the virtues of Lady Fineux. The rather poor canopied figure of *Nicolas Ridley*, in the south aisle, was erected in 1857. The martyr was appointed to the incumbency of Herne in 1538, by Archbishop Cranmer, a remnant of whose house may still be seen at Ford, a mile or so to the south-east. One of Ridley's acts at Herne was to direct that the *Te Deum* should be sung in English, a revolutionary proceeding which at once aroused the ire of the authorities.

Modern development is depriving Herne of its ancient appearance, but many attractive little houses remain to remind the visitor of the past.

Adjoining the Church, and bordering the Canterbury road for a considerable distance, is the finely timbered estate of **Strode Park.** The fine mansion and some eighteen acres of the surrounding parkland and gardens are in the hands of Cripple-craft, which is a Home for severely physically handicapped men and women. Visitors are welcome, but prior arrangements should be made with the Superintendent.

Walks and Excursions from Herne Bay

To Reculver. The twin towers are clearly visible from the sea-front and walkers have only to make the slight ascent to the Downs at the eastern end of the town and follow the broad asphalted path over Beacon Hill, along the Lees and through the charming **Bishopstone Glen.** For motorists the direct road branches from Mickleburgh Hill a short way past St. Bartholomew's Church, passing through pleasant Beltinge, and after nearing the coast at a point commanding wide views makes a sweep inland again at Hillborough, then again turns seaward to Reculver.

The sister towers of Reculver are a familiar landmark between London and Margate. In ancient times Reculver, under its Roman name of Regulbium, guarded the north entrance to the channel of the Wantsume as did Richborough the south. Lying somewhat out of the direct line, it is not referred to by Latin writers so frequently as the other fort, although recent excavations indicate that Reculver was built as a stone walled fort before Richborough was given walls.

Reculver

Admission. – The Saxon church and Roman fortress are in the care of the Department of the Environment. The church is open daily, *fee*. The walls of the fort may be seen at all times, *free*.

Car Park and Caravan Site. – Under Municipal control on high ground overlooking the sea. There are also privately operated caravan sites.

The **castrum**, when entire, occupied about eight acres, and at one time was garrisoned by the first cohort of Vetasii from Brabant. Considerable portions of the south and east walls still remain, and below ground many valuable relics have been found. The north wall has long since disappeared under the sea, and but for the protecting sea-wall and groynes the rest would not be long in following. In Leland's time Reculver stood "wythin a quarter of a myle or little more of the se syde."

Reculver has Saxon as well as Roman memories. Ethelbert retired here with Queen Bertha in 597, after his baptism, and built a palace for himself. In 669 King Egbert gave leave to Bassa, a "mass priest", to erect a monastery; which foundation was, in 949, granted by Eadrad to Christ Church, Canterbury. A copy of this charter, which was drawn up by Dunstan, then Abbot of Glastonbury, may be seen in the Library of Canterbury Cathedral. Old St. Mary's Church, which stood within the castrum, was almost entirely destroyed in the early part of the last century. Much of the material was used in the construction of the present St. Mary's Church, a mile inland at Hillborough.

Fortunately the value of the towers as a landmark led to the tardy intervention of the authorities of Trinity House, and the western portion of the church was spared and restored. Notice below the connecting gable the fine Early English doorway.

The footpath eastward and a turn right leads to the still massive **Roman Walls.**
The modern parish church of St. Mary the Virgin at **Hillborough** serves a growing population, and is largely built of the materials of old Reculver Church.

To Whitstable (4 miles). The walk to Whitstable by the cliffs is much shorter than that by road. From the Pier follow the Western Esplanade over Hampton Hill, descending steeply to the suburb of **Hampton,** with its ancient oyster pier. The path is then through the Studd Hill estate, and along the low cliffs or on the new sea-wall to the esplanade at Tankerton, the eastern suburb of Whitstable. The coast road goes past Hampton pier and Studd Hill estate on to Swalecliffe, Tankerton and Whitstable.

To Blean Woods. A mile or two south-west of Herne are the extensive **Blean Woods.** Only here and there is it possible to penetrate these leafy recesses, but several public roads lead through parts of the woods, and a fair idea of their beauty and extent is gained by motorists. The most open portion lies to the east of the Canterbury Road, and is reached by taking the leafy lane just beyond the Fox and Hounds, rather more than a mile south of Herne, leading in the direction of Hoath (*see* below).

To Chislet, Upstreet and Grove Ferry. Leave the town by Mickleburgh Hill and the Margate Road. Cross the railway by Blacksole Bridge and bear left to **Hunter's Forstal,** a pleasant little village said to owe its name to the fact that it was long the rallying-place of the huntsmen in the district. Then turn right to **Broomfield,** with a large pond in which tradition declares that many a voluble scold has been soundly ducked. At the pond the road bends rightward, presently dropping somewhat steeply to **Ford,** a picturesque one-street hamlet with a modern interest as the site of the Herne Bay waterworks, and a more alluring old appeal as the site of Archbishop Cranmer's manor house, the scanty remains of which can be seen to the rear of the farmhouse on the left-hand side of the road.

Ascending the hill, continue by the straight road through picturesque **Maypole** to four cross-roads. The road to the right is one of the most delightful in the locality, and should on no account be missed, leading as it does through an unenclosed portion of the leafy Blean Woods to the main Herne Bay-Canterbury road *(see last excursion above)*. The road on the left climbs up to **Hoath,** another delightful village, its little church – formerly a chapelry to Reculver – with its small shingled tower and spire containing several ancient brasses and a fine modern oak reredos. The winding road continues eastward for another mile and a half to **Chislet.**

Chislet Church is of far greater interest than the ugly wooden excrescence that caps its massive Norman tower would lead one to suppose. There is a fine Norman chancel arch, and the square, carved and panelled font, canopied sedilia and stone carvings in the chancel are of great beauty. Other interesting features are the two-roomed priest's chamber and some Roman pottery of the first century found in the churchyard in 1949. The ancient south doorway to the tower has now been restored after being closed for many years. The Dog Whipper's Marsh in the neighbourhood commemorates in its name the man who used to be paid ten shillings a year for whipping dogs out of church. (This sum is still paid!) The manor was another of those given by King Ethelbert to St. Augustine's, Canterbury, and is one of the largest in Kent.

Close to the church is the farm house of Chislet Court, a fine Queen Anne building.

From Chislet the southerly road leads in less than a mile up to the Canterbury and Margate and Ramsgate road. The village bordering the road is **Upstreet,** where are some fine old Georgian and Queen Anne mansions. The pleasantest route to **Grove Ferry,** which lies a little south of the main road, on the River Stour, is by the footpath beside the **Ship Inn.** This drops gently through meadows to the river. For the road to the Ferry turn leftward on reaching Upstreet, and follow the main road for a hundred yards or so in the direction of Sarre. The road will then be seen on the right, descending steeply to the level crossing and the bridge over the river.

Grove Ferry is a noted fishing centre and a popular place for picnics, with a pleasant riverside hotel *(Grove Ferry)* with tea and beer garden.

To Sturry and Canterbury (8¼ miles). From eastern end of Central parade turn inland by East Cliff Hill, which becomes the Canterbury Road. Pass under railway to Eddington and Herne (1¾ miles). At Church bear *R* and pass the leafy Strode Park. The steep descent to Sturry should be negotiated with care, as there is a *level crossing at foot*. At the foot of the hill, too, the Margate and Ramsgate road joins on the left. Cross railway, and continue straight on, leaving narrow winding High Street on right. Canterbury is entered by Northgate.

Sturry, derives its name from the river Stour, on which it is prettily situated. It is the site of the Junior King's School of Canterbury which is installed in Milner Court, formerly the home of Viscount Milner. Additional buildings have been erected between the new work and the old, of which the most picturesque features are the Tudor gateway and the sixteenth-century tithe barn, one of the largest surviving in the country. The Church of St. Nicholas, set among giant chestnut-trees, has a fine embattled tower, beautiful timbered porch and fifteenth-century font. Under the tower is buried the last abbot of St. Augustine's Abbey, Canterbury.

Fordwich, a quaint old village was once the port of Canterbury, a tidal estuary of the sea finding its way right up to it.

The diminutive **Town Hall** (Admission charge) is a gem, the overhanging upper portion half-timbered, the ground floor of brick and stone. It is believed to date from the earliest years of the fifteenth century, and is now scheduled as an Ancient Monument. Note in the panelled "council chamber" the list of Mayors from 1292 to 1884; also the press-gang drums, the ducking stool, and the ancient iron-bound trunk which contained the archives of the Corporation, now in the Canterbury Cathedral Library. (The Mace, made of gold captured from the Spaniards, and other regalia, are in Canterbury Museum.) In one corner is the "Jewry," the retiring-room of the jury.

The **Church** is a building of great antiquity, containing traces of Saxon work in the tower, Norman windows and font, a rare "heart shrine," and enclosed pews. A beautifully carved Early Norman tomb is said to be part of St. Augustine's, whose monastery of St. Peter and St. Paul was established at Fordwich and re-established at Canterbury.

The manor of Fordwich was given to the monks of the Abbey, and later the Prior of Christ Church, Canterbury, was made to pay the Abbot a red rose for land there. The monks of both communities had quays at Fordwich, and it was here that Caen stone was landed for building the Cathedral.

Boats may be hired for pleasant trips down the Stour, which is navigable all the way to the sea, and there is very good fishing, the *Canterbury and District Angling Association* preserving ten miles of river, as well as having rights on Westbere Lakes at Fordwich.

Birchington and Westgate-on-Sea

Birchington

Banks. – *Lloyds, National Westminster, Barclays, Midland.*

Bathing. – Excellent from sandy beaches with gradual slope. Water-skiing.

Bowls, Tennis. – Near Beresford Gap and by Bungalow Hotel.

Bus Services. – To Margate, Canterbury, etc.

Distances. – Acol, 2; Canterbury, 12¼; Margate, 4; Minster, 4; Monkton, 3½; Quex Park, 1; Reculver (by cliffs), 5½; Sarre, 4; St. Nicholas-at-Wade, 3; Westgate, 2.

Early Closing. – Wednesday.

Golf. – The Westgate Links are within easy reach.

Hotels. – *Bungalow*, Lyell Road; *Court Mount*, Canterbury Road; *St. Valerie Guest House*, Minnis Road.

Parking. – In the Square in old village. Also at Minnis Bay and various other places along the front, free during winter months.

Post Office. – The Square.

Public Library. – Alpha Road.

Station. – About midway between the old village and the sea.

Yacht Club. – At Minnis Bay, with Club House and own boat park.

Less than two hours by rail from London, this straggling, unassuming little place, now included in the borough of Margate, has all the essentials of a first-class holiday resort, including a healthful, bracing climate. There is a flourishing social life in the village, with something to suit all tastes. An amateur dramatic society is particularly active and stages several shows.

The front at Birchington has three bays. **Epple Bay,** the easternmost, provides an invigorating cliff-top promenade with wide sea views. Pleasant cliff-top greensward continues past Beresford Gap to **Grenham Bay,** quiet and secluded. **Minnis Bay,** to the west, is lower and more open. Both of these bays are now linked by a new promenade at the foot of the cliffs. The Minnis Bay promenade serves as a protective sea wall guarding the low-lying land in this area. A cliff path skirts the coast and marshland westward to Reculver.

Turning inland from the shore, take the road past the station to the Square in Old Birchington which as a member of the town and port of Dover, was included in the jurisdiction of the Cinque Ports.

The **Square** is a large irregular space, through which runs the Margate-Canterbury high road.

At the south-west corner stands the **Parish Church,** dedicated to All Saints, a building of great interest and antiquity. The tower, surmounted by a shingled

21

spire, stands in an unusual position, being at the east end of the south aisle. It contains a peal of eight bells. Rossetti died at Birchington on April 9, 1882, and was buried in the churchyard. In the south aisle, near the door, is the beautiful Rossetti Memorial Window. In the early thirteenth-century chancel, with an ancient panelled and painted screen, is an elaborate triptych of the Last Supper by Westlake. The font is early English. The Quex Chapel contains a number of monuments and brasses to members of the Quex and Crispe families.

Quex Park *(not open)*, lies about half a mile south. The old manor-house was, in the days of its former owners, the Quex, or Quekes, and the Crispes, the scene of several interesting historical events. William III and his consort enjoyed its hospitality on several occasions while awaiting a favourable wind to take them to Holland. The handsome **Waterloo Tower** was erected in 1819. It contains a peal of twelve bells.

The **Powell-Cotton Museum** contains zoological, ethnographical and archae-logical exhibits of exceptional interest collected by the later Major Powell-Cotton. The animals set in wide, well-lit cases give a remarkably realistic impression of wild life in African and Indian scenery. In addition, over 7,000 objects represent the arts and crafts of races all over the world. From Birchington itself of special interest is the pottery bowl discovered at Birchington with a hoard of fourteen bronze palstaves, an important relic of the late Bronze Age. *In June, July, the museum is open Wednesdays and Thursdays. From 20th July–10th September, daily except Mondays and Saturdays; for the rest of the year, Thursdays only. Hours are 2.30–6 p.m. Admission charge. Entrance by Quex Park Farm Gate, via Park Lane (B2048).*

St. Nicholas-at-Wade *(Bell Inn; Sun)* is a delightful, unspoilt village lying just off the busy main Canterbury road three miles from Birchington. Many of the houses are of a lovely mellow red brick, with Carolean gables. Its quietness and seclusion have endeared it to a considerable number of visitors.

The **Church,** standing on a slight eminence just above a farm, has a lofty embattled tower seen for miles around. It is reputed to date from the year 1100. The *parvise*, or priests' chamber, over the door, is reached by old oak steps. The carving of the Norman columns on the south side of the nave should be noted. The carved oak pulpit bears the date 1615; and the altar table and screen are also beautifully carved. In the Bridges Chapel is a remarkable sixteenth-century brass, and in the spacious west end of the nave is an ancient chest.

Sarre is rather more than a mile from St. Nicholas, on the Canterbury road. When the Isle of Thanet was still an island, Sarre was one of the two places at which ferry-boats were stationed, Stonar being the other. The channel of the Wantsume was at that time three-quarters of a mile in breadth. In 1052, a Danish fleet, after plundering the eastern coast of Kent, sailed right past Sarre and out into the North Sea by way of Reculver. When the river dried up, Sarre dried up too. Queen Elizabeth I is said to have stayed at Sarre Court. Important Saxon relics have been unearthed in the locality. **Sarre Wall,** the straight road, leading from Upstreet to Sarre village, was probably made by Archbishop Morton, who was much interested in drainage schemes in this part of Kent. He was Archbishop of Canterbury from 1486 to 1500.

The *Crown Inn* at Sarre has long been noted for its cherry brandy and has associations with Charles Dickens.

Close to Sarre, in the direction of Monkton, a turning southward from the Ramsgate road leads to **Pluck's Gutter,** where a road and bridge afford direct communication between Thanet and that part of Kent which lies south of the Stour.

Westgate-on-Sea

Banks. – *Lloyds*, *Barclays* and *National West-minster*.

Bathing. – Excellent. Tents, lock-up huts and cubicles to be hired from the Margate Entertainments Department.

Beach. – Two fiinely shaped bays, both sandy.

Buses to Margate leave the Railway Station, Westgate, or pass along Canterbury Road at frequent intervals. There are also services to Birchington, Canterbury, etc.

Cinema. – St. Mildred's Road.

Dancing. – St. Mildred's Ballroom.

Distances. – Birchington, 2; Margate Jetty, 2; Minster, $4\frac{1}{2}$; St. Nicholas-at-Wade, $4\frac{1}{2}$.

Early Closing. – Wednesdays.

Golf Links. – (18 holes) immediately out of town.

Hotels. – *Ingleton*, Sea Road; *Kimberley*, Sea Road; *Bridge*, St. Mildred's Road; *Longford*, Sea Road.

Library. – Minster Road.

Post Office. – In St. Mildred's Road, opposite St. Saviour's Church.

Putting. – Green adjoining Royal Esplanade.

Tennis Courts. – At Royal Esplanade.

Westgate is a well laid-out town with attractive houses, shops and excellent facilities for bathing and sport. There are two beautiful miniature bays, St. Mildred's Bay and West Bay, girdled by substantial sea-walls and promenades.

The pleasant Gardens, with their grass slopes, shrubs, and banked-in walks, overlook the sea. The houses are well set back and there are numerous shelters and seats. On the Green is a Pavilion, used for entertainments, etc. There is a good view from this point of Margate and its far-stretching jetty and, westward, of Reculver's twin towers.

St. Mildred's Bay is dominated at one end by the St. Mildred's Ballroom, and at the other by the West Cliff House (R.N.I.B.). **Westgate Bay,** or the West Bay, is becoming increasingly popular both for bathing and residence.

The principal building is **St. Saviour's Church,** in the centre of the town, built of Kentish rag. The foundation-stone was laid in 1883, by Sir Erasmus Wilson, who did so much to popularize Westgate with the medical profession and the public. Nearly opposite the church is the Post Office.

The **Congregational Church,** an effective spired building of red brick, has over the doorway, a statue of Wyclif.

Reculver

Margate

Banks. – *Lloyds*, King Street, Canterbury Road and Northdown Road; *Barclays*, High Street and Northdown Road; *National Westminster*, Cecil Square, High Street and Northdown Road; *Midland*, The Parade and Northdown Road; *Trustee Savings*, Cecil Square.

Bathing. – Westward of the Harbour is a large Bathing Pavilion with restaurant and cafe; to the east of the Jetty is the Lido Bathing Pool, available at all states of the tide, with terraced bars and cafes; tidal pools at Marine Terrace and Walpole Bay. There are also changing facilities at Newgate Gap, Walpole Bay, Palm Bay (below Hodge's Flagstaff) and Westbrook. Beach chalets available for daytime use only. Information from Entertainments Manager, Winter Gardens.

Beach. – Broad expanses of sand. Long stretches of seaweed-covered rock are left bare at low tide.

Boating. – Sailing boats, motor boats and speed-boats make frequent trips.

Bowls. – In Dane Park, Eastern Esplanade, Westbrook, Westcliffe Gardens and Royal Esplanade. Visitors may also play on the greens of the Margate Bowling Club, Northdown Avenue.

Buses and Coaches. – Buses to and from Westgate, Birchington, Broadstairs, Ramsgate, Sandwich, Deal, Canterbury, Dover, Folkestone, etc. Coaches make varied trips through some of the best Kent and Sussex scenery.

Car Parks. – All Saints' Avenue (close to station), Dreamland Park, Hawley Street, the Rendezvous, Palm Bay, and numerous smaller places.

Cinemas. – *Cameo*, Northdown Road, Cliftonville; *Dreamland*, Marine Terrace; *Plaza*, High Street.

Dancing. – Public ballrooms at *Dreamland*, *Winter Gardens*, *Lido*, Cliftonville, *Fort Lodge Hotel*, Cliftonville, *Orchid Room*, Cliftonville.

Distances. – Birchington, 4 miles; Broadstairs, by cliffs, 5; Broadstairs *via* St. Peter's, 3½; Canterbury, 16; Deal, 14½; Dover, 27; Herne Bay, 15; Kingsgate, 3; London, 71; Minster, 6½; Pegwell Bay, 6; Ramsgate, 4¼; Sandwich, 9; Reculver, 15½; Walmer, 16; Westgate, 2; Whitstable, 20.

Early Closing. – Thursday.

Entertainments. – Daily, Sundays included, at the Winter Gardens, Theatre Royal and the Oval. Dreamland Amusement Park. The Lido, Cliftonville. Queens Entertainment Centre, Cliftonville.

Fishing. – The sea-fishing off Margate is good – tope, mullet, bass, whiting, flatfish, pouting, cod, etc. Favourite fishing stations are the Pouting Ground, about half a mile from the Jetty, the Ledge, in the direction of Westgate, off the Longnose Buoy and from the Jetty. Fresh-water angling in the Stour; train to Grove Ferry or Sandwich. Buses also run.

Golf. – Links at Kingsgate (North Foreland) and Westgate.

Hotels. – *Endcliffe*, The Oval, Cliftonville; *Walpole Bay*, Fifth Avenue, Cliftonville; *Bicken Hall*, Edgar Road, Cliftonville; *Hereward*, Gordon Road, Cliftonville; *Fort Lodge*, Cliftonville; *Holland House*, Edgar Road, Cliftonville; *Palm Bay*, Cliftonville; *Cheddar House*, Dalby Square, Cliftonville; *Oval*, Godwin Road; *Roxburgh*, Fort Crescent; *Craven*, Cliftonville; *Greenwich House*, Dalby Square; *Norman*, Edgar Road, Cliftonville; *Royal Crescent*, Royal Crescent; *Craven*, Eastern Esplanade; *Greylands*, Edgar Road, Cliftonville; *Granville Court*, Lewis Crescent, Cliftonville; *Harvey Court*, Edgar Road, Cliftonville; *Brierdene*, Warwick Road, Cliftonville; *Berkeley Court*, Sweyn Road, Cliftonville; *Glenwood*, Edgar Road, Cliftonville; *Granville*, Dalby Square.

Inquiries. – Information Centre, Marine Terrace.

Library. – Public Library, Victoria Road.

Population. – 49,080.

Post Offices. – *General Post Office*, Cecil Square. *Cliftonville Branch Office*, Northdown Road. *Sub-Offices:* Parade, Tivoli (South Margate), Victoria Road, Upper Approach Road, Ethelbert Terrace, Canterbury Road, Ramsgate Road, Upper Dane Road.

Putting and miniature golf-courses at Hodge's Flagstaff, Westcliff Gardens, Station Approach, Royal Esplanade, Lido and Ethelbert Crescent. Beyond Palm Bay and at Hartsdown Park are approach courses.

Tennis. – Courts in Dane Park; Palm Bay, near the Flagstaff; and Hartsdown. Also at Westcliff Gardens; Royal Esplanade; and Dalby Square. Open on Sundays.

Theatres, etc. – *Winter Gardens*, Fort Promenada; *Theatre Royal*, Addington Street; *Lido Theatre*, seafront, Cliftonville; *Oval*, Cliftonville.

25

MARGATE

Margate, labelled "Merry Margate," is a charmingly laid out town with miles of green lawns and gardens fringed by golden sands, pleasant houses in the residential areas to the east, west and inland, many acres of beautiful public parks. It has almost unrivalled facilities for bathing, sport and every kind of entertainment. Liberal provision is made for the amusement of all classes and types of visitors. There are amusement parks and funfairs; bowling-greens, putting-greens and tennis-courts are numerous; there are many large car parks, while a special track has been set aside for horse-riding. The links at Westgate and North Foreland are capable of satisfying the most exacting golfers, and there are half a dozen other courses between Whitstable and Sandwich.

The bathing is ideal. Sea-trips of all kinds are available. The town is an excellent centre for excursions. In the world of entertainment first-class shows and music are to be enjoyed, and at the hotels and numerous ballrooms there are excellent dance floors. It cannot be too often insisted upon that there are at least two Margates, and that the Cliftonville and Westbrook quarters have scarcely anything in common with the regions more popular with the day visitors.

Among its natural assets is Margate's unrivalled air, clear and invigorating. All the winds, except those from the south-west blow as sea breezes, while the chalky soil absorbs moisture, so that the air has the same exhilarating effect as that, say, of the Alps but intensified by the flavour of the sea.

The district around Margate, with its far-stretching fields of wheat and barley, is a continual delight. There are few more enjoyable walks on the east coast than the five-mile tramp from Margate along the cliffs to Kingsgate, the North Foreland and Broadstairs.

The **Harbour,** formerly a busy port of call for all types of shipping and cargo, is now a centre for a popular yacht club and much used by pleasure craft generally. The **Harbour Pier,** built of Whitby stone in 1815, is 909 feet long. Though but little used by visitors, it is worth strolling down for the sake of the view at the end. At the shore end are the offices of the Margate Pier and Harbour Company. A tablet commemorates the landing on Margate Jetty of 46,772 troops of the Allied Forces on the evacuation of Dunkirk in May, 1940.

The **Jetty,** 1,240 feet long, is one of the most popular promenades in the town, a miniature railway running from end to end. The Jetty Extension is hexagonal in shape and very spacious having been designed to handle a busy steamer traffic. Most of these services, however, have now ceased to function. It is still a great attraction as a promenade and is a popular vantage point for anglers.

On the eastern side of the Jetty will be noticed the small domed pavilion housing the **Lifeboat,** "The North Foreland," a motor vessel of the Watson (Cabin) Type. *The boat is open to inspection daily,* and is well worth a visit.

Eastward from the Harbour

Leaving the Jetty, ascend the heights of Cliftonville either by Fort Road, or by the promenade at the cliff foot which leads to steps in the neighbourhood of the Fort. The Fort is formidable only in name. Whatever it may once have been, it is now merely a pleasant promenade with a fine sea-wall, surrounding –

The Winter Gardens. The building lies in an artificial hollow. Here stars from the entertainment world give performances daily and on Sunday evenings. There is a concert hall seating 2,000 persons; another for 1,000 and a covered Colonnade. Balconies overlook the sea and the gardens, and the sunken lawns and prettily laid-out circular banks give complete shelter from the winds. As it is more than a hundred feet above sea level, the Fort Green commands a wide prospect. An incline leads down the face of the steep cliff to the sea-wall and the sands.

The Cliftonville Lido is situated on the cliff top to the east along the Promenade. Terraces have been cut in the cliff-face down to sea-level. On the top are greens, putting and a car park. Below, on the first terrace, are the Lido Theatre, sun terrace, games hall and puppet theatre, a small zoo and aquarium. On the second terrace is the large Cliff Café with orchestra and entertainments. On the level of the undercliff promenade the Bathing Pool, available at all states of the tide, projects into the sea, and the Golden Garter provides "Wild West" entertainment. On this level also are the Jolly Tar Tavern, French Bar and billiards and table-tennis hall.

East of Fort Promenade is the cliff-top **Queen's Promenade,** leading to the Queen's Motel and Entertainment Centre, which bisects the Front. The undercliff Promenade runs from the Harbour and Jetty to the Queen's Motel, where it turns inland up the Newgate Gap.

In a short distance a footbridge spans a deep cutting in the cliff known as **Newgate Gap.** A few yards inland rock-lined steps lead down to the Gap, which affords convenient access to the sands. The sands can also be reached by the steps that lead to the beach chalets.

Cliftonville

Here are many excellent modern hotels, boarding-houses and private residences and flats. It is, in fact, the most popular residential part of Margate.

Beyond the Queen's Entertainment Centre there is an open space on the cliff-top picturesquely laid out with shrubs and walks, and known as **The Oval.** Here is a sunken enclosure with stage, the scene of numerous daily entertainments. Seats and deck-chairs are ranged on the slopes. A flight of steps leads down from the Oval promenade to the sands and a sun-deck café.

A short distance farther on is a quadrangular space known as The Lawns, with bowling-greens, shelters, seats and substantial steps leading down to the sands of **Walpole Bay** which has a tidal bathing-pool and another modern café.

On the Eastern Esplanade, a few yards inland, is the **Catholic Church of St. Anne.**

The footbridge over **Hodge's Gap** leads to the Bungalow Tea Gardens and Restaurant and at the eastern end of the bridge is **The Flagstaff Promenade,** popularly known as "Hodges." The protruding cliff on which the flagstaff stands is a breezy spot and commands a delightful all-round

The Esplanade, Margate

view. Close at hand are public tennis courts, putting-courses, and a car park. A sea-wall and Undercliff Promenade is approached by flights of steps. Below are convenient beach chalets which may be hired from the Corporation. A short promenade runs eastwards to **Friend's Gap**, another of these interesting gaps in the coastline. The fine walk eastward to Kingsgate, with its continuation to Broadstairs, is described on p. 30.

Northdown Park, slightly inland, is thirty-eight and a half acres in extent and provides further amenities in gardens, games and riding.

Westward from the Harbour

The Marine Parade extends in a long curve past the Children's Pool and the Bathing Pool to Westgate. Many of the buses start from this central point. Beyond is the **Clock Tower**, and then the **Marine Pool**, with a tidal bathing-pool of two acres. It is equipped with shower-baths and a hot-water supply and a sun-deck café.

Across the road is **Dreamland**, the town's principal entertainment centre, with cinema and ballroom, as well as cafés, restaurants and bars. In the 20-acre Amusement Park are scenic railways, amusement rides and shows, together with an arena for firework displays seating 4,000. There is also a 5-acre Safari Wild Animal Park in wooded surroundings.

To the west is the **Central Coach Station** and Two-Tier Car Park (entrance in All Saints' Avenue).

On the grass-plot overlooking the Parade is a statue to the memory of the men drowned on December 2, 1897, by the capsizing of the surf-boat *Friend to all Nations*.

Beyond the Bathing Station are attractive beach chalets which can be hired from the Corporation.

The district inland from this point is popular with sports enthusiasts, the extensive **Hartsdown** and **Tivoli** parks on the far side of **Margate Station** containing numerous public courts and greens, an approach golf course, and Margate football ground (Southern League football). Tivoli Park contains also a charming woodland garden and the courts of the *Margate Lawn Tennis Club*, open to visitors.

The Marine Parade now becomes the **Westbrook Promenade,** with cliff-top lawns, sunken gardens, games centre and children's playground.

Overlooking the Promenade is the **Royal Sea-Bathing Hospital,** which enjoys far more than local fame. Since its foundation in 1791 it has been the means of benefiting many thousands of persons. Patients suffering from surgical tuberculosis are received from a wide area, and the hospital has an active orthopaedic unit. The hospital also accommodates chest patients but not convalescent cases.

Other Places of Interest in Margate

Dane Park, about half a mile from the sea, may be reached by bus, or by taking any of the turnings behind the Cliftonville Promenade. The Park consists of about thirty-three acres, laid out with lawns and winding walks, and a lake backed by ferns and huge blocks of rock-work. Facilities are provided in the Park for tennis, cricket, bowls and other games.

The prominent red-brick building with the lofty tower on the height to the south-west is the **Royal School for Deaf Children**, Victoria Road. On the opposite side of the valley is **Princess Mary's Hospital** (Rehabilitation).

The **"Grotto"** *(daily charge)*. The entrance is in Grotto Hill, about half a mile from the sea.

Steps at the end of the entrance hall lead down to a passage roughly hewn out of the chalk. This is about 4 feet wide, and is serpentine in form. Passing through an arch, the visitor enters a vaulted circular chamber, known as the Rotunda, with a massive column in the centre. Column, roof and walls are alike covered with shells of diverse sorts, shapes and sizes, disposed in elaborate designs. Above is the small domed shaft by means of which the Grotto was discovered in 1835. Three gathered arches form the entrance to a second serpentine passage about 50 feet in length, its panels containing some of the finest work, which slopes down to the **Rectangular Chamber,** an apartment about 20 feet long by 11 wide. Opposite the entrance is a curious arched recess, about 4 feet from the floor. There are 2,000 square feet of this intricate mosaic, and the designs, though infinitely varied, are harmonious. The grounding throughout is in the same kind of shell – that of dog-winkle laid outwards – making a uniform surface upon which to show the designs. For the figures, including flowers, stars and suns, about twenty-eight kinds of shells are employed.

The Church of St. John the Baptist in Thanet, the parish church of Margate, once a chapel of Minster, is in the south-west part of the town, at the upper end of High Street. Built of flint, it occupies a commanding position on a hill and its spire is visible for many many miles around.

The church, founded *c.* 1050, was restored 1875–9 and given a new roof and spire; the interior was further completely restored in 1961. It possesses famous fifteenth- to seventeenth-century brasses. The long low building, and the uniform height of nave and chancel without a chancel arch gives the interior an unusual appearance.

St. Paul's Church, Cliftonville, is Early English in style; **All Saints',** Westbrook, serves the other end of the town. The original **Holy Trinity Church** in Trinity Square was destroyed during the Second World War, and has been rebuilt in Northdown, incorporating an existing chapel-of-ease as the side-chapel. Here is the War Memorial from the former church.

In Market Place, leading off Harbour Parade, is the **Town Hall,** an old flint building with Carolean gables, and hung with portraits of civic worthies. An oak tablet records the names of all Mayors, Recorders and Town Clerks since the borough was incorporated in 1857.

The **Chief Post Office** is in **Cecil Square.**

On the western side of the town are **Garlinge** and **Dent-de-lion,** the one a village, now enclosed by the modern growth of the town, the other a ruin of the ancient castle of Daundelyon or Dent-de-lion, which can be seen by turning to the left off the Canterbury Road by the *Hussar,* and then to the right. The road is private and no cars are allowed. The early fifteenth-century gateway is in excellent preservation, and is surmounted by the arms of the family, and some portions of the old battlemented mansion still remain. According to Philpott, the Daundelyons settled here in the time of Edward I. Under one side of the gate-house was discovered in 1703 a large chamber with Roman burial urns.

At the lower end of Northdown Road is the entrance to the **Margate Caves** in the grounds of a private house. The chalk caverns were variously used in the past as dungeons and by smugglers.

Rather more than a mile almost due south of the Jetty is **Salmestone Grange,** acquired by the Benedictines in 1194. It is probable a Hall existed here in Saxon times, while pieces of Norman masonry are incorporated in the existing walls. Some restoration work was carried out in the fourteenth and fifteenth centuries *(open Saturdays 2–5 p.m., June–September inclusive, or at other times by arrangement with Warden. Admission Charge).*

A little south of Salmestone along Nash Road is **Nash Court,** comprising the remains of a stately house, but chiefly remarkable on account of its curious underground chambers, which seem to be old chalk workings, though later they may have been used by smugglers. By permission of the tenant, a portion of these may be inspected.

To Kingsgate and Broadstairs

The walk along the cliffs to Kingsgate is via a broad promenade from Hodge's Flagstaff passing the Hydrophone Station, established during the 1914–18 War. At **Foreness Point** the views of the coast on either side are very fine. **Kingsgate** is a well-designed residential district, lying between the North Foreland and Foreness Point, and is included in the Broadstairs and St. Peter's Urban District.

To return to Margate, take an inland turning to Reading Street at the cross-roads by Kingsgate Castle, and reach Margate either via Northdown or via St. Peter's. The walk, however, may be continued to Broadstairs past the North Foreland Lighthouse and the return to Margate made by bus or train.

Joss Bay, Kingsgate

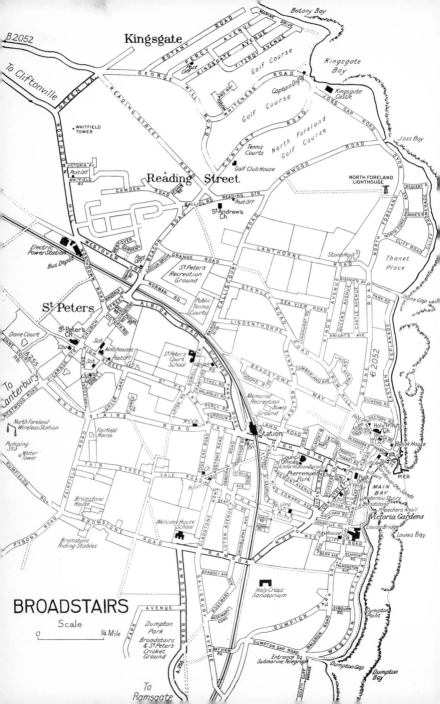

Broadstairs

Banks. – *Lloyds* (branch at St. Peter's), *National Westminster* and *Midland*, all in High Street; *Barclays*, Albion Street.

Bathing. – Excellent. Tents and chalets on the sands at Viking, Louisa, Dumpton, Joss, Stone, Kingsgate and Botany Bays. Applications for hire of sites, tents and chalets to Entertainments Manager, Garden-on-the-Sands.

Beach. – Sand.

Boating. – Viking Bay is admirably adapted for rowing and sailing. Motor-boats provide sea trips. A Regatta is held annually. Sailing Club with weekly races.

Bowls. – In the Memorial Recreation Ground, adjoining station.

Buses. – Frequent services to neighbouring resorts and good services to all parts of Kent.

Car Parks. – Victoria Parade, Eastern Esplanade, Western Esplanade, South Cliff Parade, Dumpton Park Drive, Queen's Gardens, Granville Avenue, Wrotham Road, Oscar Road, King Edward Avenue, Pierremont Avenue, Dundonald Road, Grosvenor Road and Fordoun Road; Croft's Place, Albion Street, The Pier and Joss Bay.

Dancing. – Grand Ballroom, West Cliff Road.

Distances. – Canterbury, 18½ miles; Deal, 15; Dover, 20; Kingsgate, 2; Margate, 3¼; Margate (by cliff), 5; Minster, 7; Northdown, 1½; North Foreland, 1½; Pegwell Bay, 3; Ramsgate, 2; St. Peter's, 1; Sandwich, 9.

Early Closing. – Wednesday.

Entertainments. – Music and novelty entertainment during season at the Garden-on-the-Sands Pavilion; Cinema at York Gate Hall.

Fishing. – Off North Foreland, good. Also from the rocks at certain states of tides. There is a local Sea-Angling Society while competitions and an Annual Festival are held.

Golf. – North Foreland Golf Links (bus service). Two minutes from bus-stop. Open meetings are held at Easter, Spring, and late Summer, Bank Holidays and Christmas.

Hotels. – *Royal Albion*, Albion Street; *Curzon*, Granville Road; *Castlemere*, Western Esplanade; *Castle Keep*, Kingsgate Castle; *Dutch House*, North Foreland; *Beechfield*, West Cliff Road; *Merriland*, The Vale; *Dumpton Lodge*, Western Esplanade; *Hotel Lancaster*, West Cliff; *Kingscliffe*, Granville Road; *St. Augustine's*, Granville Road; *Kingsmead*, Eastern Esplanade; *Hotel on the Jetty*, Broadstairs; *Oakfield*, The Vale; *Dundonald House*, Belvedere Road; *Waverley*, Chandos Square; *Cleveland*, Granville Road.

Population. – About 20,450.

Post Office. – High Street, near Station. Several sub-offices.

Public Library. – Pierremont Gardens.

Riding. – Facilities offered by several establishments. Annual Horse Show and Gymkana.

Station. – *Broadstairs*, at top of High Street, half a mile from sea-front. Buses pass. For the extreme western end of the town and for the Dumpton Park area, *Dumpton Park Station* may sometimes be found more convenient.

Tennis. – At Recreation Ground, Callis Court Road, St. Peter's. Hard Courts at Recreation Ground by railway station and at North Foreland Golf Club.

Broadstairs is renowned for its healthy situation in the heart of the famous Thanet holiday area. As a holiday resort for children it is ideal. There is a splendid sandy beach and the town has a high level of sunshine.

The greater part of the town stands at an elevation of from 100 to 200 feet above sea-level. Some of the older streets are inconveniently narrow, but the town as a whole is well planned. A boon to motorists is the broad road branching from St. Peter's Road just above the station and obviating the necessity of passing through the narrow streets of St. Peter's.

BROADSTAIRS

Adjoining the station is the **Memorial Recreation Ground,** with good bowling-greens, hard tennis courts and a 9-hole approach golf course. There are facilities for cricket, football and other games at **St. Peter's Recreation Ground.** The War Memorial stands at the entrance to **Pierremont Park,** a pleasant, tree-shaded spot about midway between the station and the sea. The Park may be entered by a short turning from High Street, by the side of Pierremont Hall, or from Queen's Road, a lower turning from High Street. Queen Victoria, in girlhood, spent several summers in the old mansion here, Pierremont Hall, which is now used by the District Council.

High Street and adjacent roads form the principal shopping quarter, the former coming to an abrupt termination on the very edge of the cliff.

The pretty semicircular **Viking Bay** is bounded on one side by steep chalk cliffs, and on the other by the picturesque pier. A zigzag flight of stone steps gives access to the sands, and there is also a passenger Lift and near the bandstand another flight of steps. The sands are very soft and yielding, and form ideal playgrounds for children. The seven bays which comprise the Broadstairs coast are well sheltered by the cliffs. There are tents and chalets available for hire and the bathing is all that could be desired. At low tide it is possible to walk some distance along the foreshore. A good undercliff walk extends between Louisa Bay and Dumpton Bay.

The coastline comprises nearly four miles along the edge of the cliffs and skirts a succession of bays, each with charms of its own. Another pleasant feature of the sea-front is the stretch of wide lawn, over a mile in extent. The seascapes all along are delightful, the view on clear days extending to the coast of France, and there is always the busy traffic of ships to give it movement and variety.

A few yards from the point where High Street joins Victoria Parade is **Dickens House,** with a tablet recording that here lived the original of Miss Trotwood.

The **Victoria Gardens** are attractive, with a projecting cliff upon which is placed a shelter. The view across Viking Bay shows Broadstairs at its most picturesque, with the castellated mansion known as Bleak House a prominent feature.

At the south end of Victoria Gardens the Louisa Footbridge leads across a narrow gap to the **Western Esplanade,** and so to **Dumpton Bay.**

In the opposite corner of the bay is the pleasant **"Garden-on-the-Sands,"** and Pavilion.

"The Quaint Old Pier," on the north side of the bay, was declared by Dickens to be "fortunately without the slightest pretension to architecture, and very picturesque in consequence." It resembles some great hulk, on a magnified wooden groyne. A pier seems to have stood on the site since the time of Henry VIII, various structures having been used by vessels engaged in the Iceland cod fisheries, an industry occupying much of the population in past years. The present much-tarred pier dates in the main from 1808. Because of silting, however, the harbour can now be used only by yachts and vessels of light draught.

Harbour Street, a narrow lane winding upward from the pier to Albion

Broadstairs

Street, contains an interesting relic in the shape of the **York Gate,** a flint arch beneath which once hung heavy doors that could be closed in case of threatened invasion. An inscription on the gateway records that it was built by George Culmer, about 1540, and repaired by Sir John Henniker, Bart., in 1795. Further up the street are some remains of the ancient chapel of "Our Lady of Bradstowe" (Broadstairs). This shrine, like others round the coast, was so venerated by sailors that they were accustomed to lower topsails when passing.

To Dickens lovers, one of the chief objects of interest in Broadstairs is –

Bleak House, where he wrote a great part of *David Copperfield* and other novels, but not *Bleak House itself*. In Dickens's time the residence was known as Fort House. It had previously been occupied by Wilkie Collins. A later owner, however, converted the old house, with its balcony and curiously shuttered windows, into the present castellated residence. The house stands in a commanding position on the north cliff. On the side of the house has been placed a granite tablet with a bronze bust of the novelist. The house is in private ownership but is open to the public daily from March to the end of October.

Other houses in Broadstairs associated with Charles Dickens are No. 40 Albion Street (now part of Albion Hotel), Lawn House, which he occupied in the summer of 1840, and the Albion Hotel, in which he had a suite of rooms in 1845, 1847 and 1859. A plaque on a shop in High Street marks the site of the one-time house where he stayed in 1837 and wrote the concluding pages of Pickwick Papers.

35

BROADSTAIRS

The asphalted **Eastern Esplanade** has some charming houses.

Holy Trinity Church, in Nelson Place, was erected in 1829, as a chapel-of-ease to St. Peter's, in which parish Broadstairs was formerly included. It was rebuilt in 1926 in Romanesque style and has a spacious interior.

The **Church of Our Lady of the Sea** (Roman Catholic) was built in 1931.

Antiquaries will be interested in many discoveries of **ancient remains** made in the locality. Graves have yielded Roman, Saxon and other relics, and excavations have furnished distinct proof of at least two very early settlements of considerable size. In 1911 several skeletons ascribed to the Bronze Age were discovered.

St. Peter's

Officially a part of the Broadstairs and St. Peter's Urban District, was formerly by far the more important place, with "Bradstow" as its little suburb by the sea. As a member of the town and port of Dover it is included in the jurisdiction of the Cinque Ports.

The **Parish Church,** dedicated to St. Peter the Apostle, dates, in part, from the eleventh century. It consists of nave with Norman arcade of five arches, chancel, and north and south aisles. The North aisle extends as far eastward as the chancel, and is separated from it by three Early English arches. The chancel ceiling is elaborately decorated. Several ancient brasses may be seen. A marble tablet commemorates Thomas Sheridan, father of the famous author of *The School for Scandal*. Of even more interest is an upright slab on the south side of the church, marking the grave of Richard Joy the "Kentish Samson," a worthy of prodigious strength.

Nuckell's Almshouses, in High Street, have a curious statue of Charity.
From St. Peter's Church a footpath leads to Margate (2½ miles).

Excursions from Broadstairs

To **North Foreland** (1½ miles), **Kingsgate** (2 miles), and **Margate** (5 miles). At Holy Trinity Church either turn right to Eastern Esplanade, or follow Stone Road northward. Continue to the extensive plantation surrounding **Stone House,** long the seaside residence of Archbishop Tait, and now a private school. Further along the North Foreland Road the lighthouse can be seen immediately ahead. Diverting to the left, however, Lanthorne Road leads past the **Hearts of Oak Convalescent Home,** to the picturesque village of **Reading Street,** from which Margate can be reached *via* Northdown, or St. Peter's by turning leftward.

The North Foreland Lighthouse may be seen any day, except Sundays, from 1 p.m. to within an hour of sunset. The tower is 85 feet high and is ascended by steps round the inside of its walls. The 175,000 candlepower light is 188 feet above high-water mark, and visible for 20 miles. The light is eclipsed five times in seven seconds every twenty seconds. It was off this point that the great four days' fight took place in June, 1666, between the English fleet under Monk, and the Dutch under De Ruyter and De Witt.

Kingsgate. The road from the lighthouse skirts the grounds of Kingsgate Castle, a picturesque building in a unique situation. It was once the residence of

Lord Avebury, the distinguished banker-scientist to whom we owe the institution of Bank Holidays; it is now converted into residential flats. In the grounds adjoining (originally belonging to the Castle), on **Hackemdown Point,** is the *Castle Keep Hotel,* built in the Italian style.

Holland House, the largest of the white houses facing the road and adjoining the coastguard station, is named after its original owner, Henry Fox, first Lord Holland, Secretary of War 1746–56, and subsequently Paymaster of the Forces. His house was on a very extensive and ambitious scale, copied from an Italian villa, but few portions now remain.

Steps opposite the white houses give access to the sands, where there is good bathing. At low tide there are interesting walks beneath the cliffs in either direction, with fine arched rocks and caves and several acres of seaweed-covered rock. Altogether Kingsgate is a delightful, picturesque and health-giving spot, and it is not surprising that so many pleasant houses have been built in recent years. In 1683 Charles II and his brother, subsequently James II, landed here on their way, by water, from London to Dover. A gate was erected to commemorate the landing of the King, but having been blown down during a gale it was re-erected in grounds near by.

On the northern side of the bay is the battlemented *Captain Digby Inn* with car park adjoining. This is a favourite walk out from either Broadstairs or Margate.

Broadstairs to Ramsgate

By the Cliffs (2 miles). Follow the Western Esplanade to **Dumpton Bay** ($\frac{1}{2}$ mile), where the cross-channel cables come ashore. **Dumpton Park,** a short distance inland, has been greatly developed. Leaving the South Parade the path ascends to the King George VI Memorial Park. Then the path leads between the park and the *Thanet Bowls and Tennis Club* in Montefiore Avenue. From there a path skirts the park to the Ramsgate East Cliff Esplanade.

By the Sands. When the tide is out this is a delightful walk. The steep chalk cliffs (130 to 140 ft.) are seen to great advantage from below. The rocky pools and long stretches of sea-weed are a great attraction to youthful naturalists. A curious feature is the long bank of flints thrown up by the tides below the grounds of East Cliff Lodge. Though the landward end is more or less stationary, the seaward portion – estimated at some 2 miles – is continually changing its position. The bank, known as "The Coburns," is well seen from the cliffs at low water. West Cliff Promenade extends round the foot of the cliffs between Louisa Bay and Dumpton Bay.

By Road. The Ramsgate Road starts at the foot of High Street, and passing the Thanet Technical College ascends obliquely to the railway bridge. Here turn right, and in a quarter of a mile left, passing **Dumpton Park,** with railway station and greyhound racing track. In Ramsgate, **Hereson,** is passed. For the East Cliff turn left at once; for thz Harbour, continue along King Street and turn left along Harbour Street.

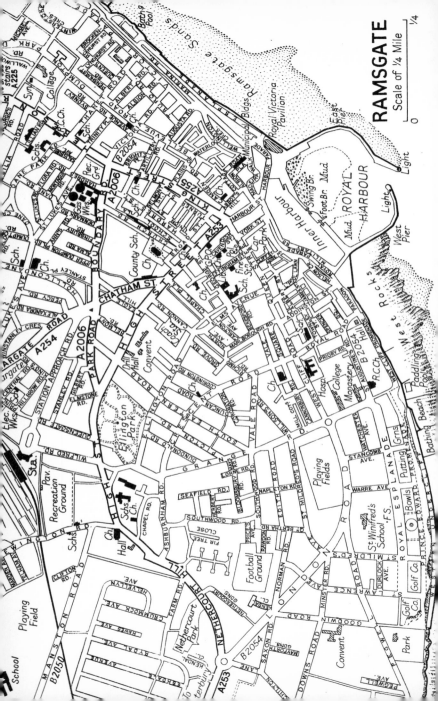

RAMSGATE

Scale of ¼ Mile

Ramsgate Sands

Royal Victoria Pavilion

Municipal Bldgs

East Pier

Light

ROYAL HARBOUR

Swing Br.
Foot Br. Mud
Mud

Inner Harbour

West Pier

Light

West Cliff Rocks

Paddling Pool

Bathing Beach

ROYAL ESPLANADE

PRINCE EDWARD PROMENADE

Golf Co.

Golf Co.

Park

Convent

CHATHAM ST.

HIGH STREET

PARK ROAD

Ellington Park

Recreation Ground

Sta.

Playing Fields

St. Winifred's School

Football Ground

Nethercourt Park

Playing Field

School

Ramsgate

Banks. – *Lloyds*, Queen Street; *Barclays*, Queen Street, *National Westminster*, High Street; *Midland*, High Street and Grange Road; *Trustee Savings Bank*, Queen Street.

Bathing. – Excellent facilities at Main Sands and along nearly three miles of foreshore. Marina Bathing Pool with cafe and sun lounges. Paddling and boating pool at St. Lawrence Cliffs.

Beach. – Sandy. At low tide a fine stretch of level sands, extending to Broadstairs, is exposed east of the Harbour.

Bowls. – Several public greens on the West Cliff, where the Ramsgate Bowling Club has its headquarters, in Ellington Park (*St. Lawrence Bowling Club*) and Montefiore Avenue (*Thanet Bowling Club*).

Buses and Coaches. – Frequent bus services throughout the town and between Ramsgate and neighbouring towns. Coach tours to all parts of Kent and Sussex from seaward end of York Street.

Camping and Caravan Sites. – Licensed camping and caravan sites are available within easy reach of the town and sea front. Particulars from Information Bureau.

Car Parks. – Queen Street, and Belmont Street (free); Cannon Road (charge); Harbour (charge); Leopold Street (charge); Staffordshire Street (charge); Meeting Street (charge). Parking is also permitted in many roads along and near the seafront.

Cinemas. – King Street and Market Place.

Dancing. – Coronation Ballroom; Granville Ballroom, Granville House; Victoria Pavilion.

Distances. – Broadstairs, 2; Canterbury, 18; Deal, 13½; Dover, 20; London, 74; Margate, 5; Minster, 5; Pegwell Bay, 1½; Sandwich, 8; Herne Bay, 15.

Early Closing Day. – Thursday.

Entertainments. – First-class production shows in Granville Theatre; two cinemas; "Pleasurama" Amusement Park and Olympia Hall, overlooking Main Sands.

Fishing. – Cod, whiting, plaice, sole, etc., are fairly plentiful off the coast. Good line and rod fishing can be had from the piers, and there are excellent fishing grounds just off the shore, well known to the boatmen. The headquarters of the Royal Ramsgate Invicta Angling Association are at Royal Harbour.

Golf. – Ramsgate and its near neighbour, Sandwich, offer almost unrivalled facilities to golf-players. St. Augustine's course at Ebbsfleet, the North Foreland Royal St. George's and Cinque Ports links are all easily accessible.

Greyhound Racing at Dumpton Stadium opposite Dumpton Park Station. Evening races on Mondays, Wednesdays and Saturdays, June to September.

Hotels. – *Court Stairs*, Pegwell Road; *Beverley*, Nelson Crescent; *San Clu*, East Cliff Promenade; *Regency*, West Cliff; *Sycamore*, Albion Road; *Savoy*, West Cliff; *Mooring's*, Albion Place; *Westbourne*, The Paragon; *Four Winds*, Victoria Parade; *Continental*, Hardres Street; *Pier View*, Rose Hill; *Royal Oak*, Harbour Parade; *Sylvan*, High Street; *St. Placid's*, Victoria Parade; *Avenue House*, Avenue Road; *Foy Boast*, Sion Hill; *Malvern Motel*, Truro Road; *Viking Ship Motel*, Pegwell Bay.

Hovercraft Services. – To and from Calais from the International Hoverport, Pegwell Bay.

Inquiries. – Information Bureau, 24 King Street. Enquiry Office opposite station in summer.

Library. – Public Library. Guildford Lawn. Branch Library, Newington Road.

Model Village. – West Cliff Promenade.

Population. – 39,220.

Post Office. – Head Office, High Street.

Sailing. – Sailing and motor-boats put out for trips to sea, to the Goodwins, etc. Ramsgate is the headquarters of the *Royal Temple Yacht Club*.

Tennis. – At the Warre Recreation Ground, near Ellington Park; in Spencer Square, West Cliff; and Montefiore Avenue.

Ramsgate is built on and between two lofty chalk cliffs. The opening is supposed to have given the place its name, *Ramsgate*, the *Gate of Ruim*, the British name for Thanet, though it possibly derives from a Saxon personal source.

RAMSGATE

The town has much to be proud of in its sunny terraces, gay gardens, and wonderful facilities for pleasure, sport and entertainment. In spite of modern developments, however, the town itself retains much of its old-time picturesqueness, the quaint grouping of houses, one above the other, with the piers and the shipping in the foreground, preventing any approach to monotony. By day, sea, sky and sands, with green-topped white cliffs in the background, set off the human kaleidoscope, while at night the illuminations pick out slopes and terraces with most delightful effect.

Ramsgate was for centuries a limb of its ancient Cinque Port neighbour, Sandwich; but in 1884, it succeeded in securing incorporation. It is now governed by a mayor, eight aldermen, and twenty-four councillors. Extensive remains have been found in and around the town.

Ramsgate is justly proud of the part it played in World War II. The Harbour became a front-line naval base as a reserve to Dover, and many of the "little ships" which sped to the rescue of the Allied troops on Dunkirk beaches set out from Ramsgate Harbour. About one-third of the troops evacuated from Dunkirk were landed at Ramsgate.

The **Harbour,** of considerable commercial importance to the town, is very popular with visitors. Formerly a centre of a flourishing fishing industry, it is now handling the import and export of motor-cars, spares and mixed cargoes. The harbour area is the busiest part of the town and a place of never-failing interest.

A certain amount of ship repairing is done. The inner basin is non-tidal. There are three slipways for such vessels as require scraping or hull repairs. The area of the harbour is about forty-six acres, the width of the mouth being 200 feet. A cross wall separates the inner and outer harbours. The greater part of the harbour was constructed by Smeaton, of Eddystone Lighthouse fame, who here first employed the diving bell for constructing foundations. Some beautiful yachts may frequently be seen in the inner harbour, Ramsgate being the headquarters of the **Royal Temple Yacht Club.** A yachting week is usually held during August and is a notable event in yachting circles. Local fishermen will readily arrange private fishing trips.

The **East Pier** is about 2,000 feet long, and the **West Pier** 1,500 feet. At the end of the West Pier is a stone Lighthouse, with powerful light. Access is gained to the pier from the West Cliff by a steep flight of steps. Both piers form delightful promenades, the East Pier being especially popular, and either provides a good sea blow.

The motor **lifeboat,** *Michael and Lily Davis,* is moored in the outer harbour. The Ramsgate station was established in 1802.

The **Royal Victoria Pavilion,** adjoining the Harbour and the sands has been developed for entertainment purposes. The upper Promenade running round the lunetted roof and above the extensions, provides undistured views of the sands and sea.

Near the foot of the East Pier is a plain **Obelisk,** set up to commemorate George IV's visit to his kingdom of Hanover from Ramsgate. On his return in November, 1821, he decreed that the harbour of Ramsgate should be styled Royal.

The **Custom House** is a dignified building of red brick, with Corinthian pillars and a small dome.

Yacht Harbour, Ramsgate

A Walk Eastward

From the harbour ascend to the East Cliff Promenade by a **Lift**, or by way of the **Madeira Walk,** interspersed with shrubs and flowers. A charming waterfall fringed with ferns looks cool on the hottest day, and at night is illuminated by coloured lights. The lawns and gardens above are known as the **Albion Gardens.** Queen Victoria lived for a time as a girl at Albion House, Albion Place, now used as municipal offices. On the seaward edge of the Gardens is a **War Memorial.**

Wellington Crescent, with its colonnade, gardens and bandstand, leads eastward to the *Augusta Stairs,* by which the sands can be gained. The **Granville Theatre,** a municipal enterprise, can accommodate over 900 people. Granville House was designed by E. Welby Pugin.

The broad asphalted promenade is connected with the lower promenade and the sands, 90 feet below, by another **Lift. East Stoke,** now a children's home, was erected by the first Lord Winterstoke (d. 1911), the head of the firm of W. D. and H. O. Wills. Over the gateway is inscribed his punning motto, "As God Wills."

The broad esplanade continues along the cliff edge and passes King George VI Memorial Park. Above are the very attractive **Winterstoke Gardens.** Below, an undercliff drive and rock garden approaches to the seashore are a charming link between the gardens and the beach. The gardens command fine views seaward. From the farther end runs a foot-

41

path leading to the **Montefiore Sports Grounds** and to Broadstairs, past **George VI Memorial Park,** at one time the estate of Sir Moses Montefiore, the philanthropist. At **Hereson,** a district on the left, is a **Synagogue,** founded and endowed by the late baronet. The adjoining **Mausoleum** contains the remains of Sir Moses and Judith, Lady Montefiore (d. 1862). A granite pillar from an Egyptian Temple stands near the tomb. **Dumpton Park** has ceased to be the name of a pleasaunce and is now that of a residential neighbourhood having its own railway station, opposite which is the Greyhound Racing Track.

From the East Cliff, descend by the Lift or stroll down the long slope to the **Marina Bathing Pool** and main sands. This pool is the third largest in the country, and with the adjoining café and sun lounges, is one of the gayest parts of the shore.

A Walk Westward

On the western side of the harbour a good main road connects the two cliffs. The **Royal Parade,** with its arches and balustrades, gives access to the West Cliff by an easy gradient. The level road beneath the upper approach is known as the Military Road, and is chiefly used as one of the Harbour quays.

At the Paragon is the **West Cliff Hall** built into the cliff and commanding fine views while farther along the top promenade is the picturesque **Model Village,** a delightful miniature village set amidst trees and gardens.

St. Augustine's Abbey Church (Roman Catholic) stands in St. Augustine's Road, beyond the Concert Hall and the Model Village, on the promenade. Designed and paid for by A. W. Pugin, the famous Gothic Revival architect (1812–52), it is regarded as his most characteristic achievement. The building was opened in 1851 but the tower and spire have never been completed. The interior furnishings are outstanding examples of early Victoria craftsmanship. In 1856 the church was handed over to Benedictine monks who today have charge of the nine Roman Catholic parishes in Thanet and act as chaplains to seven convents. Adjacent to the Church is the Grange, built by A. W. Pugin as his residence, now used as part of the College.

On the opposite side of the road are the Abbey and St. Augustine's College (Day and Boarding). Both buildings are of later date than the Church, and were designed by Edward Pugin, with additions by his brother, Peter Paul Pugin.

The West Cliff

The West Cliff forms a fine western wing to Ramsgate and is the most sheltered part of the town. Below the cliff is the long **Western Undercliff** promenade, a delightful sun-trap sheltered from cold winds. This promenade communicates with the cliff top by a lift, by sloped paths and, at the west end, by a cleverly constructed **Chine.** An artificial beach has been made adjacent to the Undercliff, with modern bathing chalets, car park and café, and a children's paddling pool.

The principal feature of the cliff-top scheme is the **Prince Edward Promenade** and the dual carriageway known as **Royal Esplanade.** These are separated by grassy plots, and on the seaward side of the Royal Esplanade is another green expanse, including bowling-greens, putting-greens and miniature golf-courses. The centrepiece of this very extensive scheme is the Children's Boating Lake flanked by two semicircular pavilions, one a restaurant, and forming windscreens.

The first left-hand turning from **Grange Road,** at the eastern end of the new promenades, leads to Pegwell Bay and the London Road running north-westward to the Canterbury Road at Nether Court. Close to Grange Road is the Southwood football ground where the Ramsgate Athletic F.C. (Southern League) play. Grange Road leads in three-quarters of a mile to –

Ellington Park. This park is a delightful open space, close to the Station, and easily reached from the front by bus. Though only twelve acres in extent, it is one of the most beautiful of its kind in the country, with its greenery and shade in pleasant contrast to the gold and blue of the shore. Magnificent trees screen north and east winds. Refreshments can be obtained at the kiosk.

Ramsgate Railway Station is served by frequent buses. The prominent red-brick building in the valley is the **St. Lawrence College,** one of the youngest of our Public Schools.

Close at hand is the **Warre Recreation Ground.** At Northwood, close to the Margate Road, is **Jackey Baker's Sports Ground,** of 41 acres, providing excellent facilities for cricket, football and hockey. Hockey festivals and International matches are events held here.

Returning to the front by way of High Street, note, in Chatham Street, the **Chatham House County Grammar School for Boys** and Townley House, where Queen Victoria lived as a child.

The next left-hand turning leads to –

St. George's Church, the tower and hexagonal lantern of which are conspicuous from all parts of the town. St. George's is the parish church of Ramsgate, and was erected in 1824, Queen Victoria with her mother being present at the consecration service. The building is in the florid Gothic style of the Georgian era. There is some modern stained glass commemorating Dunkirk. The tower, which has a certain resemblance to those of Ely and Boston, is 137 feet high. The Trinity House authorities made a contribution of £1,000 in order that the tower might be surmounted by a lantern which would serve as a landmark. It contains a peal of tubular bells.

On the right of the High Street is George Street, leading to the **Congregational Church** and the **Public Library.**

Close at hand is the **General Post Office.**

St. Lawrence is a scattered parish a short distance north-west of Ellington Park.

The ancient **Church of St. Laurence** is of great interest. It stands on a hill, and its massive square tower is prominent. The church attained its present form about 1200, a smaller building having occupied the site from about 1062. It was one of the three chapels-of-ease to Minster until 1275, when it was made parochial. The windows of the tower and the arches which support it are Norman, as are also the bays in the nave, and possibly the south porch. The tower was restored and new clock faces inserted as a memorial of Queen Victoria's Jubilee. In the South Chapel are brasses of Nicholas Manston (1444) and Joan Manston.

Viking Ship 'Hugin', Pegwell Bay

Places near Ramsgate

Manston lies two miles from Ramsgate by way of St. Lawrence. The Mansons of Manston Court were an important Kentish family, one being Sheriff of the county in the reign of Henry VI. The scanty remains of the ancient mansion are built into a farmhouse.

Manston Aerodrome, for many years a famous military air base, is now used jointly as a civil terminal for air services to and from the Continent and by the R.A.F. The Royal Air Force Station was famous in both World Wars. A Spitfire, which flew in Fighter operations during World War II, is maintained as a memorial and can be seen near the road running past the Station Headquarters.

Ozengell, a farmhouse, midway between St. Lawrence and Manston, at the junction of the Sandwich and Canterbury roads, is noted for the valuable finds made in 1845, when the railway was constructed. Among the discoveries was a pair of bronze scales, with a set of weights formed out of Roman coins, now in the Liverpool Museum.

Pegwell Bay, a mile west of Ramsgate Harbour, is finely shaped, but the flatness of the coast and the expanse of sand exposed at low water, rather spoil it. The mouth of the River Stour can be seen across the bay. Pegwell is renowned for its shrimps, which may be bought fresh, or potted and pasted. Amateur shrimpers are warned that the sands are in places very treacherous.

A modern development is the **International Hoverport** on the shore from which daily flights operate to Calais. There are spectator and refreshment facilities.

By the buses which go on to Minster, turn inland and ascend Chilton Hill, from which there is a good prospect of Richborough and the bay. Then the road descends to the sea at **Cliffsend** *(Sportsman Inn)*, where the cliffs that guard the coast of Thanet end abruptly. The main road to Sandwich goes straight on, fringing the low sandy foreshore, which is here thickly strewn with seashells. A branch road to **Minster** turns right at the *Sportsman Inn*, and then sharply left, and runs through lavender fields and cherry orchards, past the golf-links and dyked marshes with grazing sheep, to join the Minster-Sandwich road rather more than a mile from Cliffsend.

Two Historic Landings. We are now on historic ground. It was with the landing of Hengist and his war-band at **Ebbsfleet** (449) that English history began. To commemorate the 1,500th anniversary of this historic occasion a stone was unveiled in the vicinity by H.H. Prince Georg of Denmark on 29th July, 1949. Also at this spot is the Viking Ship *Hugin*, an exact replica of the vessel in which Hengist sailed to Britain.

It is curious that yet another famous landing should have taken place on this very spot. It was in August, 597, that Augustine and his forty monks arrived on that mission to the Saxon Ethelbert which was to be fraught with such momentous consequences. Although Queen Bertha was a Christian, and was attended at court by a French bishop, the King knew so little of the new religion that he stipulated that

MINSTER-MONKTON

Augustine's first interview with him should on no account be held under a roof, but in the open air, as he feared the charms and spells of the strangers. The traditional spot where the meeting took place is by some lavender gardens on the Minster road, where it is crossed by the railway line near the Golf House, and is marked by a **Cross,** erected by the late Lord Granville in 1884.

Close to the Cross are the **St. Augustine's Golf-Links,** three miles distant from either Ramsgate or Sandwich. There is a service of buses running from Margate, Westgate and Birchington past the the club-house to Ramsgate and back. **St. Augustine's Well,** a natural spring said to have appeared when St. Augustine asked for water, lies on the golf-course, but permission to visit it is readily granted by the Secretary.

Five miles from Ramsgate is –

Minster

Minster is much visited on account of its famous church, and has some lovely orchards and lanes. It has a few picturesque old houses and cottages, the oldest being an admirably preserved sixteenth-century cottage, now in use as a restaurant.

The **Church** is cruciform in shape, and consists of a Late Norman nave, two side aisles, and Early English chancel and transepts. The tower has a fine Norman doorway, and three stages of circular-headed windows. Parts of the existing building and the adjoining abbey ruins date from the eleventh century. At the south-east corner of the tower is a Saxon stair-turret traditionally said to be a watch-tower for shipping.

The monastery and church associated with Domneva and Mildred were dedicated to St. Mary, and occupied the site of the present church. In 738, St. Edburga, who had succeeded St. Mildred as Abbess, founded a second church and abbey, dedicated to SS. Peter and Paul. About the year 840 marauding Danes destroyed all the buildings with the exception of the original conventual church of St. Mary, but the foundations of St. Peter's were discovered by excavation in 1929. The lands were eventually assigned to the monks of St. Augustine's, Canterbury, under whom the present church was in great part built.

Minster Abbey lies a few yards north-east of the churchyard. It was built on the site of St. Edburga's monastery, established in the seventh century. The Abbey was given by Canute to St. Augustine's Abbey in Canterbury in A.D. 1027. Later the Manor House was built as a residence for the monks. It was described in the Domesday Book of 1086, and is said to be one of the oldest houses in England still inhabited. In 1937 the Abbey was transferred from private ownership to nuns of the Benedictine Order.

The ruins are open to inspection daily 11–12 and 2.30–5, except Sundays, and Saturday afternoons between 3 and 4 p.m. There is no admission fee, but donations to the Abbey Restoration Fund are gratefully received. The interior of the Abbey is not shown, but the site of St. Mildred's Tomb, the early thirteenth-century Doomstone in its picturesque arch, as well as the ruins of the church are of extreme interest, also several ancient trees in the beautiful gardens. The whole place seems to give an impression of peace and continuity not found in uninhabited ruins.

Monkton, about midway between Minster and Sarre, has some beautiful farms and old houses, and an interesting church, with a plain square tower and long nave, outside which may be seen the old parish stocks. In the church are a fine brass in memory of a priest, dated 1460, and a good Jacobean pulpit.

The Goodwin Sands

are about seven miles from Ramsgate in the direction of Deal, and extend parallel with the coast for about ten miles from north to south, with an average breadth of two miles. In fine weather motor-boats put off almost daily from Ramsgate and Broadstairs for trips to the Goodwins; landings are occasionally made at low water.

The Goodwins are at once a safeguard and a danger to shipping. The great sandbank acts as a natural breakwater, protecting from north and east winds a deep channel known as **The Downs.** This is open to the south, but is sheltered by the land from the most prevalent winds, except when they are of extraordinary velocity. Tradition ascribes the name of the sands to the fact that they once formed part of an island belonging to Earl Godwin, the father of Harold. A remarkable fact concerning the sands is that they are steadily moving landward and, some authorities believe, will eventually join, or rejoin, the mainland.

At low tide the sands are visible from Ramsgate to Deal as a brownish streak across the water, and in fair weather it is possible to land and walk about on them with perfect safety. Wrecks and seals can be seen, but directly the water rises, the sands become soft, and their power of suction is so strong that the largest vessel driven upon them and left is swallowed up in a few days. Several attempts have been made, notably by Smeaton, to erect lighthouses, but nothing in the nature of a satisfactory foundation has been discovered. A chain of light-ships, the beams of which are seen at night from the cliffs at Ramsgate, serve the same purpose. Many a story might be told of vessels now interned in this dismal ocean graveyard.

The Cinque Ports

The original Cinque Ports were Hastings, Sandwich, Dover, Romney, and Hythe. hence the application to them of the word "cinque," the old French equivalent of five. Later, the "Ancient Towns" of Winchelsea and Rye were added, making seven, but the old French name was retained. To each of the head Ports were attached a number of "limbs" – not always coast towns – some of which were corporate, others non-corporate. Several of the smaller "limbs" have entirely disappeared, and of the head Ports Dover is now the only one of maritime importance. The jurisdiction of the Ports extended from Birchington to Seaford in Sussex.

From the time of the Romans there was a defensive system along the exposed south-east coast, under the leadership of the Count of the Saxon Shore. William the Conqueror changed that title to Lord Warden of the Cinque Ports, but retained the function of the Confederacy. In the thirteenth century the fleet of the Cinque Ports was powerful enough to vie with the whole French navy. In 1229 Henry III prescribed that the Ports should provide fifty-seven ships, to serve the King at their own expense for fifteen days each year. The number of ships to be furnished by each Port gives a good idea of the relative importance of the towns at the time. Dover had to send twenty-one, Winchelsea ten, Hastings six, and Sandwich, Hythe, Romney and Rye five each.

As compensation for their burdens, special privileges were granted to the Ports. The towns were self-governed; their freemen bore the honourable title of "barons," and traded toll-free in every corporation in the kingdom. They were exempt from military duties and had the privilege, referred to by Shakespeare, and reasserted at the coronations of King Edward VII and King George V, of bearing a canopy of cloth of gold or silk over the King and Queen.

The last sortie of the Ports was against the Spanish Armada; but even then their era was ending, for the "Eastward Drift" of shingle and sand from Dungeness to the Thames estuary was silting up the harbours. Now those of Hastings, Romney and Hythe have long been built upon. Sandwich is now nearly two miles from the sea; and even Dover harbour is maintained only by incessant labour.

The arms of the Confederation of the Cinque Ports consists of three half lions and three half ships (the stern).

Modern legislation has shorn the Cinque Ports of most of their ancient privileges, but they are still. independent of county jurisdiction in many important particulars. The honorary office of **Lord Warden** has been held by many eminent statesmen, including William Pitt, the Duke of Wellington, Lord Palmerston, Earl Granville, the Marquis of Dufferin, Mr. W. H. Smith, the Marquis of Salisbury, Lord Curzon of Kedleston, King George V when Prince of Wales, Lord Brassey, and Sir Winston Churchill. The present holder of the office is Sir Robert Menzies. Except for a short break, Walmer Castle has been for over two centuries the official residence of the Lord Warden.

Sandwich

Access. – By bus or train from Ramsgate, Margate, Herne Bay, Canterbury, Deal, Dover, etc. Through connections from London.

Banks. – *Barclays*, The Market; *Lloyds*, 12 Market Street; *National Westminster*, 21 Market Street; *Midland*, 12 Cattle Market.

Car Parks. – The Market Place, where a market is held every Thursday; The Quay.

Cinemas. – Delf Street.

Distances. – Ramsgate, 6¾; Canterbury, 13; Deal, 6; Dover, 13; London, 69; Margate, 9.

Early Closing Day. – Wednesday.

Golf. – The famous golf-links of the *Royal St. George's Club*, the "St. Andrews of England," are a mile and a half from the station,

and are approached by a road branching from the only road from Sandwich to the sea-shore. This is one of the six courses upon which the Open Championships are played, and one of the five on which the Amateur Championships are decided.

The links of the *Prince's Golf Club* adjoin those of the Royal St. George's. North of that again, at Ebbsfleet, are the *St. Augustine's Links*.

Hotels. – *Bell*, High Street; *Guildford*, Sandwich Bay; *Fleur-de-Lis*, Delf Street; *Haven*, Harnet Street; *King's Arms*, Strand Street.

Population. – 4,620.

Post Office. – King Street.

A visit to the ancient port of Sandwich, the chief of the Cinque Ports of Kent, should on no account be omitted. The sea, now 1½ miles distant, is approached by a good road (toll for cars), and the shore has the finest stretch of sand and offers the best bathing to be found on this coast, while the lovely mellow old town has succeeded all through the centuries in retaining a pleasant flavour of the sea. The flavour, however, is not altogether that of an English port; the Flemings and the Dutch have left their mark in quaint gables and overhanging storeys, while it has also many of the characteristics of a little country market town. The huge churches – out of all proportion to the Sandwich of today – attest its former importance.

Historical Note. – The origin of the name *Sandwic*, the village on the sands, is obvious. After the Roman occupation Richborough, or Rutupiae, ceased to be the chief port, and the Saxons followed the receding sea to Stonar and Sandwich. The latter became one of the leading members of the Cinque Ports confederacy, and even during the Saxon period was spoken of as "the most famous of all the ports of England." The Danes frequently attacked and captured the place, using it as a base for further operations. Here Sweyn and Canute landed in 1013. Subsequently, as the great port of embarkation for France, and the landing-place for Continental pilgrims to Becket's shrine at Canterbury, Sandwich played an important part in many of the leading events of English history. The same cause which had ruined the port of Richborough was, however, slowly operating also at Sandwich, and towards the end of the fifteenth century the haven became quite impassible for ships of any size. The declining fortunes of the town were to some extent restored by a large influx of Dutch and Flemish refugees during the religious persecutions of the fifteenth and sixteenth centuries. These industrious folk introduced the woollen and other trades, and so flourished that they soon formed a third of the population.

The Barbican and bridge, Sandwich

The bus station and car park are in the Market Place, and Sandwich should be explored thence on foot, as it is most essentially a place for leisurely sightseeing.

The gem of the town is the ancient **Barbican** and toll-house by the swingbridge at the north end of High Street. The lower part is of alternate colours, chessboard fashion; the upper storey is of wood roofed with red tiles. A stroll of a few yards eastward along the river bank leads to the flint **Fisher Gate,** the only one left of the original five, and now scheduled as an Ancient Monument. It was through the Fisher Gate that Becket passed on his last visit to Canterbury.

Pass through Fisher Gate up Quay Lane, turn left along Upper Strand Street and round Hog's Corner to —

St. Clement's Church, with an arcaded Norman tower, justly considered one of the finest in Kent. St. Clement's was designated the parish church in 1948. The church consists of a Perpendicular nave, its fine roof ornamented with gilded bosses, two spacious aisles, and an Early English chancel. The tower arches are Norman; note the beautifully preserved carving of the tympanum over the tower staircase door, and the fine fifteenth-century font with heraldic decoration. The organ cases to the west of the aisles are fine specimens of contemporary English craftsmanship. The outer doors of the porch bear the date 1655, worked with round-headed nails.

Continue past the Church up a short lane to an asphalted path, known as the **Mill Wall,** forming part of the rampart formerly on the east, west and south sides of the town.

Pass to the right along the wall, with good views of the many-roofed town, commanded by St. Clement's Norman tower and the bulbous spire of St. Peter's, to New Street. To the left is the **Railway Station,** nearly opposite St. Bartholomew's Almshouse. A house in New Street bears a plaque "Tom Payne lived here *c.* 1759". Thomas Payne, born in 1737, was author of *Common Sense* and a major contributor to the founding of American independence.

In the other direction New Street leads into the heart of Sandwich. **St. Peter's Church,** dating from the twelfth century, is soon reached by a side turning on the right. The south aisle was wrecked by the fall of the tower in 1661, and has never been rebuilt. This church is now the chapel of Sir Roger Manwood's School. The north aisle contains three tombs, the central one a fine one to Thomas Elys, founder of St. Thomas's Hospital.

New Street ends at the **Market.** Here is the **Guildhall,** erected 1579, but having a modern face, on which are displayed the ancient arms of the town. *Admission charge:* 10.30–12.30, 2–4.

Other ancient and beautiful buildings border the Market Place, which should be left by the street named Moat Sole (*Sole-Pond*). Here is **St. Thomas's Hospital,** an ancient institution housed in comparatively modern buildings. The Hospital stood just inside the Woodnesborough Gate of Sandwich. Nothing of the Gate remains, but the Town Wall may be traced to the right, past the field still known as *The Butts.* Loop Street leads from the wall by some beautiful old houses to **St. Mary's Church,** an extraordinary assemblage of styles. Its present odd appearance is due to the collapse of the tower in 1667 when nearly all but the outward walls was destroyed. This church has recently been restored, and occasional services are held. The roof beams, now exposed, are of considerable interest. The mediaeval Peter's Pence box should be noted as also the springs of the original Norman arcading in the west wall.

St. Mary's Church projects into Strand Street, or the Canterbury Road, and those bound for the Roman remains at Richborough (*see* p. 52) should turn leftward, passing **Manwood Court,** an old building bearing the date 1564. It was erected and endowed as a free grammar school by Sir Roger Manwood (1525–92).

After being in abeyance for some time, **Sir Roger Manwood's Grammar School** was reopened in 1895, new buildings having been erected opposite the King's Field, Manwood Road.

RICHBOROUGH CASTLE

Richborough Castle

Admission charge. – March–April, 9.30–5.30, 2–5.30 Sundays; May–September, 9.30–7; October, 9.30–5.30, 2–5.30 Sundays; November–February, 9.30–4, 2–4 Sundays.

The length and even height of the massive walls of Richborough Castle, which crown the old island and overlook rich river pasture lands, make them appear low when seen from the road and railway. It is only when they loom close that their forbidding bulk is fully appreciated. They are one of the most remarkable relics of the Roman occupation of Britain and of intense interest both to archæologists and laymen, who in the carefully exposed and preserved foundations can read the story of the might and far-reaching power of the early Roman Empire. Many of the objects found in the course of excavations are exhibited in **The Museum** near the entrance.

Richborough and Reculver, known to the Romans as *Rutupiae* and *Regulbium*, guarded respectively the south and the north entrances to the mile-wide channel of the Wantsume, which at that time separated the Isle of Thanet from the mainland. Rutupiae was the principal landing place and base for the legions crossing from the opposite coast of Boulogne under the Emperor Claudius in A.D. 43. From that time it was inhabited continuously through the whole period of the Roman occupation, and served as one of the principal ports for continental traffic, from which the great Roman road, later known as Watling Street ran to Canterbury, London and the north. During its existence of nearly 400 years it passed through many vicissitudes, changing during the first century from a military to a peaceful commercial and administrative centre. The early wooden buildings of the first settlement were

Richborough Castle

destroyed to make room for a huge concrete foundation with a super-structure of Italian marble embellished with marble, bronze and gilded statues. Many fragments which have been found and are gradually being pieced together are evidence of the elaborate nature of the building, which must have had unusual distinction for a distant Roman province. Well-built flint dwelling-houses dating from this period must have been occupied by superior officers. About the middle of the third century, when the raiding Saxons first made their appearance, Rutupiae became again a military post, and the central monument fell into decay. A small fort defended by an earthen mound and stockade surrounded by three deep ditches was constructed. This, however, was soon found to be insufficient, and the fort now represented by the massive ruined walls was built in its place. The 2nd Legion was moved here from Caerleon in South Wales, and it was probably the headquarters of the officer styled "Count of the Saxon Shore." It is also probable that Richborough served as a naval base for the fleet operating against the Saxons.

This site, which saw the first coming of the invading legions, was also the last to be evacuated by them in the early years of the fifth century, and many of the troops must have passed through the port when returning to the Continent. Whether or no it was garrisoned by the British until a late date is uncertain, but it evidently continued as a landing-place for travellers and invaders until the later port of Sandwich came into existence.

The imposing walls of the Castle are still in wonderful preservation on the north and west, although on the south local inhabitants for hundreds of years took toll of the stones, as far as the marvellous Roman cement would allow, for building material.

The walls give an idea of what the stronghold must have been like in its prime, and in the west wall the remains of the gateway through which Watling Street passes is a vivid reminder of the distant past, when the walls echoed the challenge of Roman sentries. In any mental picture it must be borne in mind that the sea then flowed right up to the foot of the promontory or cliff on which the castle stands, in such a way as to make it an island at high tide, and that in addition to the castle there was here an important Roman town.

The castle walls are formed of seven courses of squared grits and Portland stone of unequal size, bonded at intervals by double rows of large flat tiles, mostly of bright red colour. Each company officer had charge of the building of one section, and all along the walls individual characteristics and small variations can be seen in the construction details of each section. In the north wall is a bastion containing a small postern gate.

In the centre of the fort will be seen a cruciform mass of concrete raised slightly above the grass; this is thought to be of the same period as the main foundation – c. 85 A.D. – and to be part of the structure of a four-way triumphal arch in marble. This cross rests on a platform of masonry, 146 feet long and 106 feet wide, which goes down to a depth of 30 feet. The upper 5 feet of the platform projects from 10 to 12 feet over a **Subterranean Passage** to which access is given by modern concrete steps.

The whole site is beautifully tended, and great care has been taken to show which parts are the original Roman work, as exposed by the excavations, and which are modern paths and steps made for the benefit of visitors and ensuring easy access to every part.

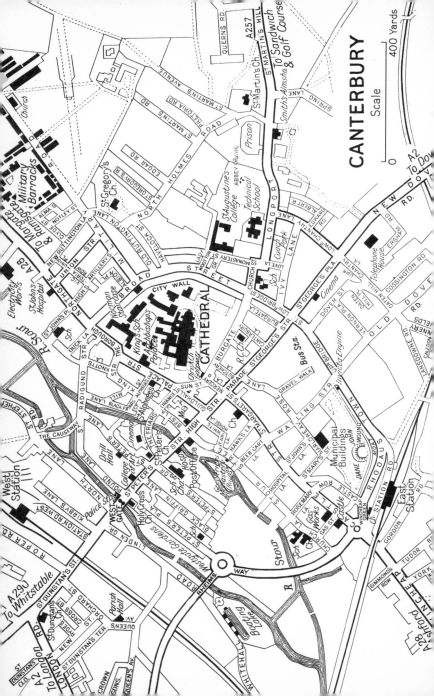

CANTERBURY

Scale

0 400 Yards

Canterbury

Canterbury, the chief cathedral city of the kingdom (its Archbishop bears the title Primate of All England), is the goal of thousands of pilgrims and visitors throughout the year.

It is a flourishing country town with busy cattle and general markets. Its ancient buildings and the beautiful Cathedral provide so much of historical interest that it is essential that one's visit should be leisurely, with time to savour the principal items.

Historical Note. – Canterbury was probably called into being by the need for a depot, in connection with the various ports on the Kent coast. Recent excavations have shown that the site was occupied in the early Iron Age (second and third century B.C.). As the road from these ports into the heart of England increased in importance, so flourished Canterbury, the first and last city upon that road. It was

Ethelbert's capital at the time of his conversion (597) to Christianity, and that monarch gave to Augustine his palace at Canterbury, as well as the Roman church of St. Martin (which had already been used for some time for Christian worship by Queen Bertha) and, according to tradition, his pagan temple which Augustine proceeded to dedicate to St. Pancras, who had a church in Rome close to the monastery from which Augustine had come.

Augustine founded the Abbey which still bears his name. (It was originally a Benedictine Monastery dedicated to SS. Peter and Paul.) For a number of years this Abbey was of much greater importance than the Cathedral, being the burial-place of the kings and queens of Kent, of Augustine himself and of various succeeding archbishops. In 758, Cuthbert, having recently built a new chapel in the Cathedral, directed that he should be buried therein – an interment which the monks did not dare announce until it was a *fait accompli* – and after this only one archbishop was buried in the Abbey. Consequently, when Becket was murdered, it was in the Cathedral that he was buried, it was to the Cathedral that Henry II made his amazing pilgrimage, and it was the Cathedral which received the priceless gifts of the pilgrims who flocked to the shrine during the ensuing 300 years.

For the accommodation of pilgrims various inns and lodging-houses were established and the city grew prosperous on an immense tourist traffic. The Grey Friars, or Franciscans, established their first English foundation at Canterbury in 1224, while some years afterwards the Black Friars and White Friars also established a community.

In 1538, however, Henry VIII issued his mock writ of summons accusing Becket (who had been dead 300 years) of treachery, and challenging the ghostly delinquent to appear and give an account of the deeds done in the flesh. The outcome of Becket's non-appearance at Westminster was that his shrine was despoiled.

Despite this, and later spoliation by the Puritans, the Cathedral remains a very beautiful building. War bombing inflicted ugly scars on the city and some of its characteristic features, including the fine old Corn Market, were destroyed, but happily most of its more precious possessions remained intact. The Cathedral suffered only superficial damage, but the Cathedral Library was destroyed, as also was the historic St. George's Church, in the main street. The library has now been rebuilt. The modern buildings which have now been erected have been the subject of commendation by eminent authorities.

Entering the city from the London road by St. Dunstan's Street, on the corner is seen the **Church of St. Dunstan-without-the-Westgate,** principally of fifteenth-century construction. At the eastern end of the south aisle are monuments to the Roper family and beneath, in the family vault, is the severed head of Sir Thomas More (1535). On the opposite side of the road from the church is a brick gateway, sole remnant of the house where his daughter, Margaret Roper, lived.

At No. 71 St. Dunstan's Street is the *House of Agnes*, now an hotel, and the house described by Dickens in his *David Copperfield*. Opposite is the *Falstaff*, a fifteenth-century inn with some old oak panelling and beautiful ironwork from which its sign is hung. It is but a few steps to the West Gate of the ancient city.

The West Gate

The massive West Gate, with its double towers, was erected on the site of earlier structures by Archbishop Simon of Sudbury and completed in 1380. Situated at the river crossing where most of the continental traffic landing in Kent converged, its position throughout history was the most important in Canterbury. The present building incorporates some Roman bricks. From about 1430 to 1829 it was used as the city gaol. Indeed, a debtor was confined here as recently as 1847. This interesting relic has been preserved as an Ancient Monument, and is

Ancient Falstaff Hotel, Canterbury

now used as a **Museum** *(small charge, daily except Sundays,* 10–1, 2–6; *Oct.–March* 2–4*)*. Among objects of interest may be mentioned the old condemned cell, a collection of old arms and armour, constables' staves, etc; a "boneshaker" cycle and a machine of the type that cyclists of 1886 called "ordinary". Visitors should ascend by the newel staircase to the top of the tower for the sake of the fine view of the Cathedral, the surrounding city and the river.

Holy Cross Church to the right of West Gate was originally situated over the former gate, but was rebuilt on its present site by Archbishop Simon in 1380. It contains some good ironwork; a fifteenth-century font with wood cover, and ancient wood-carving, and one of its bells dates from the fourteenth century.

Behind the church are the pretty Westgate Gardens overlooking the placid stream. The gardens follow in part the line of the old Roman walls of the city and near the church may be seen an embattled tower (rebuilt).

Within the city walls St. Dunstan's Street has given place to St. Peter's Street, on the left of which is the **College of Art,** founded on the site of his birthplace by T. S. Cooper, the Victorian artist. Beyond this, at the corner of St. Peter's Lane, is the diminutive **St. Peter's Church.** Incorporated in its small tower are a number of Roman tile fragments.

The main river branch is crossed by **King's Bridge,** and flanking the water are the old **Canterbury Weaver's Houses,** half-timbered Ghent-like buildings whose gables overhang the river. Huguenot and Walloon weavers set up their looms here after their persecution in 1685 and began for Canterbury a considerable industry.

On the other side of the street is –

St. Thomas's Hospital, or Eastbridge Hospital as it is now sometimes known, was founded 1180 by Edward FitzOsbold with the intention of providing temporary accommodation for the poor pilgrims who flocked to the shrine of St. Thomas of Canterbury, murdered ten years previously. The buildings were completed in 1203. The former great gateway has disappeared. The present entrance leads into a vaulted hall, on the left of which is a small fourteenth-century chantry chapel. The Refectory is somewhat shorter than originally, part of its length having been pulled down to provide space for cottages for the in-sisters. In 1879 a chimney built against the wall was removed and an early thirteenth-century mural revealed. The refectory table dates from 1630. The gallery is modern but is made from ancient panelling.

The **Royal Museum and Public Library** in High Street has an ornate facade. The **Museum** *(open free weekdays)*, recently modernised, is of great interest.

Those wishing to press on to the Cathedral should continue down High Street and turn left into Mercery Lane, which leads on to the Christ Church Gate entrance. Others who wish to see first other parts of the city should take the turning opposite the Royal Museum.

Along Stour Street on the right is the entrance to the remains of **Grey Friars,** partly strung across a narrow channel of the river. This was the first Franciscan friary in England and was built on this site about 1267. There were considerable buildings, but that seen today is the remains of the Dorter and an old boundary wall.

The building in Stour Street now occupied by the City's Health services is the much-altered **Poor Priest's Hospital,** at one time an almshouse for poor clergy. It was originally established about 1220 and rebuilt in 1373.

At the end of Stour Street, Church Lane leads to –

St. Mildred's Church, perhaps the most interesting and most ancient of the Canterbury churches. Roman tiles are built into the walls of the nave. Note the fine beams, fifteenth-century font and cover with elaborate iron pulley bracket characteristic of many of the Kent churches, and the sixteenth-century door on the north. The Thomas Cranmer commemorated on the south wall was a nephew of the Archbishop. Izaak Walton, of *Compleat Angler* fame, was married here in 1626.

In a by-road off Wincheap is the **Martyr's Memorial,** perpetuating the memory of the Kentish Martyrs (thirty men and eleven women) who suffered under Queen Mary I (1555–1558).

Near at hand is the **Norman Castle,** of which only the shell of the Keep remains. This massive square keep is generally attributed, on account of the marked similarity of design, to Bishop Gundulph, who built Rochester Castle and the White Tower, or central keep, of the Tower of London. The lower part of the walls are 11 feet thick.

Following the line of the old city walls we come to –

The Dane John Gardens, a pleasant recreation ground chiefly remarkable for its fine avenue, over 1,000 feet in length, of lofty limes, and for its huge artificial Mound, thought originally to have been a Roman-British burial site.

In the moat on the south side of the mound is displayed the capstan from Nelson's flagship *Foudroyant*. The garden also contains a monument to *Christopher Marlowe*, who was born in Canterbury in 1564.

At the entrance to the gardens in Watling Street is the valiant locomotive *Invicta*, built by Stephenson in 1830, and second only in point of interest to the famous "Rocket". The Invicta did service on the Canterbury and Whitstable Railway, the first line to be opened in the south of England.

In St. George's Street will be seen the Tower with its early twelfth-century door – the only remains of the old St. George's Church where Marlowe was christened.

In Butchery Lane may be seen the **Roman Pavement,** by far the most interesting of the remains discovered as a result of excavations after war damage. This mosaic pavement, together with hypocaust (heating chamber) also discovered, formed part of a large building erected about A.D. 100.

A little further along the Parade, Mercery Lane leads to the Cathedral. On the corner, incorporated with modern shops, is the stone arcade of the famous **Chequers of the Hope,** a celebrated hostelry which sheltered pilgrims, among them Chaucer.

THE CATHEDRAL

Admission. – All parts of the Cathedral are open free. Sunday 7–7.30; Weekdays (summer) 7–7, (winter) 7–6.15; Saturdays till 5.

Official Guides conduct visitors over the Cathedral by appointment. Arrangements to be made at least 14 days beforehand with the Secretary of the Guides Office (Tel. 63135). No charge is made for the services of the guides and no gratuities are to be given. Offerings, placed in boxes provided, are gratefully received. Guides are not available on Sundays, but the Cathedral is open to view until half an hour before each service.

Dimensions. – Length of Cathedral interior, 514 ft., exterior, 530 ft.; length of nave, 220 ft.; choir, 180 ft. Height of nave, 80 ft.; choir, 71 ft. Breadth of nave, 72 ft.; choir, 40 ft. Height of Central Tower, 235 ft. Western Towers, 156 ft. 8 in. Crypt, or Undercroft, 163 ft. long, 83½ ft. wide. For times of Services, *see* notices.

In the words of Dean Stanley, "There is no church, no place in the kingdom, with the exception of Westminster Abbey, that is so closely connected with the history of our country as Canterbury Cathedral."

During the Second World War numerous bombs fell in the Precincts, but the main building fortunately escaped serious injury. The Library was destroyed and has since been rebuilt.

Historical Note. – As already stated Canterbury was Ethelbert's capital at the time of his conversion (597). The earliest Cathedral was erected by Augustine on the site of Ethelbert's palace about the end of the sixth century.

With William came the energetic Lanfranc, and he put the rebuilding of Canterbury Cathedral in hand with so much zest that the work was completed in seven years. His work, however, did not please Anselm, his successor, who pulled down and rebuilt the eastern part, the choir itself being completed under Anselm's successor with such beauty that it became known as "Prior Conrad's Glorious Choir." Despite fire damage again in 1174 some of the outer structure of Conrad's Choir remained.

William of Sens and William the Englishman, during the next ten years, recon-

Canterbury Cathedral

structed and extended the Choir, leaving it much as we see it today. The side screens were added in 1305. Lanfranc's Norman nave, however, was pulled down about the end of the fourteenth century and replaced by the present Perpendicular nave. Finally, about a century later, Cardinal Morton added the central tower, and Prior Goldstone built Christchurch Gate.

The Exterior

Christ Church Gate, by which the Cathedral precincts are entered, was built in 1517 by Prior Goldstone II. It is a beautiful specimen of Perpendicular work, restored in 1935–7 to its former loveliness. The turrets, which in the last century were lowered to provide a local resident with a clear view of the Cathedral clock, have been re-erected, the stone-work faced and the painted heraldry revived. The oak doors date from the time of Charles II. Opposite is the Canterbury **War Memorial.**

The **South-West Porch,** the principal entrance to the Cathedral, was completed about 1420. The figures in the canopied niches are about a 100 years old. In the central space is a defaced representation of the "Altar of the Sword's Point".

The Interior

The Nave was built in the latter half of the fourteenth century, and is in the Perpendicular style. It has a remarkable resemblance to the nave of Winchester Cathedral, which was built at the same time. The series of clustered pillars have been aptly called a forest of stone. The aisles are narrow and very lofty.

North Aisle. – In the third bay from the west stands the *Font*, of extraordinary shape, dating from 1639. The *Pulpit* is of oak, with decorative gilding. Near the east end is a monument erected by the captain, officers and men of H.M.S. *Kent* to commemorate their comrades who fell in the battle of Falkland Isles (December 8, 1914). Throughout the Cathedral, indeed, are numerous monuments recalling the fighting traditions of Canterbury.

The piers supporting the central tower are the original piers of Lanfranc's church, but cased with Perpendicular work by Chillenden. The **Choir Screen,** adorned with six figures of kings, is fine fifteenth-century work.

The **Choir,** most important example of Early Gothic architecture in the country, was built 1174–1184. The pointed and the rounded arch are used almost indiscriminately. The peculiar contraction of the walls at the head of the choir was rendered necessary by the fact that the chapels of St. Anselm and St. Andrew had escaped the fire, and William of Sens had promised the conservative monks that in rebuilding he would preserve all he could of the old structure.

The Decorated Screen which surrounds the choir was constructed by Prior of Eastry (1284–1331). The north doorway, still perfect, is remarkably fine. The Episcopal *Throne* was the gift of Archbishop Howley in 1844.

The Monuments in and about the choir are best seen from the side aisles. They are all of archbishops, mostly of the fourteenth and fifteenth centuries.

The **South-West Transept** was built in the fifteenth century. Leading out of this is –

St. Michael's, or the **Warriors' Chapel,** in the Perpendicular style. It is longer than when it was built in the eleventh century, the newer east wall passing across the tomb of *Stephen Langton,* the leader of the barons who wrung Magna Carta from King John.

St. Anselm's Chapel was originally dedicated to SS. Peter and Paul, and an interesting relic of this saintly patronage is a fresco representing St. Paul shaking off the viper at Melita. Above the chapel is a small *Watching Chamber,* in which a guard was stationed at night to protect the treasures of Becket's shrine.

The **Pilgrims' Steps,** the deep indentations in which tell of countless pilgrimages, lead up to –

Trinity Chapel, specially built to receive the *Shrine of Thomas Becket.* The site of the shrine is shown by the marks worn in the stone of generations of pilgrims. The mosaic pavement is very curious, resembling that in the sanctuary at Westminster.

A more tangible historical memorial than the blank space of Becket's shrine is afforded by the adjacent **Tomb of Edward the Black Prince** (*d.,* 1376). The figure is clad in full armour, the hands clasped in prayer. The under side of the canopy is painted with a representation of the Trinity. Above hang replicas of the warrior's brazen gauntlets, the "casque which never stooped except to time," the shield of wood, and the coat of leather sewn with silk and emblazoned with the arms of France and England. (The originals are in a glass case at the foot of the Pilgrim's Steps.)

Immediately opposite the tomb of the Black Prince is that of *Henry IV* (1413), the only monarch buried in the Cathedral, and his second consort, Joan of Navarre.

The circular chapel at the extreme east end of the Cathedral is usually known as –

The **Corona,** or Becket's crown. On the left side is the tomb of *Cardinal Pole,* the last Archbishop who acknowledged the supremacy of the Pope. In the centre stands the so-called *Chair of Augustine.* The best authorities agree that it must

CANTERBURY CATHEDRAL

date from the beginning of the thirteenth century. It is of Purbeck marble, in three pieces. When an Archbishop is enthroned he is placed first in his throne, as Bishop of the diocese; then in St. Augustine's chair, as Primate of All England and Metropolitan Patriarch of the English Church; and finally in the canopied seat in the Chapter House, "to remind us of the unbroken succession in which he continues that long line of Archbishops who were Abbots of the monastery."

From the Corona the full length of the Cathedral (514 feet) is seen.

The windows in the Trinity Chapel are filled with glass illustrating cures wrought at Becket's tomb. As the glass dates from the thirteenth century, it is of great historical value.

Opposite his tomb is the **Chantry of Henry IV,** which was dedicated in 1440. It is one of the gems of the Cathedral. Down the steps on the right is **St. Andrew's Chapel,** corresponding to St. Anselm's on the other side of the choir, one of the oldest parts of the building, and now forming an approach to the **Norman Treasury** (note Dean Farrar's clock).

The **North-East Transept** is interesting as showing the skilful adaptation by William of Sens of the old work of Ernulf and Conrad, in order to make it harmonize with his own choir. In the north-east corner is the **Chapel of St. Martin of Tours,** disused since the Reformation, but now restored in memory of the late Viscount Milner (1854–1925). The altar displays the arms, on the north side, of New Zealand, Australia, South Africa, and Canada, and on the opposite side the arms of Tours. A roundel in the east window depicts the story of St. Martin and the beggar. In the Chapel are thought to be buried the Saxon Queen Ediva, consort of King Edward, the son of King Alfred and also Lanfranc, who was Archbishop in William the Conqueror's time.

The **North-West Transept,** with door leading to the Cloisters and Chapter House, is known also as *The Martyrdom,* and was the scene of the tragedy which rendered Canterbury famous through Christendom. Hardly any portion of the structure, however, remains as it was at the time of the murder, having been completely rebuilt in the middle of the fifteenth century. The doorway leading into the cloister replaces the one by which Becket and the knights entered the Cathedral. In the south-east part is the *Murder Stone,* marking the spot where Becket fell.

The Murder of Becket. – The quarrel between Becket and Henry II had virtually resolved itself into a contest between Church and Crown. The banished prelate ventured to return to England in 1170, and proceeded to the seat of his diocese. One of his first acts was to suspend the Archbishop of York, thus incurring the wrath of Henry who exclaimed in a moment of thoughtless fury, "Will no man rid me from this turbulent priest?" Four of his knights – Fitzurse, de Moreville, de Tracy, and Richard le Bret – took up the challenge and hastened to Canterbury, where they arrived on the afternoon of Tuesday, December 29, 1170. Leaving their weapons outside, they entered the Archbishop's Palace, and demanded an interview, which ended in angry altercation. "You threaten me in vain," said the valiant Archbishop; "were all the swords in England hanging over my head, you could not terrify me from my obedience to God and my lord the Pope."

The knights retired to get their weapons, and meantime the frightened monks almost dragged the Archbishop, in spite of his struggles and protests, round the cloisters and into the north-west transept. Vespers had just begun when two servants rushed up the nave crying that the soldiers had burst into the palace, and were then making their way through the cloisters. The monks barricaded the door, but Becket insisted on its being open. "The church," he said, "must not be turned into a castle." He had proceeded up four of the steps leading to the choir, when the knights rushed into the transept calling for "the Archbishop, the traitor to the king." All but three of the monks fled, but Becket turned resolutely, and saying, "Here am I, no traitor, but the Archbishop and priest of God," descended the steps and stood with his back against a pillar. Even in that hour of passion the knights seem to have felt a certain horror at the thought of committing sacrilege, and Fitzurse, throwing down his axe, endeavoured to drag the Primate from the church. A struggle ensued, in which Tracy flung Becket to the pavement. A tremendous cut from Richard le Bret fractured the skull of the fallen martyr, and the knight's sword snapped in two on the pavement. Hugh of Horsea, who had joined the knights as they entered the cathedral, being taunted with having taken no part in the deed, planted his foot on the corpse, and gave it a tremendous blow. "Let us go," cried the knights, "the traitor is dead. He will rise no more."

A wooden altar was afterwards erected on the stone of martyrdom, bearing the point of le Bret's sword and other relics, and was known as the "Altar of the Sword's Point." It is represented in the central space over the south-west porch.

A door leads from the Martyrdom to the **Dean's or Lady Chapel,** the former name being derived from the numerous monuments of earlier deans here placed.

The Crypt. The westward portion was built by Prior Ernulf in Anselm's time. It is a fine specimen of Norman groin vaulting. Notice especially the quaint devices on the capitals of the pillars.

The **French Church.** – The undercroft of the south-east transept was the **Black Prince's Chantry,** founded by the Prince on the occasion of his marriage in 1363. It is used for Sunday services in French (3 p.m.) by a few of the descendants of the Huguenot exiles from France and Flanders who were permitted to worship here by Queen Elizabeth I.

The whole crypt was dedicated to the Virgin, "Our Lady of the Undercroft." Dark and sombre as it now is, it must once have presented a very different appearance. The delicate fourteenth-century screen was probably added with other decorations at the time of the Black Prince's marriage. South of the altar is the tomb of *Lady Mohun*; and close at hand the cenotaph of *Cardinal Morton*, minister of Henry VII, and author of that ingenious method of taxation known as "Morton's Fork." "If you live well," said Morton, "you can afford something for the King's necessities. If you live ill, you are saving money and can equally afford to pay." In **St. Gabriel's Chapel** note the fine central pillar with its carved capital, and the twelfth-century painting on the roof.

The Eastern Crypt was the work of William the Englishman (1180–4). It is much loftier and lighter than the other portion and contains the earliest Early English work. Here Becket's body was placed for fifty years before its removal into the magnificent shrine in his Chapel above. Here also Henry II did penance for his crime, and chose to be scourged by the Church's representatives. Each monk present gave him lashes on his bare shoulders. The Crypt contains two columns brought to the undercroft for shelter in 1932. They upheld three arches which divided the apse from the nave in the Saxon church at Reculver. These columns are of extreme antiquity and probably date from Roman times.

The Monastic Buildings

It is important to remember that the Cathedral, majestic as it is, formed only part of the monastic settlement. In most communities of the kind the cloisters and other buildings were on the sunny south side, as at Westminster Abbey, but at Canterbury, owing to considerations of space, we find them on the north.

The **Cloisters** (144 feet square) were begun by the will of Archbishop Courtney not long after the nave, to which the tracery of the windows and the vaulting closely correspond. Portions of the earlier cloister of Lanfranc's time, which had a sloping wooden roof, may still be traced. The north wall, which formed part of the **"frater"** or dining-hall of the monks, shows some beautiful Early English arcading. In the green cloister garth flat tombstones mark the graves of *Archbishop Frederick Temple* and *Dean Farrar*. In 1924, Dean Wace were interred in the cloister, and here also is the grave of the well-loved "Dick" Sheppard, Dean 1929–31.

The **Chapter House.** Lanfranc's Chapter House was rebuilt by Henry of Eastry in 1304. The lower portion and the wall arcades of the present building are his work. The roof and windows are Chillenden's and date from 1400. The *Prior's Seat* is at the east end below the Freemasons' Window. The west window, depicting historical events connected with Canterbury, is a memorial to Dean Farrar, by whose exertions the Chapter House was restored and reopened in 1897 as a memorial of the thirteenth centenary of the landing of St. Augustine.

The **Library** is perhaps the oldest established library in the English-speaking world. The present building (1954) replaces that destroyed in the bombing. There are some 30,000 printed books and a large number of manuscripts available to accredited students.

East of this are the **Water-tower,** a picturesque building, restored by the Friends of Canterbury Cathedral, and the long row of crumbling arches which mark the site of the **Infirmary.**

At the eastern end of the precincts is the **Kent War Memorial.** This beautiful spot was once the Canon's bowling-green. In the centre stands the restored remains of a simple memorial cross, and the loopholed bastion in the old city wall which borders the garden on the east has been restored to form a memorial chapel.

Library Passage, on the north side of the Cathedral, leads from the Infirmary to the Green Court. The Norman work, with the curiously carved capitals, is interesting.

The **Green Court,** entered through the *Prior's Gateway*, is the most delightful and picturesque portion of the Cathedral precincts. Around the court were grouped the more menial offices of the monastery, such as the brewery and bakehouse.

Across the court is the excellently preserved **Norman Porch and Staircase,** forming part of the *King's School*. The school claims to have been in existence in the days of Ethelbert and Augustine, but was refounded in Henry VIII's time. The present buildings are modern. The Junior School is installed at *Milner Court*, the former home of Viscount Milner at Sturry.

From whatever part of the precincts the great Central Tower, or **Bell Harry,** is viewed, its magnificent proportions and harmonious design compel admiration. Its height is 235 feet. It was built at the end of the fifteenth century and consists of an inner core of Tudor brick faced with stone. Bell Harry, the great bell at its summit is rung every evening as a curfew and tolled on the death of a sovereign or archbishop.

The few remains of the **Archbishop's Palace,** in Palace Street, have been incorporated in the present Palace.

St. Augustine's Abbey and College

The Abbey ruins are in the care of the Department of the Environment. Visitors are shown round by the Custodian (*fee*). Open: May to September, 9.30 to 7 (Sundays 9.30 to 7). October 9.30 to 5.30 (Sundays 2 to 5.30). November to February 9.30 to 4 (Sundays 2 to 4). March to April 9.30 to 5.30 (Sundays 2 to 5.30).

The College is open to the public between 2 and 4 p.m. on Wednesdays and Thursdays.

Historical Note. – The Abbey of St. Augustine is coeval with the Cathedral, both having been founded by St. Augustine in 597, the Cathedral to be the seat of the Archbishops in their lifetime, and the Abbey to provide a burial place for them and for the kings of Kent. When Augustine died in 605 the church was not completed; it was dedicated by Lawrence, the second archbishop, and Augustine's body was buried within its walls. Succeeding archbishops were buried there till Cuthbert (the eleventh), wishing to be buried in the Cathedral, instructed the Christ Church monks not to toll the death-bell for him till after they had actually buried him in a new chapel which he had built for the purpose. After this, which occurred in 758, only one archbishop was buried in the Abbey. However, as the burial-place of Ethelbert and Bertha, as well as of St. Augustine and his six sainted successors, and later on of St. Mildred (whose relics were brought here from Minster in Thanet) the Abbey maintained its importance and prestige as a place of pilgrimage.

Old Weavers' Houses, Canterbury

The Abbey Church was completely rebuilt in the Norman style and in 1091 the bodies of St. Augustine and his companions and the early archbishops were moved to shrines in the chancel of the new church.

During the twelfth and thirteenth centuries the Abbey successfully maintained its independence of all authority but that of the Pope. But gradually it fell into a state of financial depression, though it maintained its character for learning and piety, and possessed a remarkably fine library. In 1538 John Foche (or Essex) and his thirty monks were forced to surrender the monastery to the King's Commissioners. The lead was stripped from the roofs, most of the buildings were partially pulled down and the stone sold, and the Abbot's lodgings were adapted as a royal manor.

In 1573 Elizabeth spent a fortnight here. Tradition has it that she occupied the room over the Great (Fyndon's) Gate, where Charles I and his bride are also said to have stayed in 1625, and Charles II in 1660 on his return to England at the Restoration. By the early nineteenth century everything had fallen into decay; the mediaeval precinct was divided up among farms, the Gate and adjacent buildings belonged to a brewery, and the court was a vulgar pleasure garden.

From this state of degradation St. Augustine's was rescued by the Right Hon. A. J. Beresford-Hope, who bought all that was available of the land and buildings in 1844. He became interested in the plans for founding a training college for missionaries and eventually gave the site, as well as subscribing liberally to the funds raised for this purpose. The College was opened in 1848 and here the work of training missionaries went on till the Second World War, when the buildings were considerably damaged and the College was closed. From 1952–1967 it served at the Central College of the Anglican Communion and in 1969 became a college for theological students of King's College, London, preparing for ordination.

CANTERBURY

The College is entered through a fine Gateway completed by Abbot Fyndon in 1309. Adjoining it on the west side of the court is the fourteenth-century Guest Hall of the Abbey, now the College Dining Hall. The college buildings as a whole were designed by the Victorian architect, Butterfield. The Library, on the east side of the court, is on the foundations of the Abbot's Banqueting Hall.

The **Abbey Ruins** are reached by a roadway through a brick arch at right angles to the Great Gate. Of the monk's dormitory, a gable-end and two large buttresses remain. Next can be seen the foundations of the hexagonal kitchen and of the Refectory, which bounded the Cloister on the north and was at right angles to the Abbot's Banqueting Hall immediately to the west. The Cloister area, laid out with grass and a small fountain, lies beyond the Refectory, and its west wall contains the doorway to the monks' parlour. From the south-east corner steps go up to the floor-level of the great Abbey Church.

The external length of the church, from the west door to the Tudor Lady Chapel, was 402 feet – about the size of Gloucester and Norwich cathedrals. The area has been fully excavated, and within the bounds of the Norman church brick or flint outlines show the position of the earlier Saxon buildings. Near the crossing the great piers of "Wulfric's new Work" of 1056 are seen in a hollow below the Norman floor level; and on the north side are the graves of the second, third and fourth archbishops – empty since their bones were moved in 1091. The site of Augustine's first grave is marked close by.

The north-west tower was once a magnificent example of its period, but it was largely battered down as recently as 1821. Beside it the north wall of the Norman nave, repaired at the top with Tudor brick when the Royal Manor House was formed, stands to a considerable height. The remains of the rubble cores of the Norman pillars mark the lines of the arcades. The transepts each have the lower courses of an apsidal chapel on the east side, and in the south transept the positions of the graves of four kings of Kent are marked.

The most striking part of the ruins is the crypt of the Norman church, which stands to the level of the springing of the vault. There are three chapels, each containing most of its original altar. Traces of a painted design can be seen on the wall of the eastern chapel, and a figure composition in the southern one. The eastern altar has been restored and a modern stone arch built over it. Holy Communion is celebrated here on St. Augustine's Day (May 26th) and at other times in the summer.

Beyond the crypt, at ground level again, are the foundations of a Lady Chapel added to the church in early Tudor times.

A short distance further east is the ruined **Church of St. Pancras.** The plan is clear: a rectangle, with small chapels to north and south, and a western porch, of which a high piece of wall remains. The material is Roman brick, and a broken Roman pillar is set in the east wall. The original apse was pulled down and a larger squared east end built in the fourteenth century – the great east window, empty of its tracery, is a striking feature. In the tiny south chapel are the flint and stone foundations of what is called St. Augustine's altar, where he is said to have "celebrated the Holy Mysteries."

From St. Augustine's turn left along Monastery Street and then again left into Longport. Some distance up a left-hand turning shows the lych-gate of –

St. Martin's Church. St. Martin's is almost indisputably the oldest church in use in England, though largely rebuilt. This is the church, built in Roman times and dedicated to St. Martin of Tours, which Queen Bertha was already using as a

Christian oratory when Augustine entered the city. The church was repaired by the Normans after the ravages of the Danes and the eastern end added in the Early English style in the thirteenth century. Much of the re-used Roman material may still be traced.

The chief object of interest in the Nave is the ancient *font*, made up of twenty-two stones. Near the west door is a leper squint. Near the south-east corner of the nave is a Norman *piscina* (one of the earliest in England), and on the north side is a Norman doorway 4 feet 2 inches wide, with a stoup for holy water close at hand.

From the north wall of the nave hangs a carved wooden representation of St. Martin dividing his cloak with the beggar. It dates from 1583.

The Chancel, originally only 20 feet long, is in great part built of Roman tiles, and the existing side walls and foundations almost certainly formed part of Bertha's oratory. At the east end of the church is an Early English sedile, bordered by Roman tiles. Just within the altar rails are two Elizabethan brasses.

The city may be regained by returning along Longport and thence into Church Street and Burgate where is the **Roman Catholic Church of St. Thomas of Canterbury,** containing a relic of the Saint. Close by is the tower, last ruinous relic of the Church of St. Mary Magdalene, where R. H. Bingham, author of the *Ingoldsby Legends*, was christened.

At the end of Burgate, close by the Christ Church Gate of the Cathedral, is the site of the old Butter Market and the **City of Canterbury War Memorial.**

On St. Thomas' Hill about a mile from the city and overlooking the Stour valley are the buildings of the new **University of Kent at Canterbury.**

Harbledown

(1 mile), on the Chatham road – the old Watling Street – is the "little town" of Chaucer, where the pilgrims obtained their first sight of the Cathedral.

Here is the **Black Prince's Well.** The ancient **St. Nicholas' Church,** on the left of the road, should be seen. It was built in 1085 as part of a hospital for lepers, and was such for 100 years. The parish church of St. Michael, an ancient church much restored in the last century, is on the right of the road.

The road from Watling Street to Chartham Hatch traverses **Bigbury Wood,** where is an extensive earthwork hill-fort of the Early Iron Age. This hill-fort is the native stronghold which was stormed by Caesar in his second invasion in 54 B.C.

At **Hackington,** a mile north of Canterbury, are an ancient Church and Sir Roger Manwood's Almshouses.

On the Maidstone road, just outside Canterbury, is **Thanington,** an ancient manor mentioned in Domesday Book.

The Margate road from Northgate leads in 2½ miles to the village of Sturry and its delightful little neighbour Fordwich (*see* Index).

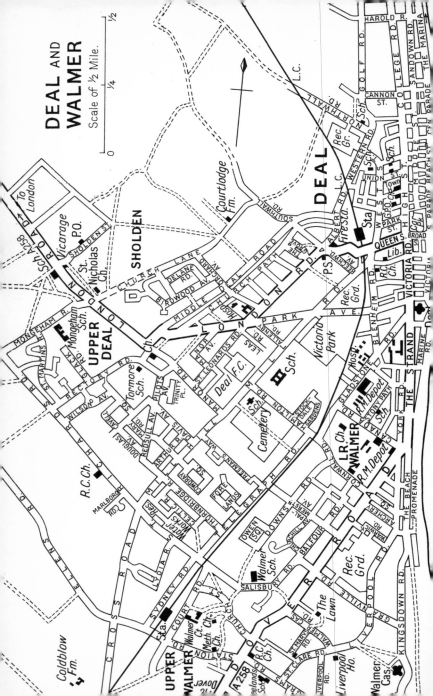

Deal and Walmer

Angling. – *See* page 70.

Banks. – *Midland, National Westminster* and *Lloyds*, all in High Street, Deal; *Barclays*, 3 Queen Street, Deal. *National Westminster*, *Lloyds* and *Midland*, The Strand, Walmer.

Bathing. – The beach is of shingle, banked by the sea in a series of steep terraces. Even at low tide deep water is reached almost immediately. A stretch of sand is exposed at low water at the north end of the town, by Sandown Castle. There is a bathing centre near Deal Castle.

Bowls. – Public greens in Victoria Park. *Deal Bowling Club* (licensed Pavilion) owns a green in Mill Road to which visitors are welcome. Also in Victoria Park is the *Victoria Park Bowls Club*. *Betteshanger Bowling Club*, Mill Hill.

Bus and Coach Services. – Terminus in Smith Street. Services cover the town and connect with other resorts. Some excursion coaches start from the sea-front, near Royal Hotel.

Car Parking Places. – Stanhope Road, Queen Street, Sandown Castle, outside Royal Hotel on front, Middle Street, Central Parade.

Cinemas. – *Classic*, Queen Street; *Royal*, King Street.

Cricket. – Excellent pitches at Victoria Park and Marke Wood Recreation Ground and the Depot, and many first-class teams are entertained.

Distances. – Canterbury, 19; Dover, 8; Folkestone, 15; London, 75; Margate, 15; Ramsgate, 13; St. Margaret's, 6; Sandwich, 6.

Early Closing Day. – Thursday.

Entertainments. – Dances, Concerts, Exhibitions and Variety Shows are held in the *Astor Theatre*, Stanhope Road, Deal. During the summer the local Amateur Dramatic societies hold a festival of plays. Dances and exhibitions are held in the *Quarter Deck* on the seafront. Band concerts are held periodically throughout the summer on Walmer Green.

Golf. – The links (18 holes) of the *Royal Cinque Ports Golf Club* are about a mile and a half from the station. Visitors are admitted as temporary members. Adjoining are the famous Sandwich links.

At Kingsdown, easily reached by bus, are the links of the *Walmer and Kingsdown Golf Club*, where visitors are welcome.

Hotels. – *Queen's*, adjoining Castle; *Black Horse*, 36 High Street; *Royal*, Beach; *Clarendon*, facing pier; *The Gables*, Gilford Road; *Aspley Guest House*, Deal; *The Glen*, Walmer; *Swan*, Queen Street; *Portland Guest House*, Sondes Road; *Winthorpe Guest House*, Kingsdown Road, Walmer; *Carter House*; *Kent House*, Gilford Road; *Adelaide House*, Beach Street; *Guildford House*, Beach Street.

Information. – Timeball Tower, Victoria Parade, Deal.

Libraries. – Public Library in Wellington Road, Deal.

Museums. – In the Town Hall and in Deal Castle.

Population. – 27,130.

Postal. – Chief Post Office is in Stanhope Road, off High Street.

Putting Greens, etc. – Miniature 18-hole golf course at Sandown. Putting course on Walmer Green.

Railway Stations. – Deal Station is in Queen Street, a quarter of a mile from the beach. Walmer Station is in Upper Walmer and is the nearest station for Kingsdown.

Riding. – The country is eminently suitable for riding. Mounts for hire from the Ringwould Riding Stables.

Steamers. – "No passport" trips to France, and Channel cruises.

The sister towns, now incorporated, of Deal and Walmer, can be recommended to holiday-makers who like a bracing air and the stir and bustle of the sea. There is even on the hottest day an invigorating breeze, while the neighbouring Downs, ever busy with shipping of some kind, provide unending interest. Walmer of the rows of sedate houses and long greensward; Deal of the fisherfolk – have their own cheerful, unaffected charm.

DEAL

There is hardly in Britain a flatter and more undeviatingly straight piece of coast than that between Sandown and Walmer Castles. In the three to four miles between the two points the impression given is one of picturesque variety rather than of monotony.

The town is regularly laid out, the three most important thoroughfares running parallel with the sea. The Dover Road strikes the sea-front at Lower Walmer, near St. Saviour's Church, and becomes successively the Strand, Victoria Road and High Street, the first-named being in Walmer, the other two in Deal. The streets immediately adjoining contain the principal shops, banks, and places of worship.

Historical Note. – Few holiday resorts have the historical glamour that belongs to Deal. There can scarcely be a doubt that it was on its beach – close to the vicinity of Deal Castle – that Caesar and his legions landed for the invasion of Britain. In August 1946, a tablet was placed near the Castle to commemorate the 2,000th anniversary of the landing.

During the Roman occupation the more convenient port of Rutupiae (Richborough), a few miles to the north, was used, and we hear little more of Deal until the time of its inclusion in the Cinque Ports as a "limb" of Sandwich.

In 1495 the Pretender, Perkin Warbeck, arrived in the Downs and made his abortive landing.

Leland, the librarian of Henry VIII, described Deal as "half a myle fro the shore of the se, a fishher village iii myles or more above Sandwic, upon a flat shore, and very open to the se."

This openness to the "se" induced his Royal master to pay the place particular attention when making those elaborate arrangements for coast defence of which so many traces remain this day.

At the outbreak of the Kentish Rising (1648) the castles were seized, with little difficulty, by Prince Charles's friends, and many of the ships then in the Downs declared in his favour. A party of about 600 Royalists landed in August from the fleet in the Downs to attack Deal, but was repulsed with great loss near Sandown Castle by Colonel Rich. On the collapse of the rising the fortresses reverted to the Commonwealth, but in the meantime the Castle at Walmer had withstood a stubborn siege.

In 1652–5 a series of naval battles was fought in the Downs between the English under Blake and Monk and the Dutch under Van Tromp, resulting in the eventual defeat of the Dutch and the death of their admiral.

Under William III (1699) the growing importance of Deal was, after much opposition from Sandwich, recognized by the grant of a charter by which the place was constituted a "free town and a borough of itself." In 1935 Walmer was amalgamated with Deal.

IN AND ABOUT DEAL AND LOWER WALMER

From **Deal Station** the nearest way to the beach is by **Queen Street,** which crosses **High Street** almost at right angles, and then becomes Broad Street. On the Front the square **Signal Tower,** in which is the Enquiry Bureau, will attract attention. The time-ball on the summit was formerly used to enable the captains of ships in the Downs to adjust their chronometers.

In 1957 a new **Pier** was opened, from which steamer trips to France and Channel cruises run in summer. It is 1,000 feet in length and has sun-lounge, café and angling cabins on the Pierhead.

Sea Angling. – The nine mile stretch of beach from Sandwich Bay to Kingsdown is much in favour with deep-sea anglers, and remarkable catches are often made, particularly during the annual festivals of the two local clubs in September and November. Deal is, in fact, by far the best place for sea-fishing within easy reach of London.

Many rods may be seen in August, but regular sport rarely begins before September, when the advent of the sprats into inshore water attracts many large cod and whiting. Good catches may then be looked for until the disappearance of the winter herring at the end of January. The whiting average about 1 lb., and cod are caught up to 20 lb. weight. Pollack, plaice, tope, dabs, dogfish, conger and many other kinds are also hooked. The baits most in use are lug worms, hermit crabs and sprat or herring.

The Beach

The magnificent shingle beach rises in a series of terraces from four to six feet in depth and often very steep, but levels out towards Sandown Castle, where at low tide a stretch of sand is exposed.

Fronting the pier is **South Parade,** southward of which is **Victoria Parade.** At the southward end and just beyond the *Queen's Hotel* is –

Deal Castle
Open daily throughout the year, *charge.*

The Castle was erected by Henry VIII in 1540, at the same time as Walmer and Sandown Castles, as part of his great scheme of coast defence. It is now a national monument, with a museum.

Deal Castle is circular in form, with a double row of six lunettes or bastions of stone, of thick arched work, pierced by fifty-four port-holes. From the centre rises a large round tower, with a cistern at the top and an arched bomb-proof cavern below. The walls of the bastions are about 20 feet thick at the foundation, but diminish to about 11 feet at the summit. The entrance is on the landward side, by means of a drawbridge and a machicolated gateway with a thickly-studded door. The Castle is so deep-seated in its grass-grown moat as to be almost invisible until one is quite close to it. There can be little doubt that such a fortification would, with the poor means of assault then available, have proved a tough nut to crack.

On Marine Road is the **Swimming Bath** of the Royal Marines. The large building nearly opposite was formerly used as a Hospital for the Marines, but was converted into Barracks in 1900–1. The present **Royal Marine Hospital** is in Blenheim Road.

The succession of deep-set grass lawns is broken about midway by the **Lifeboat House** with sheltered seats along each side, and a beautifully worded memorial to the famous Walmer luggers of the nineteenth century.

To the west of the Strand and Dover Road are the extensive barracks of the **Depot, Royal Marines.** Services at the Depot Church may be attended by members of the public, but those wishing to tour the Depot should communicate with the Adjutant.

The **Royal Marines.** A Royal Marine is a highly skilled serviceman trained for service with Commando units or in HM Ships. He is, in addition, able to specialize as swimmer, canoeist (frogman), cliff climber, parachutist, landing craft coxswain, helicopter pilot, and in many other active occupations. All Royal Marines travel around the world a great deal and they are very quickly on the scene in trouble areas. Commando ships enable the Royal Marines to use helicopters to effect speedy landings and operations.

Royal Marines first came to Deal in 1861 and they were granted the Freedom of the Borough in 1945. There is a very close liaison between the town and the Depot and many Royal Marines on retirement settle in Deal and Walmer.

Northward to Sandown Castle

Running northward from the pier are Beach Street, broad promenades, and the popular Central Parade. Beyond the old lifeboat house and the Mary Hougham almshouses for the boatmen is the Coastguard Station, standing a little back from the parade and surrounded by fascinating designs in the shingle.

The promenade and motor road, near which there is a miniature golf course, come to an end at the ruins of –

Sandown Castle. A few arched foundation walls are all that remain of the fortress built by Henry VIII at the same time, and in the same style, as Deal and Walmer Castles. In 1785 the sea broke through the outer wall of the moat, and the castle was reported "barely habitable." By 1863 the encroachments of the sea had become so serious that the War Office pulled down what was left of the structure. The site is now set out as an attractive rock garden.

From this breezy spot there is a delightful outlook over Pegwell Bay to Ramsgate and across the sandhills to Sandwich. The best bathing in the town is in this locality, for there is a fine stretch of sand at low tide.

Slightly to the left lie the golf links (18 holes) of the **Royal Cinque Ports Golf Club,** with a large and well-equipped Club House. The links adjoin the famous Sandwich courses (*see* p. 49).

From Sandown Castle, the return can be made by way of **High Street.** Facing Alfred Square, at the junction of High Street and College Road, is the **Caxton Seaside Home,** known also as the **Lloyd Memorial.**

Along the High Street beyond the modest Town Hall is civic **Church of St. George the Martyr,** erected in 1715. The corporation pew displays some fine modern carving.

In Stanhope Road, just off the High Street and close to St. George's Church, is the **General Post Office** and next to it is the **Astor Theatre** where dancing and entertainments take place.

The right-hand turn at the junction of High Street with Victoria Road is **Queen Street** up which a left-hand turn, Mill Road, leads to **Victoria Park.** Here are hard tennis courts and bowling greens.

Upper Deal

The oldest part of the town, is reached by crossing the railway bridge at the head of Queen Street.

About $\frac{3}{4}$ mile along the London Road is the old Parish Church of St. Leonard dating from the twelfth century, though altered and partially rebuilt in 1684.

Walmer Castle

The curious cupola crowning the tower was for many years chargeable as regards repairs to Trinity House, as it was a landmark for shipping. The Pilot's Gallery over the west door, was used by the Pilots of Deal. It was erected sometime after 1658, and the ship in the front was added to commemorate a great storm in 1793. The registers date from 1559, and there are many interesting brasses and monuments.

At the church the road to Sandwich turns northward by way of **Sholden,** the site of a church consisting of a nave, chancel and square tower, and containing memorials of members of the Wyborn family.

A motor road goes from the Strand parallel to the shore, passing a terrace of pleasant houses, Walmer Castle, about a mile and a half from Deal Castle, and finally reaching Kingsdown.

Seaward of the road a broad asphalted path runs along the crest of the shingle, affording opportunities for delightful breezy walks for several miles free from traffic.

Walmer Castle

Open daily through the year, charge. Except when the Lord Warden is in residence, nearly all the castle is open to view.

It is remarkable that sea-encroachments should have led to the demolition of Sandown Castle, while here, only a few miles distant, an exactly contrary process has taken place. There is clear evidence that in the seventeenth century breakers rolled on the very spot now occupied by the road in front of the castle, and the deep moat was formerly filled by the sea at high tide.

The castle became the official residence of the Lord Wardens of the Cinque Ports early in the eighteenth century. Little of the original military character of the castle remains, successive Lord Wardens having adapted it bit by bit to the purpose of a dwelling-house. The walls are 30 feet thick at the base and 15 feet above.

The apartment known as **The Duke of Wellington's Room,** is an irregularly-shaped room on the south side, and is preserved almost exactly as when the Duke occupied it. The relics include his bedstead, the chair in which he died on September 14, 1852, his washing utensils, his desk and the old camp chair that accompanied him in all his campaigns. The narrow bedstead calls to mind the great warrior's immortal remark, which has been the bane of several generations of sluggards, that "when it is time to turn round it is time to turn out."

From the ramparts, upon which the Duke was accustomed to take an early morning walk, there is a fine view through the trees and over the Downs to the French coast.

Next to the castle, the most attractive feature of Upper Walmer is the picturesque and park-like **Glen,** situated a short distance inland near the Parish Church, from which it is separated by the St. Clare Road.

Walmer Church is dedicated to St. Mary and was consecrated in 1888. It is of Kentish rag-stone, mainly in the Early English style.

Before its erection the parish church of Walmer was a venerable structure still standing in Church Street and adjoining Walmer Court. It is now commonly known as –

The Old Church, which is always open to view, and is used for services every Thursday. It is believed to have been built about 1120 by one of the d'Auberville family, probably as a chapel for the Castle which stood in the grounds of what is now Walmer Court.

The chancel was restored in 1923–4. The chancel arch and south doorway are good specimens of Norman work, with chevron, lozenge and billet mouldings. The font bowl is ancient, the cover dating from 1664. The Duke of Wellington's hatchment still hangs on the north wall of the nave.

Just outside the churchyard, a few yards to the north-east, is the **Old Manor House** comprising most of the ruined keep of the castle.

Park House, Walmer, was for four years the residence of Lord Lister, who revolutionized surgery by the introduction of antiseptic methods in surgical operations. He died there in his 85th year, in 1912. *The house is not open to the public.*

Ripple, a hamlet $2\frac{1}{2}$ miles west of Walmer and just off the Deal-Dover road through Sutton and Temple Ewell, stands in the midst of cool woods, and is notable as the birthplace of the first Earl of Ypres (Sir John French) in 1852. He is buried in Ripple Churchyard.

Walks and Excursions from Deal

To Kingsdown and Ringwold. Both places are on bus routes. **Kingsdown** is two miles from Deal Castle and can be gained along the shore, a return being made over Hawk's Hill to the Glen and Lower Walmer.

Or from Kingsdown a pretty inland road may be taken for about a mile to **Ringwould,** on the Deal and Dover road. It occupies a lofty site which commands a magnificent prospect seawards. The twelfth-century church of flint and seventeenth-century tower with heavy brick buttresses, and two wonderful old yew trees in the churchyard, are set on a hill, and the tower with its curious cupola can be seen far out at sea.

To Kingsdown and St. Margaret's Bay. From Walmer Castle continue for a mile by the asphalted walk by the surf – or the road immediately below the cliff, to **Kingsdown.** Old Kingsdown is one of the quaintest and prettiest places imaginable: its cottages all at right angles to the beach. On rising ground behind the village is the pretty Church while a short distance south of the old village is the Clubhouse of the **Walmer and Kingsdown Golf Club.**

From the top of the cliff a delightful view is obtained over the Downs to Deal and the distant cliffs of Ramsgate. The Dover Patrol Memorial, above St. Margaret's Bay, cuts the skyline ahead and, after an elevated walk of two miles, the South Foreland Lighthouse and its disused sister nearer the cliff. In the intervening depression lies the picturesque village of **St. Margaret's-at-Cliffe,** six miles from Deal by the cliff path. With **St. Margaret's Bay** it is described on pp. 86–8.

Waldershare, Barfreston, etc. Distance out and home is about 20 miles. West of the Sandwich–Dover road there are many beautiful parks and little villages joined by a network of secondary roads. The easiest route for motorists to Waldershare from Deal is to take the Dover road as far as the turning to East Langdon on the right, and follow this across the ridges of the chalk land until it meets the Sandwich–Dover road at Waldershare Park, where turn right and then left for Eyethorne. From here there is an infinite choice of routes and many charming and interesting villages to be seen.

For a description of these, with Waldershare and Barfreston, *see* pp. 86–90.

To Betteshanger, Eastry, etc. (Bus services). From the railway station follow the Upper Deal Road to the Church, there turning right, along the Sandwich road, to Sholden, where turn left to **Great Mongeham,** two miles west-south-west of Deal. The Church, with its massive embattled tower, is mainly of the Norman and Early English periods, and contains a double piscina and double sedilia, with a fine oak screen in the tower arch.

The road turns to right just south of the Church and descends steeply and ascends more steeply to **Northbourne,** where there is a fine little church originally built by monks from St. Augustine's, Canterbury. Northbourne Court, of Tudor date, was once a monastic establishment of great antiquity.

About a mile from Northbourne Church is the village of **Finglesham,** from which it is a short walk to the Sandwich main road, where turn right for Deal (buses).

EASTRY – WOODNESBOROUGH

A mile or more westward of Northbourne is **Betteshanger House,** at one time the seat of Lord Northbourne, and now a school. In the park is a pretty little modern Church built of flint in Norman style and retaining an original Norman window and doorway from the old church.

Eastry lies a mile and a half northward on the old Roman road from Dover. It is a place whose name figures largely in early Kentish annals. Many remains of the British, Roman and Saxon periods have been found in the locality. The Saxon kings Ethelbert and Egbert are said to have had a palace here. It probably occupied the site of the present **Eastry Court,** a fine square, red-brick building standing on the north side of the church.

The Church contains Norman features, notably the tower and west doorway, but is for the most part Early English with a fine high clerestoried nave.

In Woodnesborough lane, in the village, is an extensive series of caves formed by excavation work for chalk.

Woodnesborough, midway between Eastry and Sandwich, was another important Saxon station. The name is said to be derived, like our Wednesday, from the god Woden. The Church, with a curious little bell tower, probably of Flemish influence, contains a beautifully carved piscina and sedilia and three brasses.

Near the church is Woodnesborough Hill, an artificial mound that may have been connected with the sacred ceremonies of the Saxons.

About 2½ miles north-west of Eastry on the Wingham road is the farming village of **Staple.** The Church has traces of Saxon work and a Norman south wall, but is chiefly of the fourteenth and fifteenth centuries.

The return to Deal from Eastry may be made by the Sandwich road, making a detour to the little village of **Worth,** just east of the main road and two miles south of Sandwich. The small, spired church has some Norman work, Early English windows and arches and a hexagonal font carved with Tudor roses.

To Knowlton, Goodnestone and Adisham. A good walk of about 12 miles can be taken between Eastry and Wingham (both of which are in touch with Deal by bus) as follows. From Eastry go south-westward and by Mill Lane reach **Heronden.** At the top of the hill take footpath on left to the tiny old village of **Knowlton.** The little church has a fine Jacobean three-decker pulpit.

From Knowlton either continue west for a mile to **Chillenden,** where there is a windmill and a church with Norman doorway, some ancient glass, and a Jacobean pulpit; or go through Knowlton Park and Nonington Park (near St. Alban's Court) north-west to **Goodnestone.** This stands in the midst of a beautiful park, the thirteenth-century church raised high above the village street, and containing many brasses. The oldest house in the village, once the rectory, and now the post office, is a thatched Tudor building. Jane Austen used to stay at Goodnestone Park and describes it in her letters.

A left turning at the school leads through hop gardens, and by a bridle track into the road leading to **Wingham.**

Adisham (station on the Canterbury-Dover line) is reached via the hamlet of Ratling. It was on the ground formerly occupied by Adisham Mill that, in 54 B.C., Caesar's legions attacked and defeated the Celts.

The large **Church** is beautifully situated near the cross-roads at the north end of the straggling village street. The nave still has, running round the interior of its walls, the mediaeval "bench-table." An unusual feature of the nave is the slope of the floor from the west to east. The thirteenth-century *Chancel* contains fine carved stalls and book rests. A few fragments of the mediaeval screen are inserted in the present chancel screen, and there are many mediaeval encaustic tiles in the floor.

Ward Lock's
Red Guides

Edited by Reginald J. W. Hammond

Complete England

Complete Scotland

Complete Wales

Complete Ireland

Lake District (*Baddeley*)

Complete West Country

Complete Devon

Complete South-East Coast

Complete Yorkshire

Complete Scottish Lowlands

WARD LOCK LIMITED

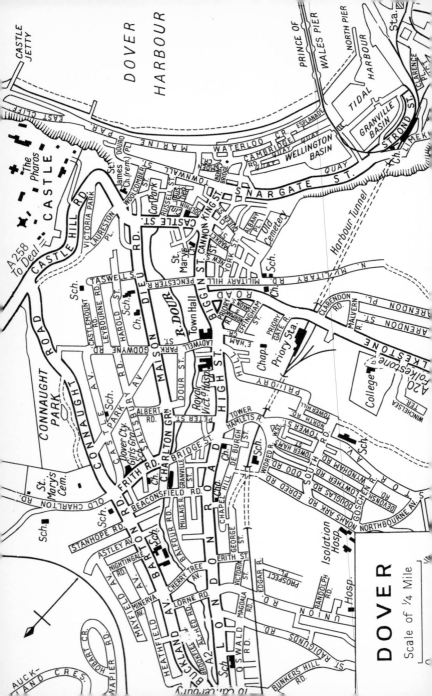

Dover

Angling. – The facilities for sea-angling are excellent with several miles of pier space. The Dover Harbour Board issues fishing tickets which give access to the Southern Breakwater and the Prince of Wales Pier. There is no charge from the Admiralty Pier. Motor-boats run daily for Breakwater. Codling, pouting, flatfish, bass, mackerel, congers, huss and whiting are plentiful. Boat fishing, usually west of Admiralty Pier, for codling, pouting and whiting. The *Dover Sea Angling Association* arranges a three-day Boat Festival in October and a three-day Pier Festival in November.

Banks. – *National Westminster*, 5 King Street; *Lloyds*, Market Square; *Midland*, 26 Biggin Street; *Barclays*, 21 Market Square; *Trustee Savings*, 10 Market Square.

Bathing. – Free bathing is permitted at all times of the day. Life Guards regularly patrol the shore. The *Dover Life Guard Club* uses the open-air pool at Folkestone on Monday evenings. During the season, swimming races, polo matches, etc, are held frequently.

Boating. – In the sheltered waters of the great Harbour sculling and sailing are popular and safe. The *Dover Rowing Club* welcomes temporary members. Motor-boats make trips around the harbour. Yachting, with weekly races and regatta, under the auspices of the Royal Cinque Ports Yacht Club.

Bowls. – Excellent public greens are available in the Maison Dieu Gardens and at River Recreation Ground.

Buses and Coaches. – The Town buses all stop in Market Square. The Coach Office and terminal point of the East Kent Road Car Company, Ltd., is in Pencester Road where detailed information of tours can be obtained. There are daily excursions to all the places of interest near Dover.

Camping and Caravan Sites. – Archers Court, Whitfield; off A.2, Hawthorn Farm, Martin Mill; off A.258, The Plough Inn, Folkestone Road.

Car Parks. – The Monument (Cambridge Road); Saxon Street; Effingham Street (near Town Hall); Bartholomew Street; Castle Hill Road (near entrance to Castle); East Cliff (bus terminus); Stembrook; Townwall Street (off sea front); Ladywell; Beach Street (near Marine Station); Connaught Road; Snargate Street; Beaconsfield Road and Buckland Terrace. The A.A.

Port Central Office is at Fanum House, Russell Street, just off the sea front.

Cinemas. – *A.B.C.*, Castle Street; *Essoldo*, Cannon Street; *Odeon*, London Road.

Cricket. – The Corporation Athletic Ground is at Crabble. County and other important matches are played here. The Dover County Cricket Week is a popular annual event. The Danes Cricket Ground is at Old Charlton Road, beyond Connaught Park and the Cemeteries. The River Recreation Ground, almost adjoining the Athletic Ground, has facilities for cricket and football as well as for tennis and bowls. The Elms Vale Recreation Ground at Elms Vale Road has similar facilities with the exception of bowls.

Dancing. – Dances are held throughout the year at the Town Hall (*see current announcements*).

Distances. – Deal, 8 miles; Folkestone, 7; London, *via* Canterbury, 72; London, *via* Folkestone, 77; Ashford, 24; Ramsgate, 19; Margate, 21; Sandwich, 13; St. Margaret's Bay, 5; Canterbury, 16; Hythe, 12.

Early Closing Day. – Wednesday.

Golf. – The nearest course is at Kingsdown – 18 holes.

Hotels. – *Dover Stage*, Camden Crescent; *White Cliffs*, Esplanade; *Central*, Biggin Street; *White House*, 27 East Cliff; *East Cliff*, East Cliff; *Webb's*, 165 Folkestone Road; *Shalimar*, Esplanade; *Mildmay*, Folkestone Road; *Channel*, Snargate Street; *St. James*, Harold Street; *Continental*, Seafront.

Information Bureau. – At the Town Hall.

Library. – Public Library at Maison Dieu House by Town Hall.

Lifeboat. – The station was established in 1837. The present boat, the *Faithful Forester*, is housed in the M.T.B. Pens in the East Dock.

Museum. – Adjoining Town Hall (entrance in Ladywell).

Population. – 35,610.

Postal. – Head Post Office in Biggin Street. Numerous sub-offices.

Putting Greens, etc. – Pencester Gardens (18 holes), Crabble Athletic Ground (Pitch and Putt) 9 holes.

Railway Stations. – *Dover Priory* for the town. *Marine* for boat travellers to the Continent.

Tennis. – Hard courts at Brook House Gardens; Connaught Park; Crabble Athletic Ground, grass courts in Connaught Park; River Recreation Ground; and Elms Vale.

DOVER

A prosperous port and busy commercial centre, Dover is situated on the shore of a fine bay. A pebbly beach is backed by high, white chalk cliffs, except in the centre where is the mouth of the river Dour and its beautiful valley.

The high ground at the back of Dover shelters it from the cold winds from the north and north-east, whilst it is open to the prevailing south-west winds and the south and south-east sea breezes.

In addition to her commercial activities, the town offers a wealth of historical interest, a bracing air, fine sea-outlook, beautiful coast and inland scenery and excellent facilities for sport and pleasure.

The sea-front is divided between the docks and the residential "seaside" quarter. The greater part of the town runs inland up the valley of the river Dour, between the lofty Castle Hill and the Western Heights. In ancient times the sea flowed for some distance up this valley and formed the haven. This haven, however, gradually silted up in consequence of the formation of a shingle bar across the mouth. For many years an entrance was kept open, but a landslip in the fifteenth century effectually stopped the mouth of the old harbour, which was replaced by the system of docks.

The Port of Dover

The Port of Dover, whose history dates back to Roman times, has grown from a little haven nestling under the cliffs on the estuary of the Dour, to one of the largest artificial harbours in the world. It is the principal port between London and Southampton and the nearest port to the Continent.

Dover Harbour today comprises an area of 850 acres, 650 acres of which are water, with low-water depths of up to 30 feet, and provides ample facilities for ocean-going, cross-channel and coastal shipping.

Of the three enclosing breakwaters or piers, two are connected with the shore. That on the East is known as the Eastern Arm, and that on the West as the Admiralty Pier, and between their seaward ends lies the Southern Breakwater. This breakwater rises 75 feet from the sea bottom and is 45 feet wide. It is formed of massive blocks of granite.

The **Eastern Arm** is 2,800 feet in length and has deep water berths. British Rail's cross-Channel Hovercraft services operate from here.

The **Camber,** originally built as a submarine basin, comprises an area of 25 acres of water. Here are situated the loading berths of the modern Car Ferry Terminal.

The **Admiralty Pier,** which protects the harbour from the west, is 4,000 feet long. The Cross-Channel passenger ferry services to France and Belgium operate from here, and there are five deep-water berths. Immediately alongside the pier is the Marine Station (British Transport Commission) which provides ample accommodation for handling the $2\frac{1}{2}$ million passengers passing through the port annually. There is a fine walk along the Upper Promenade which runs the length of the pier and gives an excellent view of the harbour, coast and channel shipping.

The **Train Ferry Dock,** adjacent to the Admiralty Pier, was built between the years 1933 and 1936. Connection is made from rail to ship by means of a link span whereby a train can be accommodated on the train deck.

The **Wellington Dock** is the oldest and largest of the docks having 8 acres of water with a depth of 14 feet. The width of the entrance is 70 feet and at the south-eastern end there is a patent slipway for the repair of craft. Apart from commercial use, it is a popular dock for yachtsmen.

The **Granville Dock** is more modern in construction and has more water than the Wellington Dock, though it consists of only $4\frac{1}{4}$ acres in area.

The **Tidal Basin** is the entrance to the Inner Harbour, and has two working berths. There are facilities for the rapid discharge of coal and stone cargoes from vessels of up to 14 feet draft. This basin partly dries up at low water.

The **Prince of Wales Pier** separates the Inner and Outer Harbours. It is 3,000 feet long and has berthing accommodation for vessels up to 25 feet draft, but is now primarily non-commercial. It provides an unrivalled view of harbour shipping and activity, and has a sun-lounge and cafeteria at the seaward end.

Dover, as the nearest port to the continent, is usually looked upon as being exclusively cross-Channel; but its trade also includes general cargo and ocean passenger traffic. In an average year some 9,000 vessels enter the port and over a million tons of cargo, import and export, are handled.

In the summer, the Harbour and docks are a favourite centre for yachtsmen of the Royal Cinque Ports Yacht Club, or visiting yachtsmen, and sailing races are held.

The sea front promenade provides a pleasant walk from one side of the harbour to the other. Its layout of gardens and fountains make it one of the most attractive on the coast.

One of the finest marine walks of its kind, stretching over half a mile from the shore and providing unsurpassed views of the channel, is that along the upper promenade of the Admiralty Pier. The promenade can be reached by the bus to the Marine Station.

The public are also allowed on the Prince of Wales Pier on payment of a small toll.

Fishing facilities are provided for the public from the Prince of Wales Pier, Southern Breakwater and the Admiralty Pier (upper promenade). For the first two a small charge is made, the latter is free.

Through the Town

A good starting point is the Rifles Monument, an obelisk standing at the sea-front end of New Bridge. New Bridge leads via Bench Street and King Street to the Central Market Square.

On the south side of the Market Place are several narrow thoroughfares known as Lanes. They form part of the oldest portions of Dover and at one time contained some of the leading commercial houses in the town.

In Market Lane is the **Old Baptists' Burial-Ground,** formerly known as *Tavernor's Garden*. It was so named after Captain Samuel Tavernor, one of Cromwell's Ironsides.

From Market Square, Castle Street leads direct to the Castle, and Cannon Street to –

St. Mary's Church notable for its fine western tower. The Mayor and Corporation have seats in the north gallery, in front of which is a fine Royal Coat of Arms, dating from the reign of William and Mary. Instead of the usual royal motto, *Dieu et Mon Droit*, this coat of arms carried William's personal motto in quaint French, *Jay Mien Tend Roy* (I will maintain [the right]). Opposite is the gallery used by the Pilots of the Cinque Ports. The Coat of Arms of Trinity House was placed on the front of the south gallery in 1947 to replace the one of the Cinque Ports. The Seafarer's Window shows the strong association of the Parish Church with the Harbour.

DOVER

With the exception of the Castle Church, this is the oldest ecclesiastical building in Dover, although the greater part was rebuilt in 1843–4, and the eastern portion has been further altered since the War. The interior is finely proportioned. At the west end are the pillars and arches of the Norman church.

Continuing up Biggin Street from St. Mary's Church, turn left at Effingham Crescent for –

Dover College, which stands on the site and includes portions of the ancient St. Martin's Priory, a Benedictine foundation. The Refectory, dating from the twelfth century, is one of the largest secular Norman buildings in the country and is used as the College Hall. The interior contains traces of ancient paintings. The Gate House now forms the Library, and the Guest House the Chapel. The school buildings stand round the Close. *(Application to see the old buildings may be made at the lodge.)*

The Municipal Buildings

In Biggin Street, facing Effingham Crescent, is the block of municipal buildings comprising the **Town Hall,** the Maison Dieu, the Connaught Hall, the Council Chamber, Mayor's Parlour, Sessions House, Muniment Room and various offices.

The **Maison Dieu Hall** *(open 10 to 1 and 2 to 5, 4 in winter, admission free)* was originally a hospital founded by Hubert de Burgh, Constable of Dover Castle, in 1203. It was a wealthy foundation and housed several permanent inmates and a master. It was used, too, for the reception of pilgrims and soldiers returning from foreign service. On the suppression of the monasteries by Henry VIII, the building was used as a brewhouse and afterwards as a victualling store for the Navy. It was restored in 1860. The Hall is renowned for its portraits and paintings and collection of arms and armour, on permanent loan from the Tower of London. The fine modern windows, designed by Sir Edward Poynter, portray events in Dover's history.

Adjoining the Maison Dieu Hall is the **Connaught Hall,** opened in 1883 by the Duke and Duchess of Connaught. This is a beautiful room used for social functions, entertainments, dances, etc. Organ recitals are frequently played on the magnificent organ.

The **Council Chamber** is noteworthy for its windows, oil paintings, pictures of old Dover and the Dover Patrol Book of Remembrance, also the Dover Book of Remembrance for the 1939–45 War. In the **Mayor's Parlour** are lists of Mayors – the earliest being in 1086 – and some of their portraits.

Maison Dieu House, behind the **War Memorial,** was built in 1665 and was occupied for many years by the Agent Victualler. It now serves as the public library.

The beautiful **War Memorial** commemorates the men of Dover who gave their lives in the two world wars.

On the balcony outside the Town Hall hangs the Bell taken by the Germans from Antwerp and erected on the Mole at Zeebrugge as an air-raid warning during the 1914–1918 War. The relic was a gift of King Albert I to commemorate the Zeebrugge expedition on April 23rd, 1918, and of the part played by the Dover Patrol.

From the Town Hall, Park Street and Park Avenue lead steeply up to **Connaught Park,** charmingly situated on the hill-side with delightful views over the town and the Western Heights. In this park are lawns, flower-beds, woodland walks, lake, tennis courts and children's play-ground.

To the north of the park are the extensive town **Cemeteries,** St. James's Cemetery containing the Zeebrugge Plot, and beyond these again, on the old Charlton Road, is the Danes Recreation Ground.

Dover Castle

From Connaught Park it is only a few minutes' walk, up the hill above the narrow strip known as **Victoria Park,** to the Constable's Tower of –

Dover Castle

Admission. – The Castle is open daily throughout the year. Charges are made for entry to the Keep and Underground Works.

Historical Note. – Though the early history of the Castle has not yet been fully worked out, excavations continue to throw fresh light on its distant past.

Probably towards the latter end of the first century the Romans built a lighthouse to guide cross-channel shipping. The remains of this lighthouse (or **Pharos**) still stand. Another lighthouse was built sometime later on the Western Heights. During the Roman occupancy of Britain a civil settlement grew up near the mouth of the River Dour, defended by a garrison.

After the withdrawal of the Roman garrison in the early fifth century little is known of Dover until, sometime before 640, Eadbald, King of Kent, founded a monastery *in castro*, i.e., within the old Roman walls. Dover gradually grew in importance as a port, but it was not until 1064 when Harold's bond came, from which William the Conqueror professed to derive his "right" to England, and expressly stipulated that he build up, on the Confessor's death, a "Castell of Dover, with a well of water in it." A few days after the Battle of Hastings the Conqueror appointed his half-brother, Odo of Bayeux, Constable, and made elaborate provision for its defence. Most of the walls and towers are late Norman work. The Keep dates from the time of Henry II. In 1216 the Castle was besieged by Louis, the Dauphine of France, and the allied barons, but was stoutly defended by the Constable, Hubert de Burgh.

83

DOVER

The Castle grounds occupy about thirty-five acres, and consist of an Upper and Lower Ward, both with surrounding walls or curtains. Entrance can be gained either by the **Canon's Gate,** or the more massive **Constable's Tower,** immediately beneath the Keep. Entering by the Canon's Gate, we cross a drawbridge from Castle Hill over the deep tree-lined moat, and bearing right have before us close to the cliff edge, the former Officers' Mess. To the left above is the platform on which stands the famous **Queen Elizabeth's Pocket Pistol,** its muzzle pointed seaward. It was said to be capable of propelling a 12 lb. ball 7 miles. Cast in Utrecht in 1544, it was presented to Elizabeth by the States of Holland.

Passing between the barrack buildings beyond the Pistol, ascend the mound by a cutting on the right for –

St. Mary's-in-Castro Church, to distinguish it from St. Mary's in the town. This building is of the greatest interest as being one of the oldest churches in the country. It is thought to incorporate re-used portions of the Roman fort, though the general arrangement and structural details suggest that it is of early eleventh century origin. The building bears traces of the various modifications it has undergone during the centuries since.

South of the nave of the Church is **Harold's Well.**
Adjoining the Church is the roofless Roman **Pharos,** or light-tower, which, with its companion tower on the Western Heights, served to guide vessels across the Channel from Gaul.

The **Keep.** – The massive Keep, built by Henry II about 1180–86, is one of the best preserved in the country. The walls are about 20 feet thick, and the towers rise to a height of over 90 feet. There are three storeys. The other sides of the enclosure are eighteenth-century reconstruction of medieval buildings.

On ascending the stone staircase to the porch, note the finely-moulded archway. Some of the apartments of the Keep are used as an **Armoury.**
The **Upper Chambers** are reached at the head of the grand staircase, and close at hand in the Well Chamber, is the **Well,** nearly 300 feet deep. Pipe holes near it would seem to be part of the elaborate Norman system for carrying water to various parts of the Keep. On the south-west side of the fortress is a loop-hole, in its original condition, with arched roof and steps for the bowman.
Of the many towers and gateways which break the line of the Curtain Wall the most important is the **Constable's Tower,** forming the principal entrance. It is defended by a drawbridge and portcullis, and was built by Henry III to replace the old north-west gate destroyed in 1216.
Peverell's Tower, farther seaward, is later in style. It has also an arched gateway and once had a drawbridge. On the north-east wall the principal building is the **Avranches Tower** (twelfth century).
The **Underground Works** were cut out at various times, the first being when Hubert de Burgh was in command of the Castle. The most interesting are those connected with the former main entrance through **St. John's Tower** at the north end of the castle.

Slightly to the north of the Castle is the obsolete Fort Burgoyne. The parade ground adjoins. Close at hand is the **Duke of York's Military School.**

Northfall Meadow, immediately below the northern side of the Castle, extends to the cliff. Here is was that M. Bleriot descended after his historic flight by monoplane across the Channel on Sunday morning, July 25th, 1909. The spot is marked by a granite representation of the ground plan of his aeroplane but is fast becoming concealed by trees and undergrowth.

In returning to the sea-front from the Castle the ruins of **St. James's Old Church** are passed. The church was badly damaged during the 1939–45 war and is retained as a "tidy ruin." This and St. Mary's in the town were the only two remaining of the four original churches of Dover.

Snargate Street probably takes its name from a sort of grating – a snare-gate – across the Dour to catch the rubbish brought down by the stream. Later a gate in the wall, near the same spot, was called the Snargate, as is commemorated by a tablet, next door to a printing office, on the northern side. There were fifteen ancient gates, all now demolished.

The Western Heights

With a magnificent view from the top, are traversed by the Military Road which climbs steeply from Worthington Street.

The remains of the **Knights Templars' Church** on the Western Heights were un-covered in 1806 and were repaired in 1913. This church, which is a short distance to the left of the Military Road passing close by a tunnel was not only one of the smallest in the country, but it is one of the very few round church sites remaining in England. Here was held the ancient Court of Shepway, composed of the Mayors, Barons and Jurats of the Cinque Ports. The Court has been revived with all its pageantry on the installation of recent Lord Wardens, but the proceedings are now held in the pictures-que grounds of Dover College.

Car Ferry Terminal, Dover

Walks and Drives around Dover

To Shakespeare Cliff. The first object for which a Channel voyager approaching Dover looks is the sharply-pointed peak, a little westward of the Admiralty Pier, known as **Shakespeare Cliff.**

The railway from Dover to Folkestone runs along the shore until it reaches the foot of the slope, when it tunnels right through the Cliff.

To reach the Cliff turn right into Snargate Street – from the market – continue over the railway bridge to Limekiln Street, then turn up Archcliff Road, passing various military depots.

A footway along the edge of the cliff leads to a footpath which ascends steeply to the summit. A bus may be taken as far as Ropewalk.

To the South Foreland and St. Margaret's Bay. By bus direct or on foot. For walkers the most interesting route is that by the cliffs. Proceed along the Esplanade to the foot of the East Cliff. Here, where the terrace road begins to climb above the Harbour, an open path leads up to the summit, from which a fine view is obtained of the Harbour. A turn to the left from the East Cliff Path leads to Northfall Meadow, and the Dover Castle entrance on the main Deal–Dover road. Continue up the cliff pathway, to the South Foreland, about three miles, and St. Margaret's Bay, about four miles.

There are several semicircular depressions in the cliff, between Dover and Kingsdown, known as **Fan Hole,** round which it is necessary to walk warily. It is possible to clamber down to the beach by way of a laborious winding path known as Langdon's Stairs.

Motorists go along the Deal Road past the Castle, turning right in two miles to the West Cliffe, with its tiny church and so to **St. Margaret's,** turning right for the Bay.

The **South Foreland Lighthouse** *(not open)*, where Marconi carried out some of his experiments has existed in one form or another since 1634 when the "light" was a coal fire. The present optic revolves over a mercury bath. This light flashes three times every 20 seconds, while the companion light, twenty miles across the Channel, on Cape Gris Nez, which shares the guardianship of the Channel, flashes once every 5 seconds.

St. Margaret's Bay

Banks. – *Lloyds, National Westminster.*   **Hotel.** – *Granville*, on cliff.
Beach consists of loose pebbles.

This beautiful bay is an ideal spot for a restful but bracing holiday. From the top of the cliff a bird's eye view is obtained of a crescent-shaped, shingly strand, then trees and undergrowth, broken into patches by break-neck paths straggling up the cliff-side; and over all the dazzling glare of the chalk. A road to the left from the cliff top passes through a part of St. Margaret's, and emerges on the Leathercote Point, the highest point of the coast hereabouts.

Prominent on the point is **The Memorial to the Dover Patrol,** in the shape of an obelisk of granite, designed by Sir Aston Webb, P.R.A. A similar obelisk was erected on Cap Blanc Nez, the highest point of the cliffs across the Channel, while a replica was also placed in New York Harbour.

The Bay has good bathing, boating and fishing facilities and is famous for its prawns.

St. Margaret's is the nearest point to the coast of France; it is often the landing place of Channel swimmers, and it is interesting to recall that when the Channel Tunnel scheme was first mooted, an experimental boring was made here. The small square brick hut at the foot of the steps near the *Green Man* is a connection point for the cross-channel telephone cables. The village proper, **St. Margaret's-at-Cliffe,** is about half a mile inland.

The Church is one of the finest Norman parish churches in the country. At the north entrance is a picturesque porch containing stone seats and a holy-water stoup. Over the west door are elaborate sculptures now much decayed. The exterior of the clerestory is ornamented by an arcade, an unusual feature in a parish church. Viewed from the west door, the interior, which is of Caen stone, is very imposing. The carved Norman capitals of the massive pillars and the rich mouldings above are the most striking features. Rudely-scratched drawings of ships on some of the pillars, notably that nearest the font, are thought to have been the work of sailors of the fourteenth–fifteenth centuries. The church is believed to date from 1160, and was last restored, as a whole, in 1869, though a number of excavations and alterations were carried out in the chancel just before the 1914–18 War, when some fragments of what are thought to be remains of the original Saxon church were discovered. The curfew is still tolled here at 8 p.m. from November to March.

A mile west of St. Margaret's is **West Cliffe,** with an ancient church. The windows are Saxon, and there is a low Norman or Saxon tower by the porch.

To Buckland River, Ewell, St. Radigund's Abbey, and Old Park. Go through the town to Buckland and River. Just before the bridge over the *Dour* is crossed at Buckland an asphalted footpath will be seen on the left, running between a large paper mill and **Buckland Church** (St. Andrew's), which can be seen well from the railway. It has a lofty nave with Norman pillars and an Early English archway. In the ancient St. Thomas Chapel, a Norman window, *c.* 1170, has been discovered north of the Early English window (1400). Near the western entrance is a large and very ancient yew.

Continue by the road, and pass under the railway to the **Athletic Ground** at Crabble. Here is the County Cricket Ground. The road bends right for a few yards and then left at a mill, and runs side by side with the shady, picturesque *Dour* to the village of **River.** The prettily situated Recreation Ground at River has public tennis courts and bowling greens. **River Church** (St. Peter's), a flint and brick building, contains a font consecrated in the year 1010 by Archbishop Alphege, which was brought from an old church at Canterbury. Below the church is the start of a delightful walk along the river bank leading to Kearsney Abbey.

River may also be reached by the Upper Road, the main Dover and Canterbury road, eastward of river and railway.

ST. RADIGUND's ABBEY–WALDERSHARE PARK

St. Radigund's Abbey. At River turn to the left up Minnis Lane and proceed uphill for a mile and a half to the plateau on which stand the ruins. The Abbey may also be reached by almost any turning on the left of the London Road.

The only parts remaining are the massive tower, picturesquely draped in ivy, portions of the chapel and refectory. The moat may be traced in the fields beyond. The Abbey was founded in 1190 and covered at one time an extensive circular area. Although richly endowed, it seems to have early fallen into disrepair.

The excursion can well be combined with that to Alkham to reach which turn left on leaving the farm gate at St. Radigund's. Along this road about 1¾ miles is a nursery of hydrangeas set in pockets among the woodland. Owing to the mineral content of the soil the flowers are always blue. This sea of blue hydrangeas in full bloom from July to September is a joyful sight.

Continuing in the same direction turn right at the crossroads to Alkham and approach the Marquis of Granby and Ewell Minnis from the opposite side of the valley to that in the route outlined below.

Beyond the Minnis Lane turning, the road from River passes the grounds of **Kearsney Abbey,** now developed as a park with gardens and a marked nature trail. The picturesque Weir, with its foreground of water-lilies, lies to the right. Kearsney Station is near to the main road.

From Kearsney one road turns left along the Alkham Valley and then right to join the main Canterbury road at **Temple Ewell,** which owes its name to the fact that the Knights Hospitallers had a home here, now represented by **Temple Farm.** The church has a Norman doorway and window and a wealth of seventeenth-century stained glass brought from the Continent.

From the main road, half a mile south-east towards Dover, the Waldershare road turns left to the north-east, skirting the beautifully wooded **Old Park.**

To Ewell Minnis and Alkham. The deep lateral depression of the Alkham Valley, served by buses from Dover and Folkestone, is extremely picturesque. The hills on the right of the road may be climbed to **Ewell Minnis,** a breezy upland village surrounded by a wealth of wild flowers, out from whence a pleasant woodland footpath leads down to **Alkham** (*Marquis of Granby*), 2½ miles from Kearsney along the valley road (B2060). This old village, sentinelled by lofty elms, lies in the deepest recess of the valley. The Early English church, standing high above the road, is of flint, with a square tower capped by a tiled, pyramidical roof.

Beyond Alkham is the Drellingore Spring, the source of one of the most important intermittent streams in the district; its river joining the *Dour* near Dover. The road climbs to the head of the valley and joins the Canterbury–Folkestone road about two miles north of Folkestone.

To Waldershare Park and Barfreston. Waldershare Park is most easily visited from Dover by bus from Pencester Road. Motorists take the main Canterbury road, turning to the right along A256 just before Ewell and left at the roundabout at the top of Whitfield Hill.

At **Church Whitfield,** a mile to the east of the road (turn off at either end of Whitfield), there is a beautiful little church with Saxon windows, arch and masonry, as well as Norman and Early English work.

The pleasant red-brick village of **East Langdon,** has an ancient flint church of some interest. Its particular treasure is a fifteenth-century red velvet cope-hood.

Waldershare Park is a seat of the Earl of Guilford. The mansion was built after a design of Inigo Jones in the reign of William III by Sir Henry Furnese, a wealthy London merchant who bought the estate. It is surrounded by an extensive park noted for its lovely trees – beeches, limes, yews and Spanish chestnuts – in which stands the **Belvidere Tower,** of the same date as the house.

88

Waldershare Church is not visible from the road. It is reached from the Dover road by a lane having a letter-box at the corner, about ¼ mile south of the signpost "to Eythorne." The church contains a number of curious monuments to members of the Monyngs and Furnese families.

At the south-west corner of the park is **Coldred Church,** a tiny building with a good deal of pre-conquest stonework remaining. It stands within a Roman entrenchment of about three acres. **Sheperdswell** station, on the Dover to Canterbury line, is 1½ miles north-west. The name of the parish is *Sibertswold,* i.e., Sibert's-downs, but the place has been variously called Sheapardswell, Sibertswalt and Shepherd's Well.

Sibertswold Church, about five minutes' walk from the station, was rebuilt in 1863. The parish is rich in earthen relics of a long-past age, notable being three large tumuli and an ancient camp, on a hill known as **Three Barrow Down.**

Eythorne is a curious mixture of rural seclusion and industrial activities. On one side of it are the wooded acres of Waldershare, and on the other the *Tilmanstone Colliery.* At Upper Eythorne is the oldest Baptist Chapel in this part of Kent. It was built in the days of the Stuart persecution, in order that the worshippers might avoid the penalties of the "Five Mile Act," but there was a meeting-house here as early as the reign of Queen Mary.

Barfreston. Barson, as the place is commonly called, although its official name is Barfreston or Barfreystone, lies in the middle of open, breezy down country interspersed with parks and beech woods, glorious at all times and especially in autumn. A huge yew of great age in the churchyard contains the belfrey.

The lovely little Norman Church is dedicated to St. Nicholas and is as beautiful inside as out. The length is only about 43 feet 4 inches. The nave is 16 feet 8 inches wide; the choir, 13½ feet; the thickness of the walls, 2 feet 9 inches. Built of flint and stone, it is said to have been erected about 1170 as a thank-offering by a nobleman who nearly lost his life while hunting in the forest. Both inside and out it is richly decorated with grotesque carvings. The south door is particularly fine, with elaborate and amusing pictures of human and animal life. At the east end is a very fine Norman wheel window with fine carving and decoration. Between the nave and the chancel is a beautiful arch supported by four twisted shafts.

Just beyond Barfreston is the beautiful **Fredville Park.** The seventeenth-century house stands on the site of an ancient manor belonging to one of the eight branches of the Boys family, who had seats in Kent. They came over with the Conqueror and many are buried in the churches in this region.

Along the Dover–Canterbury Road. The road follows the railway through Buckland and Ewell beyond which it veers away to **Lydden,** past which the road climbs the long and steep Lydden Hill (455 feet).

At 6½ miles from Dover, a road goes off leftward to the pretty villages of Wootton (1¼ miles) and Denton (¾ mile further). Wootton church dates mainly from the thirteenth century but the base of the tower is Norman. **Denton** is a peaceful place. Its church stands in a fine park surrounding **Denton Court,** with magnificent topiary.

South-west is **Tappington** (generally called Tapton) or Tappington Everard, an oak-panelled Elizabethan Manor House, for many years in the possession of the Barham family, and made famous by the author of the *Ingoldsby Legends.*

At eight miles from Dover the road from Folkestone (A260) joins the Dover Road (A2), having passed through Denton, about a mile and a half south. The junction of the two roads is on the eastern side of **Broome Park,** a beautiful estate owned and loved by the first Earl Kitchener. The house was built in the reign of Charles I.

A quarter of a mile north of Broome Park a left-hand road leads to **Barham,** with a fine church surrounded by beautiful beeches. It has an unusual green copper spire, a fine roof, a fourteenth-century font with Jacobean cover, and fourteenth-century and later brasses. Lord Kitchener's name is the first on the Roll of Honour.

Near the church is **Barham Court,** where one of Becket's assassins lived. Coal was found in 1899 by boring at Ropersole, near Barham.

A very pleasant extension of the detour may be made along the Nailbourne valley from Barham, *via* Kingston, to Bishopsbourne. Near **Kingston** an important Saxon cemetery was found in the eighteenth century. The church, dating from Saxon times, has several features of interest, including two brasses in the chancel, dated 1600 and 1584, and armour hanging on the south wall of the nave. From Kingston field paths lead to Bishopsbourne (*see* below).

Between Barham and Kingston several roads to the right climb steeply up to the main road, which runs for three and a half miles over **Barham Downs,** and, though undulating, is so straight as to be obviously part of the old Roman highway known as Watling Street. (A few miles to the west is another of their great highways, **Stone Street,** also converging on Canterbury.)

There are many fine parks on both sides of the road. Eleven miles from Dover, a narrow road to the left leads in half a mile to –

Bishopsbourne. It is of interest through its association with *Richard Hooker*, the English Church theologian of the sixteenth century. He held the living from 1595 until his death in 1600.

The large and stately **Church** with high tower has a wealth of glass, some of the fourteenth and seventeenth centuries, and the rest modern, including a west window by Burne-Jones and William Morris. The east window is blazoned with the arms of Hooker and of the sees of Canterbury and Rochester. The latter are in commemoration of Bishop Waring, who was rector of Bishopsbourne from 1619 to 1638. In the chancel is a monument to Hooker.

Skirting Bourne Park the main road drops to the village of **Bridge,** from the vicinity of which fine views are obtained.

The spired **Church** is mainly Early English, but incorporates part of the original Norman building. Under an arch in the north wall of the chancel is the recumbent effigy of a man in robes. On a stone let into the wall close at hand are Norman carved figures.

Bridge is ecclesiastically united with Bekesbourne and **Patrixbourne,** a pleasant little village of Tudor and Carolian houses, which clusters upon the north bank of the *Nailbourne,* about a mile eastward of the Canterbury road.

The extensive Saxon cemetery discovered at Patrixbourne Hill is evidence that Patrixbourne was populated at a very early date. Patrixbourne possessed a church at the time of the Domesday Survey, when the parish was named "Bourne" only.

The most remarkable feature of the church is its elaborate Norman doorway, one of the most richly moulded in Kent, with a second round arch framed by a pointed one above it.

Other beautiful features are the horseshoe-shaped Norman chancel arch, the Swiss glass in the Bifrons Chapel and the east window, a triplet of Norman lights, above the central one of which is a marigold-window of eight lights, radiating from a circle. The east-triplet is filled with old Swiss painted glass. In the chancel are two aumbries, a hagioscope, and a remarkable piscina – the arch of which is surmounted by a thirteenth-century triangular canopy, now mutilated.

Folkestone

Angling. – The long Harbour Pier is a favourite resort of sea anglers (Fishing tickets). Fishing also from the sands and beach. Boatmen make special provision for anglers and provide bait and tackle. Catches include dabs, cod, plaice, pollack and pouting. The most important event is the annual Sea-Angling Festival, consisting of pier fishing in October and boat fishing in November.

Banks. – The principal branches of the main banks are in Sandgate Road, with sub-branches in other parts of the town.

Bathing. – The main (west) beach is shingly, but at low tide a fair stretch of sand is exposed, and this has now been increased by clever placing of groynes.

There is a fine **Open-Air Bathing Pool** between The Leas Lift and the Harbour Pier. There are beach huts on Marine Parade.

On the East-Cliff Sands, there is a fully-equipped bathing station. Men in boats are stationed off the shore in case of need.

In Foord Road are Public Baths, open on Thursdays, Fridays and Saturdays.

Boating. – Dinghy sailing is a very popular sport locally, and the *Yacht Club* has its Club House in North Street. The local *Rowing Club* welcomes temporary members. Regatta and gala during July.

Every morning and afternoon in the season short cruises are made by speed-boat.

There is safe and pleasant boating on the boating lake in Marine Gardens.

For inland boating take bus from Sandgate Road to Seabrook, at the western end of Sandgate. Here begins the Royal Military Canal. A pleasant pull can be had to Hythe, and on towards West Hythe.

Bowls. – Greens are open to the public, including Cumberland turf greens at the Sports Ground in Cheriton Road, at Radnor Park and near the East Cliff Pavilion.

Bus and Coach Services. – An excellent service within the town and nearby district. Folkestone is also linked by bus with all the main centres in Kent and with the coastal towns of the south and west.

Car Parking Places. – Cheriton Gardens; Pleydell Gardens; West Cliff Gardens; Lower Sandgate Road; the Bayle; and at the Harbour.

Cinemas. – *Odeon, Essoldo,* both in the centre of the town.

Cricket. – Cricket is played on the beautiful ground in the Municipal Sports Ground on the Cheriton Road, midway between the Central and West stations. County and First Class cricket matches are played. The *Folkestone Cricket Club* welcomes visitors.

Croquet. – There is a club at the Folkestone Lawn Tennis, Squash Rackets and Croquet Ground, Bouverie Road West.

Dancing. – At the Leas Cliff Hall, and at the Continental Wampach and other hotels.

Distances. – Ashford, 17 miles; Canterbury, 17; Deal, 15; Dover, $7\frac{1}{2}$; Hastings, 38; Hythe, $4\frac{1}{2}$; London, 70; London (rail), 71; Maidstone, $35\frac{1}{2}$; Margate, 27; New Romney, $14\frac{1}{2}$; Ramsgate, 26; Rye, 26.

Early Closing Day. – Wednesday.

Hotels. – *Burlington*, Earls Avenue; *Grand*, The Leas; *Continental Wampach*, Castle Hill Avenue; *Lyndhurst*, Clifton Gardens; *Garden House*, Sandgate Road; *Esplanade*, The Leas; *Prince's*, Bouverie Road; *Barrelle*, Marine Parade; *Highcliffe*, Clifton Gardens; *Riviera*, Lower Sandgate Road; *Aston*, Trinity Gardens; *Adelphi*, Augusta Gardens; *Avondale*, Clifton Gardens; *Bethersden*, Langhouse Gardens; *Cravenhurst*, Trinity Crescent; *Cavendish Court*, The Leas; *Devonshire*, Marine Parade; *Didsbury*, Marine Crescent; *Chilworth Court*, Earls Avenue; *Lismore*, The Leas; *Manor Court*, Manor Road; *Gresham*, Clifton Crescent; *Greystones*, Clifton Crescent; *Greenwold*, Clifton Gardens; *Ingles Court*, Ingles Road; *Kia Ora*, Longford Terrace; *Norfolk*, Langhorne Gardens; *Pier*, Marine Crescent; *St. Heliers*, Clifton Gardens; *Salisbury*, Clifton Gardens.

Information. – Information Centre, Castle Hill Avenue.

Library, Museum and Art Gallery. – At Grace Hill. In the Art Gallery, loan exhibitions of pictures and objects d'art are organized throughout the year.

Lifts. – A lift at the eastern end of the Leas provides an easy means of reaching the beach and the Lower Sandgate Road.

Music. – Military and other bands play daily at the bandstand on the Leas during the summer.

Population. – 45,270.

FOLKESTONE

Postal. – The Head Post Office in Bouverie Place, and the principal Branch Office in Tontine Street.

Races. – The Folkestone Racecourse is at Westenhanger Park, six miles westward. One of the prettiest in the country, it is used for both flat-racing and steeple-chasing.

Railway Stations. – Folkestone has three Railway Stations; the **Central,** for the Leas and central part of the town; the **Harbour,** for Continental traffic only; **West,** serving the west end of the town and Sandgate. The Central Station, where all trains stop (except the boat trains), is conveniently placed for most parts of the town.

Squash Rackets. – Two courts at Bouverie Road West.

Tennis. – Public courts at Radnor Park; Sports Ground, Cheriton Road; and East Cliff.

Theatres. – *Leas Pavilion* – Repertory (closed November–Easter); *Marine Pavilion* – summer concert party; *Leas Cliff Hall* – concerts, variety and recitals.

Few seaside resorts have been developed on such admirable lines as Folkestone. While private enterprise still plays its important part the Corporation uses all the powers vested in it to safeguard and improve the amenities of the town, which is distinguished by its wide roads and pavements.

The best part of Folkestone stands upon a lofty plateau of greensand, with the fine advantage of a south aspect. From The Leas there is an uninterrupted view in clear weather across the Channel to the white cliffs of France, and along the coast to Dungeness on the one hand, and to Shakespeare Cliff and the Admiralty Pier at Dover on the other. A slight distance to the north the town is hedged in by a range of chalk hills, from 400 to 600 feet high, which screen it from cold winds and add greatly to its beauty. The Lower Sandgate Road, the cliff walks, and the beach are further screened by the wooded slope of The Leas. The cliffs and their aspect combine to give Folkestone two climates at all times, generally bracing above, mild and genial below.

Modern Folkestone dates from the opening of the railway in 1843, and is on the popular route to the Continent via Boulogne and Calais. The service of steamers also was started in 1843, and the first passage between Folkestone and Boulogne occupied four hours. Now the magnificent turbine steamers, each capable of carrying over 1,400 passengers, accomplish the journey in an hour and a half.

IN AND ABOUT FOLKESTONE

From the point of view of scenery, the best approach to Folkestone is by road from the high Dover road. As soon as the seaward shoulder of the Downs is turned, Folkestone and a vast sweep of sea and land are revealed.

Far beneath are the town, its harbour, and the sea stretching away to the horizon. Towards the right, in a graceful curve, the coast goes sweeping round by Hythe and Dymchurch to Dungeness, and the prospect is closed by the dimly-seen Fairlight Hills near Hastings.

From the Central Station turn right for the sea. On the right are the **Kingsnorth Gardens,** with lily-ponds and fountains and a wealth of flowers.

Southward from the Gardens runs **Castle Hill Avenue,** a wide thoroughfare leading directly southward to The Leas and the sea and opening up a delightful prospect that extends right up to the sea-front. The eastward end of the avenue becomes Langhorne Gardens, where is a finely-placed bronze *Statue of Harvey*, who discovered the circulation of the blood.

The Leas

Indisputably forms one of the finest marine promenades in the world. The Leas has a length of about a mile and a half, and its distinguishing feature as a promenade is its unusual breadth, especially towards the western end. A spacious roadway, overlooked by terraces, crescents, and squares of dignified mansions, extends the whole distance, and between this and the cliffs are wide, grassy walks and a glorious display of flowers. Beyond the grass again is an asphalted footway. The promenade varies in height from 130 to 170 feet above sea-level with superb views seaward.

For some distance west of The Leas Cliff Hall is a second pathway about 20 feet below the cliff edge known as the **Madeira Walk.** Part of the walk has been roofed over to form a Sun Trap Shelter, where comfortable chairs may be hired and wonderful views enjoyed with full shelter from the wind.

At the eastern end of The Leas is **The Road of Remembrance,** forming part of the town's war memorial and planted with many rosemary bushes. At the top is an inscribed tablet.

Near this end of The Leas is the **Leas Pavilion,** approached by a sunk court lined with shops. The hall is the local home of repertory. A resident company performs from Easter till October.

The Leas Cliff Hall is constructed in the face of the cliff almost opposite Castle Hill Avenue. The principal feature is a fine concert hall where celebrity and orchestral concerts are presented, as well as occasional variety shows. Dancing to well-known bands on a superb maple floor is available. Beneath the main hall is the Sun Lounge Restaurant, used as a restaurant in summer and for private functions and dinners during winter months.

Upon The Leas, just west of the Leas Cliff Hall, is a bandstand where, during summer months, bands entertain the crowds of visitors. On the face of the cliff opposite the Bandstand, is a broad, gently sloping **Zigzag Path** with shelters at intervals. It forms a convenient means of communication between The Leas and the Undercliff.

Near the eastern extremity of The Leas, a hydraulic **Lift** built in 1890, connects The Leas and the lower promenades, a distance of 100 feet.

The **Undercliff,** below The Leas, has sloping walks and stepped paths through pines and shrubs to the beach. However scorching the sun or strong the wind above, shade and shelter can always be found below.

Running along the base of the cliff is –

The Lower Sandgate Road,

for which there is a vehicular toll, and so called to distinguish it from the higher road, or Sandgate Road proper. It is the private property of the Folkestone Estate Trust, but is freely open to pedestrians. Completely screened from north winds and facing south, the road is a favourite promenade and drive in winter and summer alike. On each side it is fringed by winding paths, which on the land side are shaded by pines, and on the seaward side pass through a series of shrubberies and gardens with

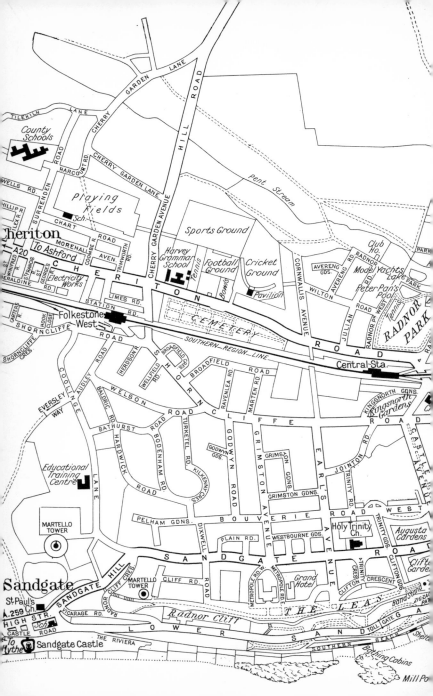

FOLKESTONE

Scale of ¼ Mile

0   ¼

alcoves and arbours. Adjoining is the **Marine Walk,** serving both as a protective sea-wall and a parade.

At the western end is a row of picturesque beach cabins and a restaurant.

From nearby, one road ascends steeply to the Parish Church, while another, the **Marine Parade,** continues on the level to the Harbour. The foreshore has been reclaimed and converted into –

The Marine Gardens

Well-kept lawns and colourful flower beds adjoin the Marine Pavilion, which provides roller skating, concert parties, and children's entertainments. A wide promenade gives access to the excellently equipped open-air **Bathing Pool.** It is 165 feet long by 75 feet wide, with a depth varying from $2\frac{1}{2}$ feet to 10 feet, and filled with purified sea water. East of the bathing pool is a large Motor Boating Pond, overlooked by a restaurant and kiosk shops, while just beyond it is the Games Rotunda.

The Harbour

Although as a fishing port Folkestone can claim a more than respectable antiquity, its modern development may be said to date from the purchase of the old harbour in 1842 by what was then the South-Eastern Railway Company. The "eastward drift" of shingle which still causes so much anxiety to all towns on the south-east coast, has rendered the harbour, designed by Telford in 1807, wellnigh useless. The directors of the newly opened Railway were prompt to see the advantages arising from the possession of an alternative through route to the Continent, and the Government, to whom the harbour had been mortgaged for £10,000, were glad to be rid of their security and its attendant liabilities for £18,000. The material which had blocked the harbour was soon cleared away, landing-stages were erected and a service of boats was established between Folkestone and the Continent. The first steamer went from Folkestone to Boulogne on June 28, 1843, and a regular service was inaugurated on August 1 following. In less than twenty years the population of the town doubled, for the foundations of its prosperity had been well and truly laid. Further development of the port has followed so that today Folkestone holds a high position in Cross-Channel traffic.

The Folkestone–Boulogne route from London to Paris is shorter by twenty-eight miles than that via Dover–Calais.

The Harbour Pier. There are three steamer berths on the east side of the Harbour Pier, which is 1,480 feet long, the average depth at low water of spring tides being 22 feet. The railway platform extends the whole length of the pier. The Customs office adjoins the berths. Above the platform runs a raised promenade which forms a magnificent vantage-point for views of the town and coast to Dover Harbour in one direction and the whole stretch of Dungeness Bay in the other. The promenade is open to the public from 6 a.m. to dusk. Fishing is permitted from the upper promenade of the pier during daylight hours and from the pier lighthouse area only, to 10 p.m.

East of the Fish Market are the East Cliff Sands, where at any but high tide a fine stretch of sand, the only one in Folkestone, is laid bare and is consequently extremely popular with the crowds of children who gather there.

Folkestone Harbour

The East Cliff

From the vicinity of the Inner Harbour, by passing under the railway to North Street and ascending the flight of steps on the right which leads up to a paved path passing in front of St. Peter's Church and Schools, the East Cliff is reached. The area has been developed somewhat on the same lines to The Leas. There is a fine broad, turfed promenade with shelters overlooking the paths below the cliff top, bordered with rock gardens.

This extends from the W.T.A. Hotel to the entrance of the Warren. Close to the hotel are the small **St. Peter's Church** – the Mariner's Church – and Sir Philip Sassoon's model cottages for fishermen's families. This part overlooks the winding streets of "Old Folkestone," the Cross-Channel traffic and the fishing industry, while the view from the eastern end embraces the whole panorama of the Warren, East Wear Bay, the famous white cliffs, the pier at Dover six miles away, and the never-ceasing stream of vessels compelled by the narrowness of the Channel to pass close to land.

The eastern end has been developed as a sports and social centre, with the handsome **East Cliff Pavilion** (refreshments), the miniature golf course,

97

putting and bowling greens, and tennis courts; while beyond is the Warren.

At the back of the promenade the Wear Bay road runs east from Radnor Bridge Road as far as the Pavilion, where it turns north, skirting the golf course and tennis courts, crosses the railway by the road leading to the Warren, bears round to the west and joins the Dover road.

There are several roads radiating from the Harbour to the upper parts of the town. The most important of these is **Tontine Street,** a modern thoroughfare. In the trough of the valley lying to the west is the quaint little **High Street** – fully six feet wide from kerb to kerb – which runs steeply uphill to the neighbourhood of the Town Hall. Formerly it was the principal business thoroughfare and it still contains many important business establishments. Turn to the left at the first opportunity, before reaching the highest part of the High Street, for the Bayle, where once stood a Saxon castle.

The Parish Church bears the double dedication of the former twelfth-century Priory Church of St. Mary and St. Eanswythe. The present chancel dates from about 1217. The upper stages of the tower were built in the fifteenth century, a work rendering necessary the strengthening of the piers by masonry casing, the raising of the aisle roofs, which made useless the circular clerestory windows, and led to the introduction of Perpendicular windows. The tower contains a fine peal of eight modern bells.

Westward of the central tower all is quite modern with the exception of the responds of the original nave arcade, but there remains much of the walling of the transepts.

The large west window is a memorial of Harvey, the discoverer of the circulation of the blood.

The Early English chancel, with its fine roof, three eastern lancet lights, well-moulded windows and doorways and Capello's mosaics of the Apostles, is the best part of the church.

From the Church it is a walk of only a minute or two by way of Church Street to the **Town Hall,** which occupies a prominent position facing the **Sandgate Road,** one of the most important thoroughfares of the town running parallel with The Leas.

From the Town Hall, Rendezvous Street leads to Grace Hill where are the **Public Library, Museum and Art Gallery.**

Radnor Park, close to the Central Station, about three-quarters of a mile from the sea, is a delightful open space prettily laid out and surrounded by dense shrubberies. On the north side are two miniature lakes and there are facilities for tennis and bowls.

Westward of Central Station is the **Municipal Sports Ground.** The cricket ground is one of the best in the South of England. There is excellent provision for tennis and bowls, and a section of the ground is appropriated to football and hockey. The Indoor Bowls Centre, open seven days a week, is one of the largest of its kind. To the north of Radnor Park Avenue a new Sports Centre is being developed.

Sandgate

Banks. – *Lloyds*, 78 High Street; *Midland*, 60 High Street.
Bathing is excellent.
Bowls. – A good green in the Recreation Ground some distance inland up Military Road.
Early Closing. – Wednesday.
Hotels. – *Royal Norfolk*, High Street; *Wellington*, Sandgate Road.

Library. – Branch of the Folkestone Public Library in High Street.
Post Office. – High Street.
Tennis. – Public hard and grass courts in the Recreation Ground some distance inland, up Military Road. There is also a hard court at Seabrook.

Sandgate is a restful little place nestling at the foot of the Shorncliffe heights, about a mile from the centre of Folkestone. It now forms part of the borough. Being within easy reach of the amusements of Folkestone, it is popular with those who, though fond of quiet, like an occasional distraction.

The town consists principally of a long, straight thoroughfare parallel with the sea, until a slight bend of the coast at Sea Point brings the road down to the shore.

Bordering the shore is an asphalted Promenade, over which the shingle is often dashed at high tides. From Sea Point the motor road, bordered by walls and banks covered with tamarisk, runs westward just behind the Promenade.

The Lower Sandgate Toll Road ends in the very delightful residential part of the town, where the Radnor Cliff Gardens and the Riviera provide pleasant views and shade.

Sandgate Castle. The ruins stand on the shore at the end of the Riviera and facing Castle Street, and are not open to the public. Though so plain in outward appearance, the Castle is of more interest than is generally supposed. Like Walmer, Deal, and Sandown Castles, it was built by Henry VIII in 1539–40. The circular keep alone remains today, and that is in great danger of being undermined by the sea, which has severely damaged it during abnormally high tides in recent years.

Opposite Castle Road, near the foot of the hill, Military Road runs inland to a Recreation Ground, with public tennis courts and bowling green, and **Shorncliffe.** The Parish Church is reached by steps from the High Street.

At the western end of Sandgate is a centennial **Memorial of Sir John Moore,** erected in 1909.

West of Sandgate is **Seabrook.**

Walks and Excursions from Folkestone

To the Warren. The Warren, the coastal area north-east from Folkestone, is as wildly beautiful as the famous Landslip between Shanklin and Ventnor in the Isle of Wight.

Motorists can follow Wear Bay Road at the back of the East Cliff. Pedestrians can go along the East Cliff or take the bus up the Dover Road as far as the *Valiant Sailor Inn*, at a height of 546 feet above sea-level. Here a footpath leads along the cliff to the end of a zigzag path cut in the cliff and leading down to the Warren. At low tide it is possible to go along the sands and boulders at the foot of the Wear Bay Cliffs.

Folkestone's most beautiful natural attraction is a scene of picturesque confusion caused by the undermining action of the sea and underground springs on the soft chalk, which has beneath it beds of almost impervious gault, or clay. Great masses are thrown down from time to time, and become covered with tangled undergrowth and grass.

Broad paths give easy access to the seashore and to some of the most beautiful spots. Whole days can be spent exploring its lovely corners, while naturalists of all kinds will find treasures in plenty.

Hewn in the face of the cliff are several reputed "smugglers' caves." Many rare plants and insects may be found in this natural playground, and fossils are numerous where rock faces are exposed.

To Caesar's Camp and Paddlesworth. Caesar's Camp, the conical knoll immediately north of the by-pass, is the most prominent and the best known of the chain of hills girdling the town. By the nearest way the distance from The Leas is about a mile and a half, but ample time should be allowed for the climb and a good look round.

Caesar's Camp, 400 feet high, commands by far the best view of Folkestone and its surroundings, comprising a wide stretch of the coast and a great expanse of undulating country. Only the last part of the climb is at all stiff. It is generally considered that the hill has no real title to the name it bears; that the great earthworks and entrenchments, which can still be clearly traced, were constructed between 1000 and 1150.

At the base of the hill, on the western side, is the series of three Reservoirs, from which Folkestone is supplied with water. An additional covered reservoir was constructed near the ridge of the hills in 1924. Seen from above, especially if the water reflects a blue sky, the spot is one of great beauty.

From the Waterworks and the northern slope of Caesar's Camp, a straight road following the municipal boundary leads eastward to the Canterbury road, near

Sandgate Castle

the Holy Well, and westward by Cheriton Hill, presently dropping down to Newington. From this road two roads lead northward over the hills to Paddlesworth, the highest village in East Kent (611 feet). The better road branches off about half a mile east of the Camp, and passes **Hawkinge Airfield,** the one-time famous Battle of Britain R.A.F. station. On the other side of the airfield, in the village of Hawkinge, note the unusual "Skylon" on the church of St. Luke in the stead of a normal steeple. Turn right on reaching the airfield and in a few yards left again. The alternative road starts northward from a point about three-quarters of a mile west of Caesar's Camp. It is a narrow road going first down hill and then steeply up. At the top of the rise the road bends right to Hawkinge, where turn left for **Paddlesworth.**

From the centre of the village, a path leads left over a field to the tiny Church, dedicated to St. Oswald of Northumbria. It has Saxon and Norman features, and includes a small nave and smaller chancel, separated by a Norman arch.

The return from Paddlesworth can be made by a very pleasant and narrow country lane passing to the west of the inn and dropping steeply down to Etching-hill, thence home through Beachborough and Newington. (Distance, out and home, about 11 miles).

To Creteway Down, etc. A pleasant circular stroll is to follow the Canterbury Road as far as Lord Radnor's Drive (bus service). Then follow the path bearing right from the main road and climb the Down immediately ahead. Keep along the ridge to the Dover Road at the *Valiant Sailor Inn* and descend the path past

CHERITON–ALKHAM VALLEY

the Martello Towers to the East Cliff, and back to the town by Wear Bay Road and the Radnor Bridge Road.

To Cheriton, Newington and Beachborough. In this excursion footpaths are forsaken for the road, so many will prefer to make the journey by car or by the bus going to Newington or to Canterbury via Lyminge or via Stelling Minnis. The Cheriton Road leaves Radnor Park, opposite the Central Station, and passes on the right the Municipal Sports Ground, and on the left the Cemetery and West Station. **Shorncliffe Camp** is on the plateau above.

Cheriton is a rapidly growing district, now in the borough of Folkestone, with a modern Church (All Souls') on the main road. The ancient Parish Church lies a quarter of a mile south, and is reached by turning under the railway and then taking the first to the right.

It possesses Saxon features in the western portion of the nave and in the tower. The square embattled tower with a Saxon window, contains a peal of eight bells. In the interior are three recumbent fourteenth-century figures and some ancient brasses and stained glass. The chancel is specially fine, and has three brasses of ancient date.

The main road goes westward from Cheriton to a signpost pointing north to –
Newington, just off the main road and less than four miles from Folkestone. It is one of the most charming villages in the district, with many and varied subjects, including the picturesque *Frogholt Cottage* with its thatched roof and overhanging storey, to offer artists and photographers. The **Church** stands at the corner of the village, and has a quaint wooden bell turret. It contains some ancient glass and a number of memorial brasses.

Frogholt Cottage can be reached in ten minutes from the Church by the footpath running west immediately beyond the barn. On reaching the road bear right. If proceeding by road, return to the main road and take the next turning on the right. Frogholt Cottage is on the left.

The mansion-house of **Beachborough** gleams white amid the trees. It is plain, but beautifully situated. Towering above it is the symmetrical **Beachborough Hill,** with a magnificent view from the summit.

To Shorncliffe Camp. Shorncliffe Camp occupies an extensive area on the ridge above Sandgate, about two miles west of the centre of Folkestone. Its name signifies the bare or shorn rock.

Walkers approaching the Camp by way of Shorncliffe Road should follow it to the end, then turn left into Risborough Lane which leads into the Camp.

Sir John Moore, the hero of Corunna, trained his troops at Shorncliffe in 1794; it remained a military station until 1815, and after a period of disuse was re-established during the Crimean War. The Camp is now the Headquarters of 2nd Infantry Brigade and of the Dover/Shorncliffe Garrison. It is also the home of the Junior Infantrymen's Battalion, whose modern buildings stand high on the cliffs overlooking the English Channel, with a fine view of the French coastline on clear days.

The Alkham Valley. The Alkham Valley is a depression running at a distance of from two to four miles approximately parallel with the coast between Folkestone and Dover. The Canterbury Road is followed to the cross-roads beyond the Sugar Loaf and Caesar's Camp. Then turn to the right. The road passes the outskirts of **Hawkinge,** whose pretty little Norman church is to be seen on the hill to the left. The church, which contains a fine Royal Arms of Queen Anne dated 1713, is also an excellent vantage point with views of the Channel and Alkham Valley. About 2½ miles farther and six miles from Folkestone is the village of Alkham, (see p. 88).

The **Drellingore Spring,** in the Alkham Valley midway between Hawkinge and Alkham is the source of one of the most notable of the intermittent streams near Folkestone. After a considerable period of inactivity they flow in great volume. The stream from the Drellingore Spring increases until it becomes a river flowing over a part of the main road near Alkham village. It joins the River Dour near Dover.

To Lyminge and Elham. These historic spots can be reached by the road through Cheriton, Newington and Beachborough. The Canberbury via Elham buses will aid walkers, while motorists can have a pleasant run outward by the Elham Valley, as described below, and back by the road skirting the eastern side of Broome Park, and passing over Swingfield Minnis.

Lyminge, seven miles north-west of Folkestone, was the *Villa Limenoea* of the Romans. Its pleasant situation, proximity to the sea, and bus facilities have made it popular as a place of residence.

The **Church,** dedicated to SS. Mary and Ethelburga, is built of flint. It contains tiles, probably taken from early Roman buildings, and traces of Saxon masonry, and affords specimens of the architecture of various periods down to the Perpendicular.

In 1862, the foundations of the early Saxon Church were laid bare. They run parallel to the later Church, on the south, and show a church with rectangular nave, the north wall of which is contained under the present porch, and a semicircular apse at the east end, a plan which seems to have been that usually followed in the seventh century in the south-east of England.

Northward of Lyminge the road for several miles keeps company with the *Nailbourne*, a tributary of the Little Stour. After one mile there is a turning to the right for Acrise, where the Church, mentioned in the Domesday Book, is of Saxon origin, and was extended in Norman times. Note the carved Royal Arms of William and Mary with escutcheon to the effect that they were placed there after the death of Mary. *Acrise Place*, is of Tudor origin, the north front being mainly Elizabethan. In two miles road and river arrive at –

Elham (pronounced Eelham), a one-time market village, picturesque and interesting alike for its ancient church and its quaint old dwelling-houses.

The **Church,** which is partly Norman, mostly thirteenth-century, replaces one mentioned in Domesday Book. It has a massive tower and spire containing a clock and eight bells. The fourteenth-century oak roof is magnificent, and the porch also contains some good woodwork. Among the objects of interest are a very ancient chest, hewn out of a single piece of wood, an ancient round font, a very beautiful alabaster reredos in the south aisle, and the magnificently decorated modern chancel and screen of the side chapel.

The wonderful Tudor house in the High Street contains magnificent carving both inside and in the oak brackets upholding the eaves.

From Elham the road continues through the beautiful Elham Valley to Barham and Bishopsbourne described on pp. 89–90.

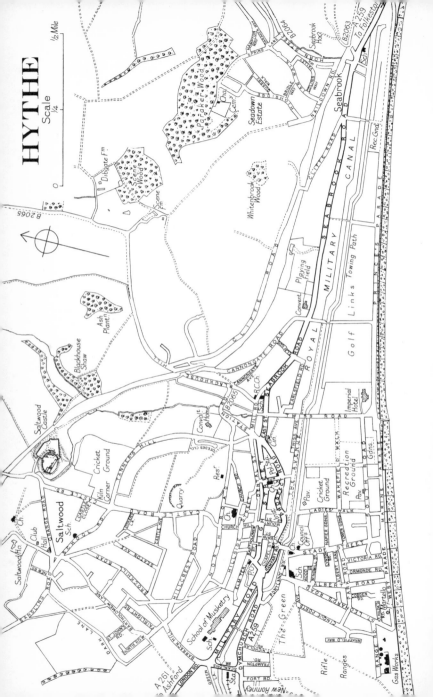

Hythe

Angling. – The Royal Military Canal is well-stocked with roach, bream, tench, rudd, carp, perch, and is strictly preserved. Tickets and information may be obtained from Mrs. A. Masters, Hon. Secretary, Cinque Ports Angling Society, 1 The Bogs, Hothfield, Ashford; or from Mr. J. P. Webb, 440 Hythe Road, Willesborough, Ashford.

Sea-angling off the foreshore for codling, whiting, conger, bass and flatfish. Boats may be hired.

Banks. – *Barclays, Lloyds, Midland, National Westminster;* all in the High Street.

Bathing. – The beach is of shingle, but a stretch of clean sand is exposed at low water and bathing is safe. Beach-chalets can be hired on application to the Borough Surveyor, Municipal Offices, Stade Street.

Boating. – Boats can be hired daily on the Royal Military Canal, at the Boat Stages adjoining Ladies' Walk Bridge and at Scanlons Bridge.

Bowls. – The Hythe Bowling Club has a good green adjoining the Ladies' Walk. Visitors are welcomed. Annual competitions.

Bus and Coach Services. – Town service and connections with neighbouring centres. Bus and coach stations in Red Lion Square and Portland Road.

Car Parks. – South Road; Beaconsfield Terrace (south end of Twiss Road); Prospect Road; Theatre Street; The Green; Military Road. Limited waiting in parts of High Street and Douglas Avenue.

Cricket. – The ground of the Hythe Cricket Club adjoins the Ladies' Walk and Recreation Grounds. Hythe Cricket Week, which follows that of Canterbury, is in August.

Cricket can also be played on the Corporation's Recreation Ground.

Distances. – Ashford, 12 miles; Canterbury, 17; Deal, 18; Dover, 12; Dymchurch, 5; Ferryfield (Lydd) Airport, 13; Folkestone, 5; London, 66; Lympne, 3; Maidstone, 30; Romney, 9; Rye, 21; Sandgate, 3; Sandling, 2; Sandwich, 18; Sellindge Church, 5; Tenterden, 19; Westenhanger, 3.

Early Closing Day. – Wednesday.

Flying. – Ashford Airport is $3\frac{1}{2}$ miles west of Hythe. Private aircraft are allowed to use the airport.

Golf. – Sene Valley Golf Course (18 holes) on high ground north of Cliff Road – entrance from Blackhouse Hill. The Hotel Imperial has a private 9-hole course on the eastern end of the sea-front. For information about play for visitors, apply to the Professional.

Hotels. – *Imperial*, Princes Parade; *Stade Court*, West Parade; *Seabrook*, Seabrook Road; *White Hart*, High Street; *Swan*, High Street; *Sutherland House*, Parade; *Red Lion*, Red Lion Square; *Duke's Head Inn*, Dymchurch Road; *Marina*, Marine Parade.

Library. – The Public Library is at Oaklands.

Museum. – The Borough Museum is at Oaklands. It contains an interesting collection of local maps, prints and ancient documents.

Population. – 11,700.

Post Office. – Main Post Office at west end of High Street. Several sub-offices.

Putting Greens. – The Cricket Club has a private green (18 holes) on their ground adjoining Ladies' Walk.

Tennis. – The Corporation courts adjoin Ladies' Walk. The Hythe Lawn Tennis Club has grass courts adjoining the Hythe Cricket Club field. Visitors welcome.

A little less than five miles west of Folkestone, Hythe is a pleasant and quiet resort which at one time enjoyed considerable importance as a port. Though the buildings are for the most part modern, there is an unmistakable air of antiquity about the place. The name is derived from *hithe*, the Anglo-Saxon for a strand or haven. Londoners are familiar with the word in Rotherhithe, Greenhithe and, less directly, in Lambeth, anciently written *Lambhithe*.

The older part of the town lies on the hillside, the newer portion on land reclaimed from the sea. The narrow High Street which is restricted to eastbound traffic only is about half a mile from the front. Between the old and the new the tree-lined Royal Military Canal pursues its placid way. Facing south, the town is largely protected by the hills which rise behind the lower town.

IN AND ABOUT HYTHE

From every point of view Hythe is dominated by the stately –

Parish Church

The church is finely placed about half-way up the hill, and is reached from High Street by either of the turnings near the Town Hall. Midway is the old **Manor-House** of the Deedes family of Saltwood, now converted into separate units.

The church is dedicated to St. Leonard, and is cruciform in shape, with a square pinnacled tower, the upper part rebuilt in 1750. The most imposing feature is the magnificent east end. The original church was built about the year 1100 and consisted simply of a nave and a small chancel.

In the early years of the thirteenth century the rebuilding of the church in the Gothic style was undertaken and the present magnificent chancel with its ambulatory, aisles, triforium arches and clerestory were erected.

When the new chancel was completed, the rebuilding of the nave was begun. The Norman arches were pulled down with the exception of one, and the roof was raised to its present height.

The bowl of the font belongs to the fourteenth century; the base is modern.

A spiral staircase of eighty-three steps gives access to the roof of the chancel, from which there is a fine panoramic view.

The **Crypt,** *(weekdays, free)* is an architectural gem dating from 1225 and is actually the ambulatory referred to above. Here are stacked some eleven hundred skulls, and at the farther end an additional pile of bones. Nearly 8,000 thigh-bones have been counted, besides fragments. It was once thought that the remains were those of men who had fallen in some great battle, but that theory has been disproved. It is now thought that the bones were placed in the Crypt in the fourteenth-century, probably when the "Black Death" swept away so many persons in 1348 and many fresh graves had to be dug in the already crowded churchyard.

There is a similar collection at Rothwell, near Kettering, Northamptonshire, and at St. Bride's, Fleet Street. Other collections of the kind have been found at Folkestone, Dover, Ripon, Upchurch, etc.

The **Town Hall** in High Street dates from 1794. Towards the east end of the street is **St. John's Hospital,** founded in 1348 for the relief of poor townsfolk and still so used. The private residence at the corner of Church Hill with Bartholomew Street was at one time a similar institution and known as St. Bartholomew's Hospital.

South of the High Street is –

The Royal Military Canal, by far the most attractive physical feature of Hythe – and giving it at least one point of superiority over all other seaside resorts in Kent. At Hythe both sea and river boating can be enjoyed, for the Canal is practically a river. It has a width of about 60 feet, and was originally about nine feet deep and, though running parallel with the sea, contains fresh water. It runs from Seabrook through West Hythe, Appledore, Rye and Winchelsea, and thence, much diminished, to Cliff End, a few miles east of Hastings, a distance of twenty-three miles. The banks are beautifully wooded.

The canal was constructed early in the nineteenth century, about the same time as the Martello towers, for the better defence of the South Coast. Its purpose accounts for the zigzag course taken by the Canal. At every angle of the bank embrasures for cannon were constructed. At intervals of about a mile and a quarter and at every bridge a signal house or station for artillery was erected. At the head of the Canal was a battery and a drawbridge. By means of the latter, communication could be cut between Folkestone and Hythe. The north bank was raised several feet above the Canal level, for defensive cover.

Every two years, in August, the famous Venetian Fete is held on the town stretch of the canal.

In addition to the canal bank there are many shaded and flower-banked walks and gardens, especially south of the Canal, where they border and cross the Recreation Ground. From Ladies' Walk Bridge, Ladies' Walk extends to South Road. It is a beautiful wych-elm avenue planted in 1810 to commemorate George III's Jubilee. The **Grove** runs parallel with the canal on the north side from Nelson's Head Bridge, at the northern end of Stade Street, to Ladies' Walk Bridge.

Giving access to the sea front from the town is **Stade Street,** in which is **Oaklands.** Here are the Municipal Offices and the town's Public Library and Museum. The grounds of Oaklands consist of a lovely tree-shaded lawn with central bandstand, surrounded by paved pathway and flower borders, with exits to the Canal Bank.

On the seafront at the southern end of Twiss Road is the *Hotel Imperial*, standing in grounds of fifty acres, which include a golf course and a number of excellent tennis courts.

A solidly constructed **Sea Wall and Promenade** extends throughout the length of the front by the various names of West Parade, Marine Parade and Princes Parade, the latter leading eastwards to **Seabrook.** A fine road gives direct access from Hythe front through Seabrook and Sandgate to Folkestone. Seabrook is charmingly situated at the foot of the cliffs and, well sheltered from north and east winds, is a favourite residential quarter. Seabrook is also the starting point of the Royal Military Canal.

Towards the west end of Hythe front may be seen Martello towers, relics of the Napoleonic scares, when many such defences were built in the Channel Islands and along the south coast of England as a defence in case of invasion. The tower on the West Parade has been converted to an attractive residence.

The shore around is the scene of much activity, and here are to be found the huts and boats of the local fishermen.

To the south-west of Hythe lies the vast amount of shingle and marsh-ground known as **Romney Marsh** (p. 112).

The Romney, Hythe and Dymchurch Railway

Although the Romney, Hythe and Dymchurch Railway is sometimes regarded by holiday-makers as having been built solely for their pleasure, it affords an interesting example of the possibilities of miniature lines as feeders to standard-gauge systems.

There is a double-track permanent way (15-inch gauge) from Hythe to New Romney, and a single track from there to Dungeness, with stations at Hythe, Dymchurch (at the western end of the village), St. Mary's Bay, New Romney, Greatstone, Maddieson's Camp, and Dungeness. Trains run frequently between Hythe, Dymchurch and New Romney, less frequently to Dungeness. From New Romney to Dungeness the line runs almost along the seashore.

There is only one class, the coaches ranging from 8-seater to 20-seater. Luggage is carried as on other railways.

The railway is the conception of one man and affords a fine example of a small boy's ambitions being fulfilled in later life. Captain Howey wanted not merely to become an engine-driver, he wanted to build his own railway. In spite of opposition he devoted his whole time to the study of railways, even becoming a cleaner in the former L.N.E.R. engine sheds the better to acquire experience. His knowledge and his own finances, helped by a few friends, produced this railway, the smallest public railway in the world.

In the summer of 1927 it was opened to the public between Hythe and New Romney stations; in 1928 it was extended to the Pilot, and by 1929 the line was completed as far as Dungeness Lighthouse, making a total distance of line of $13\frac{3}{4}$ miles.

The railway's Lilliputian accessories are all, as far as is practical, exact reproductions of those used on a full-size railway system.

At New Romney station is a cafe, and "Model land," a working "0" and "00" railway lay-out.

Excursions from Hythe

To Seabrook. From the east end of High Street, Station Road leads in to Black-house Hill, a right turn from which is Cliff Road. A short distance along this on the left a track leads to Sene Farm, where bear right and follow cart track. Over the hill, on the left, down in the hollow under the shade of Paraker Wood, is Hythe's peaceful little cemetery. Farther east on the neighbouring hill is the Canadian Cemetery. The track later leads to Horn Street, where turn right to the main road. There are three ways back to Hythe, by Seabrook Road (bus or afoot), by the canal bank, or along the sea front, on Princes Parade.

To Saltwood. Take the churchyard path up the hill to the road beyond (Castle Road). This runs due north to Saltwood Castle, which is plainly seen about a mile ahead. A short distance along the road is a footpath on the left, which leads across fields directly to the village of **Saltwood,** and is more pleasant than the road. The village stands on the hill a mile north of Hythe. Several roads converge on the picturesque village green, with its War Memorial, and the whole place, beautiful with trees and pleasant houses, new as well as old, set in shady gardens, is most attractive.

Saltwood Castle *(open to the public on Wednesday afternoons* 2.30–6 *in July and August, Admission charge)* is picturesquely situated, low wooded hills stretching away on each side and the sea opening in front. There is a tradition that the four assassins of Thomas a Becket rested here on the eve of their deed. A great part of the original Norman castle, long the manor-house of the Archbishops of Canterbury, is in ruins, but the Hall, which dates from 1300, has now been restored and is used as a library. The two handsome towers of the gateway are among the earliest examples of Perpendicular work and constitute one of the most perfect old gate-houses in existence. They were erected by Archbishop Courtenay, who reconstructed the place in 1390.

When the property was acquired by William Deedes in 1791, the gatehouse and walls remained intact. In 1884 a descendant of his had this structure restored and additions made. The castle stands today as a charming country residence formed out of a fourteenth-century gatehouse.

Part of the outer wall is Roman, dating from the time when the sea covered parts of Romney Marsh and Saltwood was a Roman port, subsidiary to the harbour at *Portus Lemanus.*

A short distance from the Castle grounds is the **Church,** set in a charming position and consisting of a western tower which shows traces of its Norman origin, a nave with one of its original windows, Norman doorways, an Early English north aisle of two bays, and a chancel. In the churchyard is the grave of Sir Wm. Henry Lucy ("Toby M.P." of Punch).

To Pedlinge and Newingreen. In spring the woods and hedgerows bordering the Ashford road between Pedlinge and Newingreen, about two miles from the town, are thickly carpeted with primroses; later, there is a wealth of wild hyacinths to delight the eye. **Pedlinge** may be reached by a footpath leading to the Forty Steps, or by the path which leaves the Ashford road on the right, a short distance farther up the hill. From Pedlinge Church a path runs northward to the Sandling Road, which is reached at Slaybrook, half a mile south of Sandling Station.

At **Newingreen** there is a popular motel.

To Sandling Park and Westenhanger. Sandling Park is a large wooded area and has a well-known woodland garden open to the public in May (*see* local notices). The park entrance to be used on this excursion is on the left of the road from Hythe, and faces the approach to the down platform of the main line at Sandling.

From Sandling station a footpath runs on the north side of the line towards Stanford and Westenhanger and runs through the northern edge of the Park past the main entrance. Following this cross the main A20 road to a stile on the north side of the road just short of the railway bridge. Thence the route is through the corner of Honeywood and down the railway line to Westenhanger.

Westenhanger is chiefly associated in the minds of many with the adjoining Folkestone Racecourse.

An object of interest is the remnant of the fourteenth-century **Manor House,** which replaced a Saxon palace and Norman castle, and which received Elizabeth I on her progress through Kent in 1573. Westenhanger House, built in 1700, stands on a portion of the site; three towers together with a short length of the wall, are almost all that remain of the old work.

A splendid view of the house, now privately occupied, can be obtained from the railway. There is a path running westward from the station, on the south side of the line. This path may be followed as far as the bridge. Here turn left from the railway along the cart track to the cottages, cross a stile to the left of these, follow the path across the racecourse, and so to the main road, where turn left for Newingreen and Hythe.

Through Westenhanger runs the old Roman highway from Lympne to Canterbury, known as **Stone Street.** Except for a bend round Horton Park, it stretches in a straight line northward from the *Royal Oak* at Newingreen to Street End, three miles from Canterbury.

To Monks Horton, two miles north of Westenhanger, and reached by way of **Stanford** (the stone ford), or by turning from the Ashford road at Sellindge, near the stone "5 miles from Hythe". The remains of the fine old Cluniac Priory, founded by Robert de Vere, Constable of England in the reign of Henry II, have been converted into a dwelling house. The Manor house, called *Kite Manor,* is one of the best examples of domestic Tudor architecture in the district. Two miles north-east of the Priory is the **Church.** It is only about 70 feet in length, including the chancel, and contains some ancient painted glass and fine wood work.

To West Hythe, Stutfall and Lympne. West Hythe and Stutfall are situated on the north bank of the Canal, and are best visited by boat; but along both banks of the Canal there are footpaths which can be entered at Scanlon's Bridge, which unites the Ashford and Dymchurch roads, immediately west of Military Road. About one and a half miles from Hythe are the ruins of the *Church of Our Lady of West Hythe.* **Stutfall** is about a mile farther.

Stutfall Castle. – The Roman fortress covered about ten acres. Huge masses of its masonry lie at the foot of the cliffs, having been overthrown by landslips, to which this part of the old cliff has been subject for centuries. The stones, pebbles, and bricks contained in the ruins are still so firmly cemented, although the work is seventeen hundred years old, that the materials cannot be separated by ordinary means.

Lympne is a little north of the castle and about two and a half miles west of Hythe. The village is the modern representative of *Portus Lemanis*, one of the four important stations of the Romans on the coast of Kent, the others being at Richborough, Reculver and Dover. It stands on a lofty cliff above Romney Marsh, which was the bed of the sea when the Romans came to Britain. But for the great embankment known as Dymchurch Wall (p. 112), there would even today be water seven feet deep beating against Lympne cliffs at high tide.

The **Church** with its massive central tower is of Norman origin, once a West tower to a church partly destroyed. Architecturally interesting, the church is well worth a visit.

Lympne Castle is a mediaeval building, rebuilt on the foundations of an earlier Norman castle. The East Tower dates from the twelfth century, built on the probable site of the Roman Watch-tower for the Roman fort 300 feet below. The Castle was modernized in 1360, when the Great Hall was reconstructed, retaining some of its earlier doorways. The West Tower was built, as an extra fortification, during the 100 Years War. The Castle was owned by the Archdeacons of Canterbury, (including Thomas a Beckett), for 800 years; and, in 1905, it was faithfully restored by the famous architect, Sir Robert Lorrimer, who enlarged it with the addition of the New Wing. *Open April to October, Wednesdays, Sundays and Bank Holiday weekends; June to September daily,* 10.30 *a.m.*–1 *p.m. and* 2.30 *p.m. to* 6 *p.m.*

The road running westward reaches in three-quarters of a mile Ashford Airport. Formerly named Lympne Airport and used by the Royal Air Force during the war, the airport is now used for cross-channel flights to Beauvais, Paris, and many other places. Private aircraft also may use the airport.

A mile westward of Lympne is the hamlet of **Court-at-Street**, "so-called," says Leland, "by reason of the place or court that the lord of the soil kept there," an explanation which requires to be supplemented by the statement that it stands on the Roman road – the "street" – which ran from Lympne to Pevensey. The hamlet is historically interesting as the site of the chapel which was the scene of the prophesying of Elizabeth Barton, the "Holy Maid of Kent," who had the temerity to denounce Henry VIII's divorce of Catherine of Aragon, and suffered at Tyburn in consequence.

Part of the walls of the chapel can still be seen. Passing the *Welcome Stranger Inn*, turn left through the stack-yard, just before reaching the farm-house. From the far end of the yard it is possible to look down the hillside upon the ruins.

Retracing our steps towards Lympne, about half a mile beyond the Lympne turning is **Shepway Cross**, the meeting-point of cross-roads, at the top of a very steep hill (1 in $7\frac{1}{2}$) which rises from West Hythe. Here the Cinque Ports *Court of Shepway* was held and the Lord Warden was installed.

Romney Marsh

The great tract commonly called Romney (pronounced *Rumney* and derived from the Saxon "Rumn-ea" – the "marsh water") Marsh, comprises Walland, Guildeford and Denge or Dunge Marshes, as well as Romney Marsh proper. It consists of alluvium and shingle, extends from Hythe, on the east, to the Sussex border on the west, is twelve miles across at its widest part, and its length is half as much again. The Royal Military Canal and the sea together virtually make it an island.

The sea is prevented from taking ownership over the land by a great embankment, called –

Dymchurch Wall, which extends for about four miles, and is more than 20 feet high and from 15 to 30 feet wide. It is a great sloping bank of earth, faced on the seaward side by huge blocks of stone, succeeded by a series of steps, with far-reaching groynes every few yards. In its course are three great sluices to aid the draining of the Marsh. A walk along the embankment is a novel experience, and a strange effect is experienced in motoring or walking about the Marsh at high tide, for the sea appears to be, and indeed is, higher than one's head.

The Marsh is one of the most deserted regions of England, notwithstanding the fact that the seclusion of Dymchurch has been invaded by the Light Railway connecting it with Hythe, New Romney and Dungeness; while there is a regular service of buses from Folkestone and Hythe to Dymchurch and New Romney, and a concrete road following the coast right round from Littlestone, practically to the Point. Except on the main roads, scarcely a soul is to be met. There are endless stretches of meadows, poplars here and there, occasional fences and dykes everywhere.

Dymchurch

Banks. – *Barclays*, *Lloyds*, both in High Street.

Buses daily from and to Folkestone, Hythe and New Romney. Dymchurch also has a station on the Light Railway.

Caravan Sites, etc. – There are several sites near the village and many permanent holiday camps.

Fishing. – Sea and in the Military Canal.

Hotels. – *Ship; Victoria; White Gables Guest House; Old Rectory Guest House; Shepherd and Crook,* Burmarsh.

Sports. – Cricket and Football are available at the Recreation Ground.

Dymchurch is a quaint mixture of modern bungalows scattered among picturesque half-timbered villas and attractive old cottages. The village owes it popularity largely to its fine five-mile stretch of firm, clean sand, in such marked contrast to the pebbly beach of Hythe. The bathing is

Priory remains, New Romney

delightful, though a long walk to the sea is necessary at low tide. In contrast with the new parts of Dymchurch is the little Norman Church in the centre. With its conical, red-tiled tower, it is surrounded by beautiful trees and dignified houses. It is strikingly broad, with no side aisles, and a west gallery stretches right across it. There is a very beautiful Norman chancel arch. Opposite the church is the "New Hall" built by Queen Elizabeth I's reign to replace an earlier one destroyed by fire, and next to it is a small prison with padded cell, used until 1866. Buses stop at the quaint *Ship Inn*, reputed to be formerly a resort for smugglers. The Martello Tower *(fee)* in High Street is a replica of the original tower.

New Romney

"New" Romney is an ancient town, a Cinque Port, and a municipal borough, now about a mile from the sea, the prefix "New" only appearing at a comparatively recent date. It is probably older than **Old Romney** – a mile further inland. According to Domesday Book, Romney was a very important place in 1086 with three churches, of which only one now remains. Its importance was brought to an end by the great storm which changed the course of the Rother, more than six centuries ago. The **Church** (dedicated to St. Nicholas) is a magnificent combination of Norman and Early English architecture.

Over the Town Hall is a small **museum.**

A beautiful avenue – visible for miles across the Marsh – leads past the railway station to the seaward extension of Romney –

Littlestone-on-Sea

Littlestone, rapidly increasing both in popularity and population, is famous for its **Golf Links.** There are facilities for tennis, fishing, and bathing, but boating is apt to be dangerous. The beach is pebbly, with sand at low tide. The prominent tower of red brick, seen for so many miles in approaching Littlestone, was built in 1890, in connection with the waterworks, but is no longer in use.

About a mile south of Littlestone there has sprung up along the line of sand-dunes at **Greatstone,** a settlement of bungalows, a popular holiday camp and the like. There is a station on the Light Railway.

Beyond Greatstone the line of holiday houses continues to **Lydd-on-Sea.** Here one of the chain of Napoleonic forts along this coast is in use as a Coastguard Station.

A mile or so west of New Romney, and higher up the ancient course of the Rother, is **Old Romney,** once a seaport, a status which it lost through the silting-up of the mouth of the river. Now it is but a hamlet, with little to see except the Church with its curious cap-like tower.

Farther north and west is **Ivychurch,** standing in the midst of the marsh, some three miles from New Romney. Its magnificent Church is dedicated to St. George.

On the road between Old Romney and Appledore, rather more than three miles from the former and about a mile from the latter, is **Snargate,** of which "Ingoldsby" was rector.

"Ingoldsby" lived in the parsonage at **Warehorne,** about three miles to the north, and a mile west of Ham Street (station). The lofty church contains some beautiful stained glass medallions of the thirteenth century and coeval with the building. At Warehorne Bridge begins the three-mile stretch of the Military Canal, extending to Appledore.

On the Rye road, six miles west of New Romney, is the very old village of **Brookland.** It may be reached by the Folkestone-Hastings bus.

The church, *c.* 1250, is remarkable for a detached bell tower, solidly built of timber and resembling three cones placed one upon the other.

From New Romney a fine modern road leads across the Marsh for about four miles to –

Lydd

Lydd is of pre-Saxon origin, and a Corporate Member of the Confederation of the Cinque Ports. Its military connections are well-known; "Lyddite", a powerful explosive, having been tested on the ranges between the town and the sea, derives its name from the town.

114

The ancient **Church,** dedicated to All Saints, is widely known as "the Cathedral of Romney Marsh," because of its size, richness and imposing appearance. It is one of the longest in Kent, with a length of 199 feet, and has a pinnacled tower rising to the height of 132 feet built at the time Cardinal Wolsey was Rector of the parish.

In the High Street are many interesting old houses and shops and the Guild Hall, with its wonderful collection of archives, including a four-teenth-century charter. There are some fine seventeenth- and eighteenth-century houses and farms on the outskirts of the town.

Ferryfield Airport is situated about $1\frac{1}{2}$ miles from the town and occupies approximately 240 acres. The Airport was built by Silver City Airways in 1954 and now houses the air ferry and passenger terminals of British Air Ferries Ltd. There is a Spectators' Enclosure with buffet.

From Lydd a road runs south-east to the new *Pilot Inn* at the coast, more than a mile north of Dungeness Point. Here the Lydd road forks left to Littlestone – and right to Dungeness Lighthouse.

Dungeness

The **Ness** is the most southerly point of Kent, and is only twenty-six miles distant from Cape Gris-nez, on the French coast. It is a steep-sided promontory formed of shingle, which the steady eastward drift has brought to the spot from the foreshore of the channel to the westward of the Point.

The promontory is of wonderful interest to students of sea-life. Those interested in shipping may spend a pleasant afternoon, for all the vessels going up or down the Channel pass within what appears to be a stone's throw of the shore. Anglers, too, find the spot rewarding, and many big catches are recorded.

To shipping, Dungeness is one of the most dangerous points in the English Channel. As fresh accumulations of shingle regularly advance the beach about nine feet a year, the Lighthouse has had to be moved forward again and again. The present modern Lighthouse was completed in 1960. Visitors may climb the steps to the top of the old lighthouse. Dungeness has a very fine motor lifeboat, the *Mabel E. Holland.*

Dungeness "A" Power Station, the fifth nuclear power station in the Central Electricity Generating Board's programme for increased supplies, was completed in 1965.

Winchelsea and Rye

The "ancient towns" of Winchelsea and Rye were the Gosport and Portsmouth of their day. Rye is now a quiet little place, parts of it so strangely antique that it has been declared that "nothing more recent than the cavalier's cloak and hat and ruffles should be seen" there. Winchelsea, once a busy and important maritime town, is but a shadow of its former self, and is now included in the rural district area of Battle. Both are included in the confederation of the Cinque Ports, and each has a most interesting history, retaining vestiges of antiquity which cannot fail to appeal to the visitor. In the same excursion may be seen Camber Castle, a fortress erected on the shore by Henry VIII.

Winchelsea

Hotels. – *New Inn; Petronillas Plat.*
Post Office. – Open from 9 a.m.

Winchelsea Halt, 9 miles from Hastings, is a mile from the town. The willow-fringed road leads directly from the station, the wooded hill on which the town is perched being in view the whole way, though at a distance no one would suspect the existence of roads and terraces behind the trees.

Winchelsea has a long and a strange history. The present town, or rather the portion that remains, is not the original Winchelsea at all. That was situated 3 miles in a south-easterly direction. It may have been a place of importance in Roman days; it certainly was so in the time of the Saxons, from whom it received its name, signifying, according to Professor Burrows, "the shingle isle on the level." In 959 it possessed a mint; and in the following century was conferred by the Confessor on the monks of Fecamp, together with Rye, part of Hastings, and many other manors. It was here that William the Conqueror landed on December 7, 1067, when returning from Normandy for the first time after the Conquest. The town was added to the Cinque Ports in, or before, the thirteenth century.

Like Hastings, Winchelsea rapidly grew in importance on account of its connexion with Normandy; and it attained an even greater degree of prosperity. But shingle gradually silted up the mouth of the harbour, and successive gales wrought such damage that the place was nearly destroyed.

Since Elizabeth's day the once mighty port has dwindled, a laudable effort, in the eighteenth century, to retrieve its fortunes by the introduction of the manufacture of cambric proving a failure.

In 1790 John Wesley came to Winchelsea, and preached his last open-air sermon under what was known as Wesley's Tree, an ash at the west side of the churchyard. The present tree replaced the original one, which was blown down in 1927.

Until 1832 the place, small as it was, returned two members to Parliament. It still has its mayor, jurats, town clerk, chamberlain, sergeant-at-mace and other functionaries, and, with the exception of the City of London, is the only unreformed corporation in the kingdom. The mayor is elected annually on Easter Monday.

It is a good plan to leave the main road where it turns left into Icklesham and approach Winchelsea by the lane crossing Hog Hill. The advantage of this approach is that one is presented with a good view of the inverted pear-shaped island which the ancient city covered and one enters by the **New Gate** – the farthest from the town's centre. Outside the gate stood the Holy Cross of Winchelsea, and just within was St. Bartholomew's Hospital.

Hardly a house is in sight from this picturesque old ruin, but by passing through the gate and following the pretty lane to its junction with the main road one does at last come to another relic of old Winchelsea – a venerable wall and a doorway, all that is left of the hospital of St. John.

Going north with the main road for another quarter of a mile we suddenly realize we are in Winchelsea. The square before us is one of the thirty-nine which comprised the seaport 500 years ago. It presents a curious scene. The roadway is of noble proportions, but except for the cars drawn up by the roadside has a sleepy, deserted appearance.

The Parish Church is but the easternmost portion of the building erected between 1288 and 1292, in honour of St. Thomas the Martyr, Archbishop of Canterbury. In its pristine state the church was a cruciform building of considerable size. It has been said that the nave extended as far as the sundial in the churchyard. The ruins of the transepts exhibit two fairly complete doorways, of later date than the original edifice; but nothing else, save a slight fragment of an adjoining wall, exists to tell the glory of other portions of the church, which were probably burnt by the French in 1380 and never rebuilt. It would probably be towards the close of the fifteenth century when the choir took its present form to serve as an entire church.

The beauty of this wonderful old church has been transformed by the addition of **The Nine Windows,** gifts of Lord Blanesburgh. These form three memorials to men who, in varied ways, have given their lives to further the ideals of the British Commonwealth of Nations.

Apart from the windows, the chief attraction of the church is the **Alard Chantry,** in the south aisle, a memorial of an old-time Winchelsea family of renown. The sedilia and piscina of the altar still remain. One of the family, Gervase Alard, the first British Admiral, was Warden of the Cinque Ports at the beginning of the fourteenth century, and his elaborate monument is the principal feature of the chantry.

The **Alard Tomb** has a recumbent effigy of an armed man, with hands clasping a heart, and legs crossed. At his feet crouches a lion; and over all is a fine arched canopy, at the angles of which are sculptured heads of Edward I and his second wife, Margaret. The whole tomb is richly decorated. Another admiral, Stephen Alard, lies buried under a second canopied tomb close by, and his monument, dating from about 1340, is similar in design to, though not so grand as, the other, which is certainly one of the finest in the country.

Facing the north-west corner of the churchyard is the **Old Court House,** or **Water Bailiff's Prison,** a modern restoration of an ancient structure rebuilt in Tudor days. It exhibits a few traces of great antiquity, such as the round-arched doorway and the niches in the masonry and the four-

Camber Castle

teenth-century tile floor. Note also the fine oak rafters. The lower floor, once occupied by prison cells, is used by a Youth Club and the upper chamber occupied by the **Court Hall Museum** and for council meetings.

Reached by passing through a gate across the end of a short road leading out of the opposite (south-east) corner of the square is the mansion known as **Greyfriars.** Now an old folks' home it is built of the material from a former monastery of 1327 on the site.

Near the modern house are the beautiful ruins of the **Chapel of the Blessed Virgin,** founded in 1310. After 600 years only the choir remains, but it is an exquisite fragment. It is entered at the west end, where stands a lofty, frail-looking arch with a 25-feet span. The east end has a very picturesque appearance.

Another of the old religious houses, the **Black Friars,** was built in the reign of Edward II. It fell at the Reformation, and no attempt seems to have been made to preserve the building. In what is now locally known as the Chestnut Field may be seen a fragment of its walls, incorporated in some farm buildings.

It is not until one has explored the byways of Winchelsea that the spell of the place is felt to the full.

To the north-west the town overlooks the Brede Level, and at this corner is –

The Land, or Pipewell, Gate. Formerly this guarded the only road to Rye (that which now leads to the station), and was the means of communication with the "inner harbour" extending at the foot of the declivity. At the bottom was a stream which served as a moat. It was crossed by a ferry – hence the name of Ferry Gate, by which this time-honoured defence is still sometimes called. In 1380 the gate was destroyed by the French, and in 1404 the present structure was erected. To John Helde, then mayor, was due its reconstruction; his worship's name and coat-of-arms are sculptured over the arch. Close by, Edward I built a castle, remains of the entrance-gate of which still exist. The watch-tower stood on the crest of the slope until 1828.

A more imposing relic is **the Strand Gate,** at the seaward end of the road in which the Court House stands. The Strand Gate guards the Rye road, which here curves northwards and runs down a steep incline towards what was once Winchelsea Harbour. It is the finest of the three gates – a picturesque old pile, having a wide gateway, with groined roof, flanked by bold circular towers. The archway was fortified by a double portcullis, the grooves of which may still be seen.

Close to the Strand Gate is an open court and shelter, known as the **Look-Out.** It occupies the site of one of the old public greens, and the miniature terrace commands a pleasing and extensive view of land and sea.

Such is Winchelsea – a strange skeleton of an antique town which does not attempt to assume a modern appearance, though it is yearly increasing in favour as a place of residence, especially among people with an artistic bent. Here Turner loved to rove, and Millais and Thackeray, as well as Ruskin, have lent the charm of their genius to delineate its attractions. In *Tower Cottage*, adjoining the Strand Gate, Dame Ellen Terry for many years spent her hours of leisure, and here the Duke of Wellington stayed when he reviewed his troops during the Napoleonic wars. The nail-studded oak door giving admission to the garden originally enclosed a prison cell in the Town Hall.

Rye lies 2 miles away, and is reached by the **Military Road,** which proceeds straight across the marsh. Camber Castle, looking like a conglomeration of martello towers, lies but a short distance off the road.

Camber Castle

was one of the fortresses erected by Henry VIII, between the years 1539–1540, for the protection of the southern shore. It was purely a fortress – not a castle-residence – and consisted of a large central keep, with smaller circular towers running into its massive wall, with which they are connected by curtains. At that time the sea washed close up to the fortress, but shortly afterwards the water receded, and is now severed from it by a considerable tract of marsh land. It is now a rough and massive ruin, possessing heavy windows – glassless, of course – thick walls, overgrown with lichen and moss, and dark underground passages.

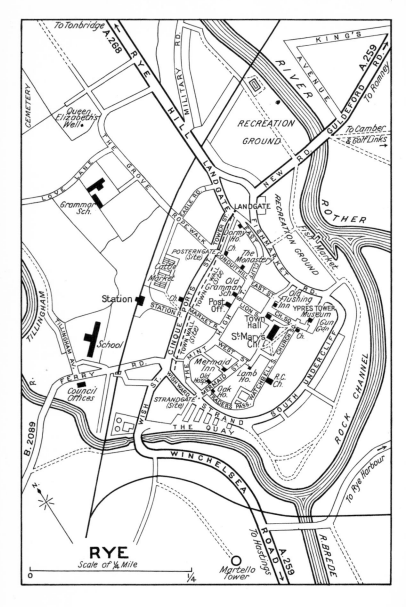

RYE

Scale of ¼ Mile

0 _____ ¼

Rye

Cinema. – *Regent*, Cinque Ports Street.
Early Closing Day. – Tuesday.
Golf Links. – Rye Golf Club along banks of the Rother.
Hotels. – *Durrant House; George; Hope & Anchor; Mariner's; Mermaid.*

Museum. – Ypres Tower, Gun Garden.
Post Office. – Cinque Ports Street.
Bus Terminus and waiting-room adjoins the railway station.

The ancient and romantic town of Rye has a history similar in some respects to that of Winchelsea; but the visitor will find it a populous and busy place in comparison with its once more mighty neighbour. After a strangely buffeted career, Rye still presents the appearance of a town, though a quaint and quiet one. It stands about 2 miles from the Kentish boundary, on a rocky eminence which was in times gone by "surrounded on all sides, and at all times, by the waters of the ocean, and unapproachable except by ships or boats." But a very different sight now presents itself. The hill, of course, remains and the town still covers its slopes, but the sea has receded 2 miles, and a broad stretch of rich marshland appears in place of the rolling tide. Across this plain flows the *Rother*, which, reinforced on the outskirts of the town by the *Brede* and *Tillingham*, runs on its sinuous course to the sea and forms the harbour.

Rye was one of the places bestowed by Canute upon the monastery of Fecamp in Normandy. By Henry II it was added with Winchelsea to the confederation of the Cinque Ports. His grandson, Henry III, "redeemed" the town from the monks in 1246. Walled in, fortified by gates and towers and a fosse, and in the enjoyment of the privileges of a Cinque Port town, Rye became a port of considerable importance, and was for a long period one of the chief points of departure for the Continent. Prosperity brought with it a curse; for the French paid several uninvited visits and wrought great havoc.

It would be difficult to say exactly when the sea began to leave Rye, but we may roughly assign that event to the fifteenth century. In Elizabeth's reign its dwindling population was augmented by the influx of nearly 700 French Protestants, who had fled hither after the massacre of St. Bartholomew in 1572. In 1573 the Virgin Queen paid a visit to the town; and in 1590 and 1596 we read that Rye was decimated by the plague.

From this time onwards the place appears to have pursued the even tenor of its way, the sea receding steadily and the harbour being gradually silted up.

Rye attracts a large number of visitors, including artists, writers, and photographers, who find the picturesque ensemble of houses, inns, shops, castle, gateway and hilly streets, climbing up to the apex of the twelfth-century church still give a picture of the town which has not changed in essentials since Van Dyck drew it in the seventeenth century. The holiday season apart, Rye also is much in evidence with its November 5 celebrations, when a torchlight procession, huge bonfire and fireworks display attracts visitors from all parts.

The **Parish Church** has been known as "The Cathedral of East Sussex". Notice in approaching the quaint old clock with its attendant "quarter boys", and the appropriate inscription, "For our time is a very shadow that passeth away". The clock is one of the oldest in England, and its great pendulum, 18 feet in length, protrudes through the ceiling of the church and swings to and fro in the face of the congregation.

The existing church dates from about the year 1120, and is one of the largest parish churches in Sussex. It consists of a chancel, nave, with clerestory and aisles, transepts and a central tower.

The east end contains some of the most interesting architectural features, notably the flying buttresses. These unusual structures (it is rare to find flying buttresses springing from the ground) fulfil a purpose other than decorative when the sag of the east end of the Church is seen. The utilitarian buttress at the south-east angle of the building is *c.* 1400–1450; the very handsome pinnacled one to take the thrust of the south chancel arcade – is of a little later date. The twin to this latter buttress is a replica built when St. Mary's was restored in the nineteenth century.

On the north side of the choir is a massive mahogany altar-table dating from about 1740. A collection of curios in the south transept includes a "Breeches" Bible, a "Vinegar" Bible and eight stone cannon-balls said to be French found in the walls.

Adjoining the church is the **Town Hall,** built in the eighteenth century, where meetings of the Council and Magistrate's Courts are held. *(Admission by arrangement with Town Sergeant.)* The open lower floor was formerly the market. The first floor is occupied by the court room, where are displayed lists of mayors and town clerks from the year 1289 and a copy of the "Engagement" of the inhabitants of Rye at the time of the Commonwealth. The old ceremony of throwing hot pennies to the assembled children takes place here on Mayoring Day. There are a number of constables' staves, Elizabethan silver-gilt maces, and other antiquities, but most visitors find a more thrilling interest in the gibbet chains and carefully preserved skull of Breeds, a butcher who murdered Mr. Grebell, a former mayor, in 1742. Next to these is the pillory. The sundial on the side of the building facing the church was removed from Peacock's Grammar School, in High Street.

In Market Street, just beyond the Town Hall, is the **Old Flushing Inn,** formerly one of the famous old smuggling inns of Rye. The removal of some panelling in the front room, in the course of repairs in 1905, brought to light a remarkably fine sixteenth-century fresco covering the whole of the wall on one side of the room.

Not far from the church, and approached by the cobbled lane between the Town Hall and the Flushing Inn, is the **Ypres Tower,** a venerable watch-tower and fortress. A few yards down this cobble lane, near the old public water cistern, a metal plaque attached to the wall gives some interesting extracts from letters that passed from the Mayor and Jurats of Rye to Lord Wilmington.

Formerly called Baddyngs Tower it acquired its present name through its sale, by the Corporation in 1430, to John d'Ypres, who used it as a residence. It is a quadrangular building, having a round tower at each corner, and, being placed on the summit of a rock which rose almost sheer out of the sea, it was of great strength. There are three rooms in the building, from all the corners of which massive doors communicate with towers, the walls of which are 4 feet thick. Having survived the sieges and sackings of Rye, it was, with some modern additions, used as a gaol until 1891, when it was condemned as unfit for the purpose. It was damaged by enemy action during the war, but now houses the **Rye Museum** *(open Easter to mid-October, charge)*.

Mermaid Street, Rye

Steps lead down from the Ypres Tower to the **Gun Garden,** long used as a battery, but now a public promenade. The view along the coast on either side, with the winding Rother in the foreground, is very picturesque. The **Town Salts,** an open space under the shadow of the east cliff, is used as a recreation ground.

In Church Square, near the south-west corner of the churchyard, will be found the **Old Stone House,** the oldest inhabited house in Rye. This venerable structure, easily distinguishable by its ecclesiastical appearance, is but a remnant, consisting of the refectory and entrance hall of the original buildings of the Friars of the Sack. It dates from the middle of the thirteenth century.

Pass up the west side of the church square and in the north-west corner take the lane leading west, past **Lamb House.** For many years this was occupied by Henry James, the author, and was also the residence of the late E. F. Benson. The house is the property of the National Trust but is in private residence. *The Henry James room and garden are open to the public (Wednesdays and Saturdays, March to October.).* From here is a view of the church and the old house with the "crooked chimney", which is a much reproduced picture. A few yards farther, on the left, is Mermaid Street; here is the old *Mermaid Inn,* now a modern hotel. The Dutch tiles and oak panelling have been preserved.

The frontage to the street shows recently revealed timbering and the whole building with its miniature court is the largest wood-framed structure in the town. Below, on the same side of the street, is Hartshorn House, a fine half-timbered building with huge gables.

At the foot of the hill once stood the **Strand Gate.** Some of the old wall still remains on the right, and in it is fixed a stone bearing the arms of the Cinque Ports.

Turn right, ascend the thoroughfare whose name – the **Mint** – recalls greater days at Rye, and so to the High Street, where note the former Grammar School, erected in 1636, with its massive projecting pilasters. Opposite is the *George Hotel,* which is older than its name implies. It contains a banqueting hall, musicians' gallery, old oak beams and ancient fireplaces.

High Street, having changed its name to East Cliff, proceeds to justify the change by throwing open a wide view across the Marsh. Then it descends somewhat steeply and narrowly to the **Landgate,** the only survivor of the three portals which guarded the town. It was erected *c.* 1360, and consists of a broad archway flanked by massive towers, with upper chambers.

On the north side of the railway, reached by the Ropewalk (which tells its own tale), is **Queen Elizabeth's Well,** at which that monarch rested and drank before entering "Rye Royal" in 1573.

Splendid views of the town and its surroundings can be had from **Point Hill,** leading to **Playden,** a popular residential neighbourhood.

To Camber

South of Rye is marshland intersected by dykes. Near the mouth of the Rother are fine sands, dunes, and the well-known Rye Golf Club, which is easily accessible by bus. The golf course (18 holes) is one of the finest in England, and covers about $3\frac{1}{4}$ miles. About $1\frac{1}{2}$ miles beyond the Golf Club is the village of **Camber,** a rapidly expanding holiday resort with shops, service station, caravan parks and holiday chalets. In the village accommodation is available at the *Royal William Inn* and the *Green Owl Inn.* Good bathing is to be had from the wide sandy beach. On the opposite bank of the estuary is the little hamlet known as **Rye Harbour.**

Hastings and St. Leonards

Banks. – Branches of *Barclays, Lloyds, Midland, National Westminster* and *Trustee Savings Bank.*

Bathing. – Bathing tents may be placed on certain parts of the foreshore. Changing on beach at certain points.
The *Hastings Seagulls Club* have their headquarters at the White Rock Baths.

Baths. – *Hastings Baths*, White Rock. Sea-water swimming, sauna, medical and private baths.

Beach. – Shingle. At low tide a wide stretch of firm and clean sand is exposed all along Hastings front.

Boating. – Motor boats can be hired from the foreshore and a speed boat from Hastings Pier. The *Hastings and St. Leonards Rowing Club* has headquarters at White Rock.

Bowls. – In the White Rock Pleasure Grounds in Alexandra Park, and in West Marina Gardens, St. Leonards. There are several Bowling Clubs; headquarters of *Hastings Bowling Association* is at White Rock.

Bus Services. – Buses serve the town and other neighbouring places. The East Kent services start near White Rock Pavilion.

Car Parks. – Underground car parks (open 7 a.m. to 11.45 p.m.) at Carlisle Parade, Hastings Pier, and Grand Parade. There is ample garage accommodation in the town, together with multi-storey park in Priory Street, and Marina Gardens, the Stade.

Coach Station. – The coach station is by the Central Cricket Ground.

Cricket. – The Cricket Ground is in the centre of the town, close to the station; entrance in Queen's Road.

Dancing takes place regularly during the season at the White Rock Pavilion. Falaise Hall, the Dolphin, on the Pier, and at some of the hotels.

Early Closing Day. – Wednesday.

Entertainment. – White Rock Pavilion, Hastings Pier Pavilion, cinemas, dancing, etc.

Football. – Pilot Field, Elphinstone Road.

Hotels. – *Queens; Royal Victoria*, Marina; *Warrior*, Warrior Square; *Yelton*, White Rock; *Fairlight Cove*, Fairlight; *Medlow; Russell; Kenrith*, St. Helen's Road; *Chatsworth*, Carlisle Parade; and many others.

Information Bureau. – York House, York Buildings.

Libraries. – Public Library, Claremont. Newspaper Road. 3 Robertson Terrace.

Model Village. – White Rock Gardens. Open throughout the year.

Museums. – In John's Place and at Old Town Hall, High Street. Fishermen's Museum, Rock-a-Nore Road.

Music. – Concerts in White Rock Pavilion; orchestra in the Sun Lounge; band performances at Warrior Square and Alexandra Park (*Sundays*); concert parties in White Rock Pavilion.

Population. – 69,110.

Post Offices. – Chief Office, Cambridge Road; St. Leonards, London Road. There are numerous sub-offices in the town and suburbs.

Putting-Greens at White Rock Gardens, West Marina Gardens, and Alexandra Park.

Railway Stations. – Hastings Central, West St. Leonards and Warrior Square.

Regatta. – This is held annually towards the end of June. There is also an annual Carnival week, usually in July.

Squash. – Courts at the Bathing Pool.

Speedboat trips from the pier.

Tennis. – Public courts, grass and hard, at White Rock Gardens, Alexandra Park, and West Marina Gardens.

For picturesqueness of situation, salubrity, historical associations, handsome buildings, beautiful surroundings and splendid parades, Hastings ranks amongst the finest of the holiday resorts of England.

Hastings and St. Leonards, once distinct, are now merged and controlled by the same Corporation. The town has a southern aspect and lies on the Sussex shore, amid the valleys and hills which form the "cliffs of old England." At the east end the hill of Ecclesbourne rises almost a sheer precipice from the sea; and beyond the intervening valley the cliffs mount

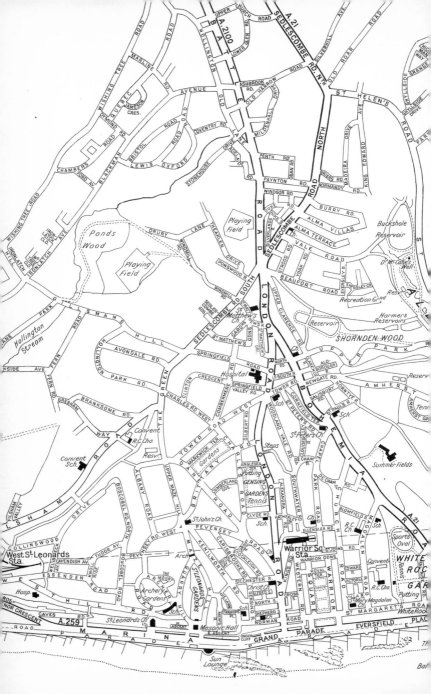

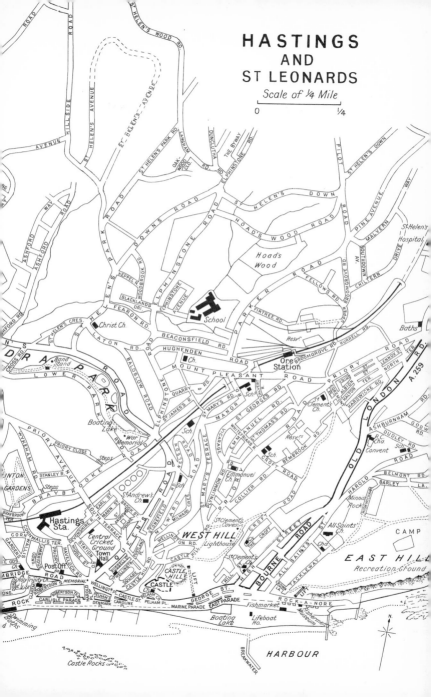

to a height approaching 600 feet – the highest point of the Sussex coast. The town itself is built upon an undulating range of hills, the streets rising tier above tier as they recede from the strip of valley by the shore; St. Leonards, at the west end, making a gradual slope towards Bo-Peep. Old Hastings lies in the valley between the East and West Hills, the latter of which bears the time-wrecked ruins of the famous Castle. This is the fishermen's quarter, and still offers specimens of old-fashioned streets, quaintly picturesque, but inconveniently narrow for traffic.

Hastings has many historical associations, the chief, of course, concerning the landing of William the Conqueror at Pevensey and the famous battle which changed the current of our island story. The Old Town can still show its Castle, its smugglers' caves, some old houses, and two ancient churches. The visitor will find much of interest in these. From the lofty elevation of the encircling hills a variety of splendid views is obtained.

Hastings offers a wide selection of modern attractions. Some of the finest music is heard in the magnificent modern Pavilion at White Rock; there is a pier; the beach, of shingle and sand, affords safe and pleasant bathing. Facilities are provided for sports, there are numerous public parks and gardens, and there is no lack of indoor entertainment.

Historical Note. – St. Leonards is of modern growth, the first stone of the now populous town having been laid on March 1, 1828. But it would puzzle the most erudite of antiquaries to discover the exact date of the laying of the first stone of Hastings. We are told that Haesten, a Jutish pirate, visited the place in the fifth century and settled here.

Under the Saxons, Hastings rose to be a place of note. Like the mighty Roman fortress of Anderida (Pevensey), it fell to the prowess of the Saxon chieftain Ella, about the time when Hengist and Horsa were subduing Kent. The site of the Saxon town is a matter of dispute.

So the Saxon succeeded the Dane, and for a time we lose sight of the town. It emerges from obscurity under Edward the Confessor, when the confederation of the Cinque Ports was established.

For a note on the Cinque Ports, *see* p. 48.

Though the momentous struggle which changed the current of English history is known as the Battle of Hastings, the fight took place some 6 miles away; and it will be better to treat of it when we go to the Abbey of Battle (*see* p. 140). The famous Bayeux tapestry records that William at once commenced to harry the country round Hastings, in order, no doubt, to draw Harold down to fight him. But he was careful not to antagonise the local inhabitants of his base. Only one house it seems was burnt, and that by accident (see Bayeux Tapestry), but compensation was paid.

Immediately upon establishing himself, William set to work to build the massive castle the ruins of which tower over the town.

IN AND ABOUT HASTINGS

Although the town itself is more interesting than many other seaside resorts, the most popular feature of Hastings and St. Leonards is still –

The Sea-Front

Hastings and St. Leonards possess between them one of the finest parades in the world, stretching from end to end for upwards of 3 miles, every foot open to the sea breezes and within view of the waves, yet sheltered from northerly blasts by the hills which in parts rise sheer above. In recent years the Parade has become notable for the way in which underground car parks have been introduced and part of it converted into a double-decker, the lower portion of which provides a sheltered walk.

Hastings Pier stretches out to sea for a distance of 300 yards.

At the eastern end of the front is the Old Town. The Castle Hill is a prominent landmark; and farther away lies the East Hill, offering to the waves a steep but crumbling wall of rock. The "Stade" will be recognized by its fishing boats.

The busiest part of the Parade is that known from the adjacent cliff (now masked by buildings and long since discoloured) as **White Rock.**

On the seaward side are the **White Rock Baths,** well-designed and well-equipped buildings containing swimming, medical, sauna and private baths, spectators' gallery and café lounge. The large swimming bath is one of the finest tepid sea-water baths in the country.

White Rock Pavilion

This Pavilion is not only an asset to Hastings but a notable contribution to its class of architecture. The principal feature is the main Hall, with accommodation for some 1,300 people, and remarkably fine acoustics. Concerts and stage entertainments take place here throughout the year. It is used, too, for dances, conferences, etc. Below the main hall is a smaller one, also used for dances and conferences in winter, but which houses the entrancing *Hastings Historic Embroidery*, commissioned from the Royal School of Needlework to rival the Bayeux Tapestry and to mark the 900th anniversary of the Battle of Hastings. Refreshments are served in the Pavilion café, overlooking the Parade.

Behind the White Rock Pavilion are –

The White Rock Gardens. Here 100 feet above sea-level commanding a fine open view of the Channel, are public bowling-greens, an indoor bowling-green, tennis courts, putting-greens, model village and children's play park. There is the Falaise Hall, used for dances and various events during the year. Licensed bar and café. Behind the Gardens is the Games Oval.

Opposite the north-eastern corner of these grounds and divided from them by Cambridge Road are the buildings of the Royal East Sussex Hospital. Here too in John's Place is the –

Hastings Museum. *(Open* 10 *to* 1 *and* 2 *to* 5 *daily,* 3 *to* 5 *Sundays; admission free.)* The museum is devoted to the history and natural history of East Sussex, the Old Town Museum in High Street being confined to the history of Hastings. There is a fine collection, with useful models, to illustrate the ancient Wealden ironworking, and one of the most representative collections of iron firebacks in the country. In addition to local and agricultural bygones and models of fast-vanishing windmills, one room is devoted to Old Sussex Pottery, in which the museum specializes.

There is a small Art Gallery in which temporary art exhibitions are regularly staged, and the Durbar Hall devoted to ethnology.

Hastings Pier. The pier is 900 feet long, 40 feet in width, and 30 feet above high-water line. At the far end is a large ballroom, used for dancing and for concerts, etc., above which is a lounge bar and balcony café affording magnificent views. Elsewhere on the Pier are refreshment rooms, amusement arcades, and solarium. The Hastings and St. Leonard's Angling Association has a club-room on the Pier.

Westward from White Rock and the Pier extends The Double-Decker Parade. On the upper parade, facing the fine private residences, hotels, and boarding-houses of **Eversfield Place,** there are well-laid-out flower beds. Below is the covered promenade where one can exercise on the wettest day or escape the heat of the sun on the hottest. The Parade extends westward to **Warrior Square,** with its green lawns, shady trees and pretty rock gardens. On the side adjoining the Parade is a popular putting-green, whilst on the second lawn is the bandstand. In St. Margaret's Road, on the east side of Warrior Square, is the **Church of St. Mary Magdalen,** with a fine peal of tubular bells. The church was opened in 1852, the sandstone used in its construction being quarried on the site. The nave corbel-heads are copies of figures depicted in Leonardo da Vinci's *Last Supper*.

Just beyond, in Magdalen Road, is the extensive **Convent of the Holy Child.** Farther up this road is the **Roman Catholic Church of St. Thomas of Canterbury.**

In the valley below the church is **St. Leonards (Warrior Square) Station.** Passing this, and climbing the opposite slope, we come to London Road, a short way up which are the **Gensing Gardens,** well laid out with lawns and flower beds. Here are shady thatched arbours, children's recreation ground with swings, and a small pond for toy boats.

Returning down the road, we pass the **Congregational Church** and then **Christ Church,** which stands in a commanding position at the junction of London and Silchester Roads, and was designed by Sir Arthur Blomfield.

Westward along the sea front is the *Royal Victoria Hotel*, the home of the exiled Bourbons in 1848–1849. Behind the hotel is the **Masonic Hall,** unmistakably a "Burton" building, and beyond, and entered by a most portentous archway are the **St. Leonards Public Gardens,** a pretty scene of copse and dell and a pond with swans. At the extreme end of the gardens is a memorial to James Burton, the "founder of St. Leonards."

Leaving by the northern entrance we see a picturesque building *North Lodge*, once the northern boundary of St. Leonards and home of the novelist Rider Haggard. Over the centre of the arch on either front is carved in stone a shield bearing the St. Leonards arms – a fouled anchor.

A few steps farther is the rebuilt **St. John's Church.**

One may continue westwards towards Bulverhythe along **The Marina,** with its towering block of modern flats and rows of tall houses, most of which are either hotels or boarding establishments, or let off in flats or apartments. No. 57 Marina is of interest as the house occupied by Queen Victoria when, as Princess, she stayed at St. Leonards with her mother, the Duchess of Kent, in 1834.

St. Leonards Parish Church was dedicated in 1956, the former building having been destroyed by enemy action in 1944. A unique feature is its pulpit which was made on the shore of Lake Galilee, and is in the shape of the prow of a boat. This very modern church well repays a visit.

Hastings and the Pier

At the end of the Parade are some pretty rock gardens and beyond the triangular **West Marina Public Gardens,** with bowling-green and putting-green. Adjoining the Gardens is a public Car Park. At this point **Bo-Peep** is reached, deriving its name from the "hide-and-seek" proclivities of smugglers in days gone by. West of the Public Gardens is a Holiday Camp and the **Open-Air Swimming Pool.**

The road which curves inland leads to West St. Leonards Station (trains to Crowhurst, Tunbridge Wells and London).

CENTRAL HASTINGS AND THE CASTLE

Running inland from the Parade, at the east end of White Rock, is **Robertson Street,** one of the principal shopping thoroughfares of Hastings. On the left, in the short byway known as **Claremont,** is **The Brassey Institute.** Of interest are the mosaics by Salviati representing scenes from the Bayeux tapestry. The Library contains over 10,000 volumes in all departments of literature. A newspaper room is open at Robertson Terrace.

Opposite is **Holy Trinity Church,** in the Gothic style, and at the end of Claremont, steps lead up to Cambridge Road, where is the **Central Methodist Church.** Turning down the hill, past Cambridge Gardens and Priory Street, and the **General Post Office,** we may bear in mind that this was the site of the ancient Priory of the Holy Trinity, from which the monks were driven by the sea in the fifteenth century.

At the foot of the hill we rejoin Robertson Street, opposite the **Clock Tower Memorial** occupying what is in many respects the "hub" of Hastings.

One of the six thoroughfares which meet at the Memorial is the busy **Queen's Road,** in which, a few yards up on the left-hand side, is the **Town Hall.** Adjoining is the **Central Cricket and Recreation Ground,** about 6 acres in extent, where good-class cricket is played throughout the summer.

A short street besides a cinema leads to **Wellington Square,** once the Grosvenor Square of Hastings with trees and lawns.

At the foot of the Square, Castle Street leads to Pelham Crescent, in which is the **Church of St. Mary in the Castle.** The church, a capacious structure, was erected in 1828, when the old town began to expand. Its Grecian front is backed by the unusual form of a semi-circular building with a gallery.

At the commencement of George Street is the **West Hill Lift.** (Operating daily at Easter and Whitsun to September) a tunnel driven through the rock for a distance of 462 feet at an incline of one in three. The tunnel affords an easy means of ascent to the summit of the Castle Hill (228 feet), the journey occupying about a minute and a half.

At the top is the tiltyard or *Ladies' Parlour*, as the hollow on the height adjoining the Castle Hill is called.

Hastings Castle

Hastings Castle

Admission fee. Open daily from 10 *a.m. in summer. On application at St. Clement's Caves in winter. Guides are available.*

The present ruins are not those of the first castle; possibly not those of the second; but they are fragments of the mighty structure which the Conqueror caused to be erected after the battle. Behind these walls the armed Norman soldier stood ready to resist foe able to cross that terrible moat, 100 feet wide and 60 feet deep. Within that chapel, of which little but the picturesque arch remains, Thomas Becket once held the office of dean, and William of Wykeham – the founder of Winchester College and New College – was subsequently a prebendary. In 1201 King John was here and promulgated his declaration of the English supremacy of the seas; but the French continued to question his assertion, and in 1216 he dismantled the Castle to prevent its capture. It was restored a few years later by Henry III. In after years the stronghold suffered much from encroachments of the sea, and by the early part of the sixteenth century was in ruins.

In 1824 the then Earl of Chichester undertook a series of excavations, and remains of great interest were brought to light. Chief among these were fragments of the old royal chapel, the chapter-house, the deanery, and portions of the prebendal houses. In 1894 the old dungeons were rediscovered.

Part of the cliff facing the sea has fallen, and part of the fortress doubtless fell with it. On this side the cliff itself formed an impregnable defence. On the east side the battered wall is slowly yielding to the ravages of time. It is nowhere perfect, but the 8-feet thick walls are interesting to look at, and afford a short but pleasant promenade. There are three postern towers on this side, the importance of which is obvious when we consider that the chief gate was situated here. Formerly a drawbridge stretched across the moat. This has entirely vanished but the portcullis grooves remain. By mounting the ramparts here we may obtain a good general view of the fosse or moat, once formidable, but now largely filled in.

Near to the Castle entrance is a door leading to the dungeons, rediscovered in 1894. These "whispering" or "listening" dungeons were carved out of the sandstone and have peculiar acoustic qualities. On account of the streaks of iron oxide running through the stone, whispers in the cells of prisoners were plainly audible to guards at the entrance.

Down on the seafront is the entrance to –

St. Clement's Caves

Open daily from 10 a.m. and Sunday from noon. Admission fee. Guides are in attendance.

These are extensive excavations, the origin of which has been variously ascribed to the Romans, the Danes, and to sand-diggers of modern times. They were probably in the first place a natural formation, but have been enlarged and fashioned by successive generations of occupiers.

The caverns are some 3 acres in extent, and consist of a series of chambers and passages hewn out of the solid rock. The tortuous passages are very impressive; but the atmosphere is equally cool, and there are plenty of lights to dispel the gloom. There are some quaint chambers and curious effigies – the latter supposed to represent St. Clement, Wellington, and Napoleon I. A modern touch is the striking likeness of Field-Marshal Lord Montgomery drawn on a cavern wall by a local artist.

By descending the steps just past the lighthouse, we should reach St. Clement's Church and the Old Town.

THE EAST HILL AND THE HARBOUR

Carlisle Parade with its huge underground car park starts at the west end of Robertson Street and terminates at Harold Place. The sands here provide good bathing. A few yards farther is Caroline Place.

We are now at the **Marine Parade,** the oldest of the series of promenades. Its eastern extremity is a good point from which to watch the fury of the waves during a south-west gale; and in winter it is a grand spot from which to view sunsets. A short distance to the east is a popular Boating Lake for children. Beyond **East Beach** is the new **Lifeboat House** with nearby a large coach and car park.

Opposite the Lifeboat House the Parade reaches its eastern limit; then we plunge into old-time Hastings and reach –

The Fishermen's Quarter

It is refreshing to leave the modern age behind awhile and to gaze on the quaint scene before us. The houses are old and uneven; the streets narrow; the beach dotted with much tarred "net-shops" – like giant sentry-boxes – used for storing nets and gear. Here and there are nets spread out to dry, or for repair. The boats are at the water's edge, and the fish are either being packed for London or disposed of in the nearby Fish Market.

The beach here is called the **Stade** (i.e., landing-place). In 1893, a limited company was formed to construct a harbour. This was intended to comprise an area of 24 acres, with 27,000 feet of quays. Large sums were sunk in the scheme, but unforeseen difficulties arose and for many years the work has been abandoned leaving the unfinished western arm. Huge portions of the masonry have been dislodged by storms. But the large accumulation of shingle these have caused to be trapped has been a welcome addition to the beach.

The **East Hill Lift** *(open daily in summer)* is a useful means of avoiding a laborious climb up 272 steps to the cliff top. It is a boon for walkers making their way to Ecclesbourne and Fairlight Glens.

A small building at the foot of the Lift covers the ancient **East Well,** from which neighbouring residents have long drawn a plentiful supply of pure water. The road here carries the quaint name of Rock-a-Nore. On the opposite side is the **Fishermans' Museum** *(free)* containing the oldest Hastings luggers and some interesting oddments. The building was originally the Fishermens' Church and services are still held occasionally. The main interest beyond this point are the sandstone cliffs, with numerous caverns, towering over the beach.

The groynes and harbour remnants hereabout act as breakwaters, weakening the force of the waves, which would otherwise ravage the coastline for some distance westward.

THE OLD TOWN

A short walk up the old world High Street from the Fishmarket leads to –

St. Clement's Church, which lies off the main street to the left, and is reached through Swan Terrace. The present structure was erected about 1380. It is a Perpendicular building, comprising a chancel, nave, north and south aisles, and a massive, though not lofty, west tower. It is one of the two survivors of the original seven parish churches of Hastings, and the oldest in the town. The curfew is still rung in the winter months and the customs of the annual Civic Service and "beating the bounds" maintained in the district. The registers date from 1558 and are very well preserved.

In High Street is the Old Town Hall, now housing the **Old Town Hall Museum** *(open daily in summer, free)*.

At the far end of High Street, with its raised footways and medley of quaint old houses, is the Roman Catholic Church of **St. Mary Star-of-the-Sea.**

Proceeding through Courthouse Street (opposite the Old Town Hall) The Bourne is reached, at the corner of which is a Methodist Chapel, rebuilt in 1940 on the site where stood the Old Hastings theatre. The sixteenth-century gabled house (No. 29) on the opposite side of the street was once occupied by smugglers, and has a double floor which facilitated the concealment of contraband goods. The initials "HCIS" so prominently incised on its face only stand for the "Hastings Cottage Improvement Society."

East Bourne Street will take us eastwards into **All Saints' Street,** a strange, old-world thoroughfare, containing a number of antique houses and presenting a quaint appearance, the footpath on one side being some feet above the level of the other. Not the least interesting feature of the street is the sudden glimpses afforded by the narrow lanes and alleys opening right and left. In one alley is the unique *Piece of Cheese* cottage *(museum open daily)* so named as it is shaped like a wedge of cheese, all rooms being triangular. A memorable building still remains at the bottom of the street, though an amusement arcade partially obscures its south front. This is **East Cliff House,** built by Capell, a Shakespearean editor of the eighteenth century.

Turn left up All Saints' Street. Crown Lane, which turns off to the right in a line with Courthouse Street, leads into Tackleway, where a plaque denotes the summer residence of the Duke of Sussex in 1794, and is the way to the steps up the **East Hill.**

At the top of All Saints' Street is **All Saints' Church,** erected about 1430, in the Perpendicular style, It consists of a chancel and nave, north and south aisles, and a western embattled tower. In the latter is the chief entrance; but there is also a south porch, in which is a piscina.

Near the church The Bourne, High Street and All Saints' Street converge. There centuries ago was the *Slough*, an open pond where the waters of the Bourne stream were penned to provide drinking water.

Leave Old London Road and Harold Road on the left and take the path which bears to the right up the side of the hill, towards a group of houses bearing the name of High Wickham. Shortly before reaching the top a diverging path on the left leads to the **Minnis Rock,** an ancient landmark.

Several courses are now open to the visitor. Continuing the walk past High Wickham, the summit of the **East Hill** is quickly gained. Here the outline of an Anglo-Saxon promontory fort may be traced.

Or from the foot of Minnis Hill we can proceed along **Old London Road,** beyond which, on the right-hand side, is a French convent, formerly the Hastings Hydro. Two or three hundred yards past this a road to the left leads to the district of **Halton,** whence a bus will carry us to –

The Alexandra Park. It is a narrow but lengthy strip running in a north-westerly direction from Queen's Road to Bohemia and Silverhill. Its 100 acres are diversified with lakes and woodland scenery, flower-beds, tennis, bowls and putting, and pleasant lawns. Originally known as St. Andrew's Gardens the Park was enlarged by the addition of Newgate and Shornden woods. There are some safe paddle boats for children. The lakes form a home for many varieties of water-fowl, and the reservoir is well stocked with trout and coarse fish. Anglers may try their luck for a small charge.

The exit at the upper end (for those turning left at the pumping station) is close to Bohemia Road, and from this point the visitor may either return by bus to the Memorial, or bus down London Road to St. Leonards.

Those who continue to follow the stream will shortly arrive at the **Bucksole Reservoir,** (fishing) alongside which runs the boulevard-like extension of **St. Helen's Road,** constructed to provide an additional entry or exit for motorists visiting Hastings. It joins Queen's Road near the railway bridge, and at the upper end joins Sedlescombe Road, along which "circular route" buses run (the most direct return to the Memorial is by Silverhill bus, going to the left).

Excursions from Hastings

Distances by Road

Battle	.	.	7	Burwash	.	.	17	
Bexhill	.	.	5½	Crowhurst	.	.	5	
Bodiam	.	.	12	Etchingham	.	.	15	
Brede	.	.	7½	Herstmonceux Castle	14			
Brightling	.	.	14	Pevensey	.	.	13	

Robertsbridge	.	11
Rye	.	.	12
Sedlescombe	.	7
Westfield	.	5
Winchelsea	.	10

To East Hill and Ecclesbourne. East Hill can be ascended by the lift or by All Saints' Street, Crown Lane and Tackleway. The summit of East Hill is a wide expanse of heath and greensward. The surface is of yellow iron-sand, through which run layers of Tilgate clay, rich in fossils. Below this is a bit of sandstone, then shale, lignite, and iron-ore – Sussex was once famous for iron. Near the top is a breezy recreation ground. The highest point of the cliff is 342 feet above the sea and the prospect is quite magnificent. A little way inland is *Rocklands*, snugly situated in its grounds, once a favourite retreat of Canning and now an hotel and camp site and with refreshment facilities. From the crest of the hill there is a charming view down the slopes leading to Ecclesbourne.

Those who are proceeding to Fairlight can descend the steps to the mouth of the combe and re-ascend by the steep path opposite. For Ecclesbourne Glen bear leftward (inland). In wet weather, the mud on the path has an adhesive quality not easily forgotten.

Ecclesbourne Glen derives its name from "eagle's bourne." Picturesque, indeed, is the dainty gorge with its winding path, its crags, its tiny rivulet, and its miniature forest. It is still delightfully rural and unspoilt, although so near a great town.

At this point some may prefer to return, and leave the Lovers' Seat and Fairlight Glen for another trip. Those who wish to regain the main road should descend the slope by crossing the stile in Barley Lane, almost opposite the main entrance to *Rocklands*. This leads to Gurth Road, which runs into Harold Road and the bus stop. Those who wish to continue the ramble will find a description of the route in the following section.

To the Lovers' Seat and Fairlight. Fairlight is somewhat difficult of approach by way of the cliffs, except for strong walkers. But it is too good to be left unseen, and those who cannot scale the hills should go by car to the head of the Glen. Perhaps the best route for those who do not motor, and yet are unwilling to walk the whole distance, is to take a bus from the Memorial to **Ore,** alighting at Christ Church, or by bus to Fairlight Place. Follow the Fairlight Road, opposite, for rather more than half a mile, when a direction-post will be seen on the right indicating a footpath which leads directly to the Glen. The paths are very sticky in wet weather.

By far the most interesting route, however, is that over East Hill, crossing the bridge over the mouth of Ecclesbourne Glen and ascending the eastern slope. A path then leads in a mile or more to the sister ravine.

Fairlight Glen is reached by the path to the left, and is even more beautiful than Ecclesbourne. There are few spots in the south of England where rock, foliage and water combine so well, and certainly the glen is worthy of its fame. The pleasantly-winding path leads in due course to an old Dripping Well, now dry, and just above another path on the eastern side leads to the site of **The Lovers' Seat,** a legendary trysting place. The "seat" has gone from its rocky recess overlooking the sea, but the spot still affords a beautiful view.

In the vicinity is Mallydams Wood, Fairlight, an extensive area maintained by the R.S.P.C.A. as a wildlife sanctuary.

From the head of the Glen a track leads northwards past Fairlight Place. Barley Lane turns off sharply to the left and leads directly back to Hastings in about 2½ miles.

Fairlight Down lies slightly north-west of Fairlight Place and is the highest hill on this part of the coast, having an altitude of 575 feet. This is *the* ascent of the district, for those in quest of a really fine view. The summit is marked by a circular broken hedge enclosure, in the centre of which, raised on a wooden platform, is **North's Seat,** a lofty look-out with a dial indicator showing the distance to various villages and towns in the vicinity.

Fairlight Church, a mile farther eastward, on the road to Pett Level, is a modern building in the Early English style, erected in 1845 to replace an earlier edifice. From the lane north of the church is obtained a good view of **Fairlight Hall,** a stone building in the Tudor style. From Battery Hill, a quarter of a mile east of the Pett Level road, a wide view is obtained. Also worth a visit are the **Fire Hills,** so named from the blaze of gorse adorning them in spring, which stands out like a beacon fire to passing ships. Beyond is **Fairlight Cove,** a modern and fast-growing community.

For the return the Hastings-Pett Level bus may be used, or the road westward from Fairlight Church leads in 1½ miles to Ore and the bus.

To Westfield and Brede. Follow the bus route up St. Helen's Road until the turn off on the right for Blacklands, where keep to the left, skirting Alexandra Park, Buckshole Reservoir and the valley of the Old Roar Stream, which is eventually crossed, to the Sedlescombe Road, where turn right. Immediately after passing below the *Harrow Inn* take the road on the right leading to Westfield (bus service).

Westfield Church, dedicated to St. John the Baptist, includes much Norman work. Among its interesting features are the south door (dated 1542), the unusually low Norman chancel arch, with squints on either side, the old carved oak pulpit with sounding board, and the high font with antique cover.

The farm-house south-west of the church was once the manor-house of Westfield, held by Wenestan in the time of Edward the Confessor, and given by the Conqueror to the Earl of Eu. The manor of **Crowham,** to the north, is the *Croteslie* referred to in Domesday: "Godwin held Croteslie in the reign of King Edward." *Lankhurst Farm,* nearly a mile to the south-east, takes its name from the old manor of Lankhurst or Longhurst. Traces of iron-works existing at Westfield in Roman times have been found.

Passing through the straggling village, we can turn off past the schools on to the common, or moor, where gorse and heather are plentiful, regaining the road a little farther on. The road now descends to the **Brede Valley.**

Just before the bridge across the river the church is seen at the top of the hill ahead, and to the right we get a distant view of **Brede Place,** also known as the "Giant's House." Built in the time of Henry VII, with later alterations, the mansion is a typical example of a small medieval residence.

Brede Church is dedicated to St. George. The earliest part, the south arcade of the nave, is late Norman while the north arcade is Early English (*c.* 1230). There is an embattled tower with six bells one of which is pre-Reformation date. Notable features are the sundial on the south wall and the iron-bound almsbox inside the south door. The south, or Oxenbridge, chancel contains a handsome effigy of Sir Goddard Oxenbridge dated 1537. Still, older is the brass, incorporated in a canopied tomb against the south wall, to Robert Oxenbridge and his wife (*d.* 1487 and 1493).

Southward the churchyard commands a magnificent view of hill and dale. At one time large ironworks existed at Brede: they ceased in 1766, to be followed in 1770 by powder mills, which existed until 1825 – there is still a Powdermill Farm in the neighbourhood.

The walk may be extended by going through Brede village and turning to the left for **Sedlescombe** and **Battle.** Or by turning to the right at Brede, the road to **Rye** is gained.

To Sedlescombe. To the *Harrow Inn*, as described in the foregoing excursion whence a good road with pleasant views leads in rather more than 3 miles to the village. On the right just before Sedlescombe is reached is the well-known Pestalozzi village. On the left just after crossing the tiny Brede stream is a garage displaying some ancient firebricks on its wall, while a cottage close by bears the date 1590.

Sedlescombe, with its picturesque sixteenth- and seventeenth-century half-timbered houses of mellow red brick and its gardens gay with bright flowers, is justly considered one of the prettiest villages in the south of England.

Adjoining the village green is an ancient hostelry, the *Queen's Head*, with a signboard representing Queen Bess. The house at the north of the green is *Brickwall*. The Farnden family, who lived here in the seventeenth century, were great ironmasters. In those days Sedlescombe was a flourishing seat of the Sussex iron industry. On the way up the hill to the church, we pass on the left the *Old Manor House*, a fine timbered building dating from 1611. In 1876, when a drain was being dug across a field opposite the school, about 2,000 silver pennies, all coined in Edward the Confessor's reign, were brought to light. The hoard was probably part of Harold's war chest, as many of his men fled from Battle in this direction.

The **Church** (St. John the Baptist) crowns a somewhat steep hill, and is about half a mile from the green. The fine chestnut trees lining the western boundary of the churchyard are of great antiquity; in a plan of the time of Charles I their massive trunks are shown covering the same ground-space as at present. The bells hung in the short embattled tower were cast at Whitechapel between 1595 and 1607. The Early English tower arch was greatly admired by Ruskin. A feature of interest is the Tudor font, with carved "linen fold" oak cover. Over the doorway within the south aisle is fixed a visor surmounted by a stone crest.

The turning to the left a hundred yards or so beyond the church leads through **Whatlington** into Battle, a hilly but pretty route of about 3 miles. Or back through the village, a path at the side of the bridge leads westward to the direct and more level road to Battle Station, Battle Church and Abbey, passing Marley Farm.

Battle, Bodiam and the Rother

Battle

Car Parks. – Opposite the Abbey Gateway, Mount Street and North Trade Road.
Early Closing Day. – Wednesday.
Hotels. – *Beauport Park ; George.*
Museum and Library (Battle Historical Society). At Langton House Memorial Hall.

Population. – 4,800.
Sports. – Available in Battle and district are Golf, Bowls, Bathing, Fishing, Cricket, etc.
Teas, etc. – Can be obtained at restaurants facing the Green and at several hotels in the High Street.

Battle is 7 miles from Hastings, 8 miles from Bexhill and 16 miles from Eastbourne. It is a popular motor-coach excursion from the coastal resorts from which there are also bus services.

The town is the centre of local government for a large and progressive rural district. In the eighteenth century it still in a sense justified its warlike name, having the reputation of producing some of the best gunpowder in Europe. This industry has for many years been discontinued, and Battle is now mostly given over to the peaceful pursuit of agriculture.

The main street runs through the heart of the old battlefield, and is bordered for some distance on its south side by the Abbey wall. At the north end of the town is the Watch Oak, now the offices of the Rural District Council. The ancient oak from whose branches, it is said, King Harold's lover, Edith of the Swan Neck, watched the battle, stood here until a few years ago. Close to the Abbey Gateway is an ancient building – the Pilgrim's Rest – which served the monks as an Almonry. Some of its doors are said to be 800 years old.

The Fifth of November celebrations are a notable event in the town's calendar while the annual Flower Show, held in the Abbey grounds in mid-August, attracts a great deal of interest.

Battle Abbey

Open weekdays from 9–1 and 2–5, dusk in winter. Saturdays till 12.45 p.m. Also open on Saturday afternoons and all day Sunday during August and first half of September. Admission charge. Visitors are conducted round in parties.

The original Abbey was erected by William the Conqueror, in fulfilment of a vow made by him on the eve of the Battle of Hastings, to commemorate his victory over Harold.

Historical Note. – When Edward the Confessor died, on January 5, 1066, there were three claimants for the throne. One, Harold Hardrada, "the strongest and most chivalric of the kings of Norway," claimed in virtue of a compact made with the Danish King, Hardicanute. Another, William, Duke of Normandy, a relative of the Confessor, based his pretensions upon his kinship, the promise of the late King, and an oath of allegiance extorted from the third competitor, Harold, "the last of the Saxons." The choice of the nation fell upon the native prince, who at once assumed the crown and prepared to make good his position. His rivals immediately set to work to compass his destruction, and, urged by Harold's own faithless brother, Tostig, Hardrada descended upon the Northumbrian coast. At this time Harold was guarding the southern shores of his kingdom; and it must have been with considerable misgiving that he marched northward to meet the Viking foe. The conflict at Stamford Bridge left Harold victorious. Four days later the Norman duke effected an unopposed landing near Pevensey, ravaging the countryside, occupying Hastings and presumably posting his army on the heights of Baldslow. There he could block the only two routes to Hastings from London and could fight on a limited front if attacked before his forces were complete. The marshes of Pevensey to the west, and those of Pett, the Brede and the Rother to the east and north, formed elsewhere an effective barrier.

This part of Sussex was particularly loyal to Harold's family. He himself had inherited the manors of Whatlington and Crowhurst – the latter a big one. William could calculate that Harold, who all the summer had planned to fight on the coast, would hasten south to save a beloved countryside and to destroy the invasion before the build-up was complete. So events worked out, which was fortunate, for William could not afford to fight far from his base while Harold's regular army was in being.

Modern historians agree that the historic site of Battle is the true scene of the conflict. The hammer-shaped height, its head dominating for 1,600 yards the slope down to the stream (Santlache or Senlac) below, had been entrenched 200 years before. It was also a natural rendezvous for the English for the handle of the hammer – the present High Street – combined the two roads whereby the hastily summoned levies of Wessex and Surrey would approach from Heathfield and those of London and Kent from Maidstone, leaving the Roman road to Hastings at Cripps Corner, would arrive by way of Whatlington and Mount Street, after detaching a similar force to watch William's army at or south of the Sedlescombe crossing of the *Brede*.

Harold chose his position with knowledge and skill. The men of Kent occupied the eastern end, at about the present school in Marley Lane and where the steep depression behind prevented their line being effectively turned; next, the Londoners at about the Chequers Inn; and Harold's household guards – his elite troops from Stamford Bridge – held the vital summit where the Abbey buildings now stand.

Learning of the advancing host making for the Senlac ridge, William by nightfall had sent part of his army to Telham Hill and assembled the remainder there at dawn on the Saturday. With the morning sun behind him on a fine October morning, after a dry summer had freed the flat Senlac hollow of its normal marshes, he spied the flutter of the Standard and the glint of weapons amid the array of soldiers. It was there that, seeing the English position so strong, he vowed that if God gave him the victory he would erect a mighty minster on that spot.

It was nine o'clock when the battle began. Harold had exhorted his men to stand firm and on no account to quit the shelter of their wall of shields and stakes. William, like Harold, had arrayed his men in the geographical order of their homelands: Frenchmen and Flemings on the right, his own Normans in the centre opposite Harold's regulars, the men of Brittany and Anjou on the left. A trumpet sounded and a flight of Norman arrows was the prelude to the onslaught of the heavy armed foot. Now came the real struggle. The French charged up from the right, at the head of the Senlac valley and where the slope is least, following the present main road in Lower Lake. Stout Kentish battleaxes cut them down. Then came the Norman horsemen, "the choicest chivalry of Europe," charging just to the left of the defeated French and covered by flights of arrows "thicker than the rain before the wind." In turn they, too, were driven back with heavy losses; the Household troops, Londoners and Kentishmen invincibly standing their ground for several hours, though Harold's two brothers were slain. William next sent a force against the English levies in the west centre, and by feigning a retreat enticed some of the untrained Sussex and Surrey levies to leave their position and charge to the valley. Meanwhile William brought round the remainder of his cavalry, who established themselves on the gradual slopes at the west end of the ridge. The advantage was dearly bought, but it nevertheless ultimately decided the fate of the day, for it gained William a footing on the level crest, whence he brought his horsemen into play. They advanced up the gentle slope to the west of the Abbey, and the battle was waged on the level ground where the conventual buildings now stand. So long as Harold lived there was hope for the English, and Harold was performing prodigies of valour. At last an arrow pierced his eye, and he fell. A score of intrepid Norman knights madly rushed upon him; most of them paid for their temerity with their lives, but the survivors despatched him, and the victory was William's.

Mindful of his solemn oath, the Conqueror soon began to erect the Abbey in commemoration of his victory. Throughout William's reign the builder was busily employed; but the Abbey was not completed until the time of William Rufus, being consecrated to the Holy Trinity, St. Mary, and St. Martin on February 11, 1094. Its first occupants were brought over from Marboutier, in Normandy. Its possessions were extensive, including manors in many counties.

For nearly five centuries the Abbey continued to flourish; but with Henry VIII came the suppression of religious houses, and Battle shared in the general ruin. The already venerable Abbey, with its contiguous buildings and its lands, were bestowed upon a royal favourite, Sir Anthony Browne. The new owner at once pulled down much of the property, and transformed the great hall, the abbot's apartments and the dormitory into a mansion. The Abbey is now used as a boarding-school for girls.

On the Green, or Market Place of Battle, the old bull ring is still preserved. Overlooking it is the fine **Gateway** through which we enter the precincts of the Abbey. This is usually thought to date from the fourteenth century, and is one of the most perfect specimens of its kind. In the west wing is the **Porter's Lodge.** The entrance is through an archway and a postern. At an intersection of the groinings in the vaulted roof of the gateway is a carved mask said to represent William I; another shows Harold, "looking to the north for reinforcements." Two corbel heads supporting the hood mould on the south side of the archway are believed to represent either Edward III and Queen Phillipa, or Harold and Edith. A small door on the right leads to the cells of the monastic prison, and over it projects a beam which bears the dolorous name of the Hangman's Post.

From the Gateway we reach the **Terrace.** This pleasant spot covers the site of the **Guest House,** resting upon a range of handsome Early English vaults, or cells, which may have served as sleeping-chambers. Sir Anthony Browne's manor-house has vanished, although we can still trace much of its plan. Resting in the old tiled window recesses in the southern wall of the guest chamber, we have an admirable view of the battlefield. Immediately below is the **Valley of Santlache,** corrupted into Senlac; meaning "communal sandpit" or "sandy stream" and not as once though "Sanguelac, the lake of blood." As elsewhere in this ironstone country the pools of water hereabouts often have a ruddy tinge.

At right angles to this terrace is the inhabited portion of the Abbey, used as a school for girls, the **Abbot's Hall** serving as the Assembly Hall. *(This part of the Abbey is not shown.)* The house has been occupied continuously since it was re-modelled by Sir Anthony Browne. In 1931 it was gutted by fire and all the roofs destroyed. Restorations were completed by 1933.

The **Scriptorium,** or Library of the monastery, is a fine lofty apartment, its vaulting still in admirable order.

Of the once proud Abbey Church nothing now remains. The roofless and extensive ruin to the east is generally identified as the **Dormitory,** erected in the twelfth century. It is the largest remaining fragment of the original structure, and, although now isolated, was once connected with the main building.

Underneath the dormitory are three **Undercrofts,** admission to which is gained from either side by a low passage. The easternmost was the **Scriptorium** (*see* above). That we now enter is remarkable for its Norman pillars and arcading.

Beyond the Dormitory is the site of the cloisters; but of these solemn courts nothing now exists save the internal arcading of the western side running along the house-wall, and the bases of a cluster of pillars at the south-east angle, near the Dormitory. The nine beautiful arches which now form part of the east front of the abbey building will suffice to give an idea of the splendour of the passages. The first two arches, counting from the left, are the earliest and finest. Dating from 1171, they present charmingly wrought capitals of flower and leaf. The door in the second bay is modern. It opens into a vestibule called the **Beggars' Hall,** to the right of which was the dormitory, whose wall, rising above the cloister arches, is of modern date.

Hence we pass through the Yew (or Monks') Walk to the **Rose Garden** leading to the wood-yard. This occupies the site of the nave of the old Abbey Church.

Battle Church *(Sunday Services at* 8, 11, 6.30*)*. Partly Norman, but mainly Early English, with Decorated and Perpendicular additions, the venerable church of Battle consists of a chancel with two lateral chapels, a nave with aisles, and an embattled west tower. Dedicated to St. Mary, it was founded between the years 1107–1124, by Ralph, the third Abbot of Battle. Little of the original building remains; but the nave is Late Norman, its stout arches having stood since the later years of the twelfth century. The west door is Early English, of a little later date; and the clerestory and chancel are of the same period. The north aisle, widened in the fifteenth century, contains some ancient and interesting glass of older date. The Alfraye brass on the floor at the extreme east end of the aisle should be noticed.

To Bodiam

Bodiam lies 7 miles north of Battle and can be reached via Robertsbridge or Sedlescombe. From Hastings the direct route is through Sedlescombe and Cripps Corner.

Bodiam Castle

Open weekdays, 10–7 (April to September); other months, 10 to dusk. Sundays, 1.30–5.30 (April to September only). Admission charge (museum included). The Castle is the property of the National Trust.

The Castle stands almost on the boundary line of Sussex, near the intersection of the Kent Ditch with the Rother. So well have its walls withstood time's onslaught that it is not easy to discover, until we reach it, that the fortress is really a ruin; and the delusion is strengthened by the moat, which exists in the same condition as when built. The Castle was built in the reign of Richard II by Sir Edward Dalyngrigge, who in 1385 was granted royal licence to "fortify and crenellate his Manor House," about a mile away, at the time there were fears of a French invasion. He took it upon himself to enlarge the licence into a permit to build a new castle entirely. It seems never to have been besieged, but was dismantled in the seventeenth century, probably by the Parliamentary forces, and then left to decay for nearly 200 years.

Bodiam Castle, although now a picturesque shell, forms one of the most perfect examples of mediaeval military architecture. It is a rectangular structure, contained within four curtain walls, 6 feet thick, and 41 feet high, and strengthened at each angle by a circular tower, 60 feet high and 29 feet in diameter. Between these are placed square towers on each side, except the north, where a double tower forms the impressive gate-house.

A wooden bridge leads on to an octagonal island on the right of which is seen in the western bank of the moat, a stone abutment. This stonework and the octagon were formerly connected by a wooden bridge and formed the original entrance. Directly in front of the octagon are the remains of the Barbican, the gap between being originally crossed by a drawbridge. Behind the Barbican a stone causeway leads to another bridge beyond which is the gatehouse. Its top is crowned with a superb line of machicolations. The original portcullis still hangs above the doorway. Above are emblazoned the family arms of Wardeux, Dalyngrigge, and Radynden and higher still is the crest of Dalyngrigge, a helmet surmounted by a unicorn's head. Inside the gatehouse a large passage gives way to an open courtyard. The second half of this passage, once divided from the first by a portcullis, was vaulted and groined. In the intersections are circular holes, termed meurtrieres or murder holes, through which could be used those "disagreable substances."

Most of the interior wall with the exception of the south-west section, has vanished to within a few feet of the ground level. Despite this it is easy to trace out the various rooms. Looking to the left the first thing to catch the eye is the triple lancet window of the chapel, now alas, despoiled of its storied glass. The Chapel consisted of a nave, sanctuary and a small sacristy. A crypt, now filled in, existed beneath the nave. On the left of the sacristy door is a piscina. The doorway in the south wall led into the State apartments. The apartments to the north of the chapel were those of the Steward and Household and were of two storeys, each with a fireplace and garderobe contained in the wall. The north-east tower was of three storeys each with the same refinements and served by a circular staircase. Beneath these apartments were cellars. The State apartments of the owner were to the south of the Chapel, while underneath was a range of cellars. On the ground floor was the Ladies' Bower and the Great Chamber and on the floor above, the State Bedroom and the Solar. The east and south-east towers were probably lodgings or bedrooms. A tall four-light window in the south wall marks the Great Hall, used only by the owner and his personal household, the retainers having their own hall in the west range. The western extremity of the Great Hall is marked by three arches that led to the Buttery, the Pantry, and the Lord's Kitchen. Before stepping through the arches let us turn to the left through the double doors into the Postern Tower. This tower has a passage, vaulted and groined, complete with meurtrieres. Another set of doors lead out on to a small platform, from which a wooden bridge for foot passengers only, once spanned the moat. A circular stairway leads to the top of the Postern Tower. Although roofless and shorn of its battlements, its defensive value can be appreciated on looking down through the machicolations. Descending the stairway we return to the Great Hall and turning to the left through the Buttery arches. A few more paces bring us to the Lord's Kitchen with two large fireplaces, both of which could have roasted the traditional ox. In the basement of the south-west tower is the well, 10 feet deep and fed by a spring. In the top storey was a dove-cote. The western side of the Castle contained the Retainers Hall with sleeping quarters above, a small kitchen with two large fireplaces and in the north-east angle, the stables and quarters for the garrison.

In 1917 Lord Curzon of Kedleston acquired the Castle to ensure its preservation. He carried out a programme of repair, excavation, and research and on his death in 1925 bequeathed it to the National Trust.

Anglers will find excellent sport in the **River Rother.** The stream is preserved by the Rother Fishing Association.

Northiam

From Bodiam, Northiam may be reached by a pretty road passing through Ewhurst.

Northiam Church (St. Mary's) exhibits specimens of Saxon, Norman, Early English, and Perpendicular. Local ironstone has been largely used in the construction of the tower. Scratch dials on the south porch should be noted. In the chancel notice the Tufton and Beuford brasses (sixteenth century), the latter representing a former rector, also a slab commemorating Thankful Frewen (d. 1749), rector for 56 years. North of the chancel, and separated from it by a glazed screen, is the Frewen mausoleum, erected 1846. The Brickwall pew, of the old-fashioned square type, is in the north-east corner of the nave. On the village green is **Queen Elizabeth's Oak,** under whose branches that monarch dined in 1573 on her progress to Rye. Facing the oak is the *Hayes Farm Hotel* with an Elizabethan bakehouse.

No.thiam possesses many ancient timbered houses. Half a mile south of the church is *Carriers*, an old farmhouse where Archbishop Accepted Frew n was born in 1588. The conspicuous loyalty of this prelate to his unfor.unate King, Charles I, is a matter of history. *Brickwall,* an elegant mansion near the church, was the seat of the Frewen family until recently. It is now used as a school, but its north front reveals its origin. The manor-house of *Dixter* was the home of the Dixters, who are mentioned in local records as far back as 1296; **Great Dixter** was built about 1460, on the site of an earlier manor. The Great Hall is one of the largest timber-framed halls in the country and possesses a unique roof containing hammer beams with carved armorials. It was restored by Lutyens in 1911. *The house and gardens are open daily except Mondays other than Bank Holidays during the summer*. The old farmhouse known as Tufton Place, for some time known as Northiam Place, originally belonged to the Tuftons, Earls of Thanet. *Gate Court* at the north of the village dates back to 1235; *Church House*, north-east of the church, is mid-sixteenth century; and nearby is *Silvenden Manor*, timber-framed and thatched, with Tudor arches and dating originally from 1450.

South of Horns Cross is the beautiful little Catholic Church built by Sheila Kaye-Smith (*d.* 1956) at Little Doucegrove. The authoress lived in a pleasantly converted oast-house nearby.

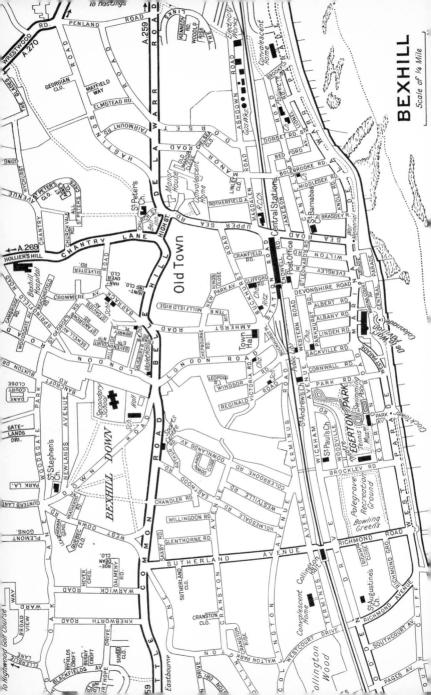

Bexhill

Banks. – *Barclays*, Devonshire Road; *Lloyds*, Devonshire Road; *National Westminster*, Buckhurst Road, near Town Hall, and at St. Leonards Road; *Midland*, Devonshire Road.

Bathing. – The shore is shingly at first, but there are good sands farther out. At low tide a rather long walk is necessary to get into deep water. Tents, cabins, etc., can be hired by the week. On the Central Parade is a bathing station with boxes fitted with shower-baths, and another in the East Parade. In Egerton Park is an open-air swimming bath.

Boating. – Paddle boats for children on the lake in Egerton Park. The headquarters of the *Bexhill Rowing Club* are on the seafront opposite Sea Road.

Bowls. – Egerton Park, Polegrove, and Sidley Recreation Ground, etc.

Bus Services to all parts of the town and to adjoining resorts. Daily coach service to London.

Car Parks. – Devonshire Square, De la Warr Pavilion and roads where marked.

Cricket. – The ground of the Bexhill Cricket Club and Bexhill Amateur Athletic Cricket Club is at the Polegrove where visitors are welcome. There are also facilities on the Down and Little Common.

Early Closing Day. – Wednesday.

Fishing. – Fishing is principally from boats, but there is good fishing for bass from the beach. Good deep-sea fishing is to be had.

Golf. – There is an 18-hole course at Cooden and a very sporting inland course at Highwoods. Putting courses at Cooden and Highwood Golf Clubs and others at Egerton Park and by the De la Warr Pavilion.

Hotels. – *Annadale*, Brassey Road; *Granville*, Sin Road; *L'Avenir*, Knowle Road; *Southlands Court*, Hastings Road; *Victoria*, Middlesex Road, and many others.

Library. – Western Road.

Music. – Band performances and concerts in the De la Warr Pavilion.

Population. – About 33,500.

Post Office. – Devonshire Square. There are numerous sub-offices.

Riding. etc. – Moor Hall Riding Stables, Ninfield; Manor Riding Stables, Lunsford Cross. Annual Horse Show.

Tennis. – Egerton Park and Little Common.

Bexhill has a following as devoted and enthusiastic as that of any holiday resort in the kingdom. It is an incorporated borough, has many good shops, and a sea-frontage of five miles. Though the town is comparatively modern, it was not unknown in very early days, for in 772 a grant of land was made by the Charter of Offa, King of Mercia, for the purpose of building and endowing the parish church.

Bexhill is just the right size for a holiday resort. It has all the conveniences of a town, without those acres of monotonous suburbs that in larger places lie between the really interesting parts and the country behind. The buses enable one to get easily from one end of the town to the other, and nowhere are the open fields far distant.

The borough – which includes Little Common and Sidley – extends along the coast from Bulverhythe to Pevensey Sluice, and has a total area of 8,015 acres, being, indeed, as regards area, the largest in Sussex.

The **Beach** is partly of shingle, partly of sand. Except for a few hours in the day, a magnificent stretch of sand is exposed along the entire front, sand clean and firm, and eminently suitable for the operations of juvenile castle-builders and paddlers. Towards the eastern end a long ledge of seaweed-covered rock, known as My Lord's Rock, is laid bare by the receding tide, and its shallow pools offer alluring possibilities to youthful investigators.

Towards the eastern end the beach is bordered by the **De La Warr Parade** stretching towards the green slopes of Galley Hill. This Parade formed the track of some of the first motor races held in England.

The dominating feature of the sea-front is the **De La Warr Pavilion,** a striking modern building consisting of two long blocks connected by the entrance hall. On one side are a theatre and concert hall; on the other restaurant and bars, and sun balconies with deck chairs. The whole of the southern front has sliding windows with a wide view of the Channel. First-rate theatrical and musical entertainment is provided throughout the year. The flat roof affords excellent facilities for sun-bathing.

The central portion of Bexhill's sea-front is known as **Marina.** The spacious roadway is flanked on one side by hotels, shops and residential flats, while on the seaward side a succession of garden plots border an inner promenade, below the level of which is a long range of Moorish buildings rejoicing in the name of the **Arcade.** On the seaward side of the Arcade is the **Central Parade,** bordered on its landward side by a series of pleasant bungalow residences. Opposite the end of Devonshire Road there is a break in the line of buildings. From this point **Devonshire Road** runs inland as one of the principal shopping centres of the town.

Now we come to the third and longest portion of the sea-front the **West Parade,** built over a stout sea-wall. It is a sunny promenade with grass verges and shelters. The **Clock Tower** commemorates the Coronation of King Edward VII. In front is a dial indicator showing the direction and distances to various places, the coast of France, London, Canterbury, etc.

Formerly a flagstaff marked approximately Bexhill's western limit, but in recent years the cliffs towards Cooden have been developed as building estates and many charming houses erected. Attractive features at this end of the Parade are the beach huts.

Immediately to the north of the West Parade is a long strip of recreation ground, of which the larger portion forms –

Egerton Park. Here are tennis courts, a bandstand, and, at the west end, a fine pavilion. Indoor bowling rinks are laid in the pavilion during winter months. A feature which endears the Park to the children is the tortuous **Lake,** spanned near the northern end by a rustic footbridge, and furnished with a fleet of boats in which they may cruise in safety. At the seaward end of the Park is an open-air seawater **Swimming Pool.** The Pavilion adjoining, formerly used as a shelter-hall, now houses a **Museum** of specimens illustrating the natural history, geology, and other features of the neighbourhood. *(Open weekdays, except Friday,* 10–1, 2.15–5; *Sundays, April–September,* 10–12, 2–4.)

The buses skirt the southern and western sides of Egerton Park *en route* to the terminus at Cooden.

Adjoining Egerton Park on the west is **The Polegrove,** another large recreation ground, with bowling-greens and ample space for cricket, Association and Rugby football, hockey, etc. Light refreshments are obtainable.

So much for Bexhill's sea-front. It remains only to add that pleasant walks can be had at either end – one over Galley Hill to Bulverhythe and St. Leonards, the other to Cooden and Pevensey Sluice – but these are more fully described later.

Before exploring the town, however, we may cross the railway by the bridge a short distance west of the Polegrove and visit **Collington Wood.** This quite unspoilt resort of 12 acres is one of Bexhill's happiest possessions.

From Collington Wood, Terminus Avenue and Terminus Road run eastward into the town. Shortly before reaching the Central Station, we find on the left the large open space over which the **Town Hall** presides, a red-brick building erected in 1895 and enlarged in 1935.

Buckhurst Road, one of the most pleasant and open thoroughfares in the town, runs obliquely uphill from the Square in the direction of the Old Town. It leads to **Sea Road,** a broad thoroughfare connecting Old Bexhill with the sea-front and forming part of the road route in and out of the town. It serves the Central Station (on the coast-line), and boasts two important churches. The first of these, the Roman Catholic **Church of St. Mary Magdalen,** is a handsome building of Kentish ragstone in the Late Decorated Style, with embattled tower, erected in 1907. Passing the station and continuing seawards, we reach **St. Barnabas Church,** erected from the designs of Sir Arthur Blomfield, and opened in 1891.

Little more than half a mile from its seaward end, Sea Road reaches the **Old Village,** now usually referred to as the Old Town, a curious medley of old and new. The road leading to it still retains in part its rural character, and with its green trees and hedgerows makes a pleasant walk. The footway is raised high above the road, and seats are placed here and there.

On the brow of the hill, to the right as one enters the village, is the Bexhill Convalescent Home, a large red-brick building, commanding fine views of sea and land.

The **Parish Church of St. Peter** is a fine structure with a low tower. The building is mainly modern but its history extends back to the Saxon period. The old parts remaining are the Norman basement to the tower, west parts of nave arcade, and parts of the Early English chancel arch and north chantry chapel.

An interesting feature of the churchyard is the ancient sundial near the path leading to the south door. The hill on which the church stands is 150 feet above sea-level; consequently the Norman tower, although at first sight somewhat squat, is seen for miles around.

The left-hand turning just beyond the church leads to the leafy **Chantry Lane,** one of Bexhill's prettiest spots.

Nearly a mile along the Hastings Road, at its junction with Wrestwood Road, is *Nazareth House*, a large building in the Scottish baronial style. It is a branch of Nazareth House, Hammersmith, and was erected in 1894 by the Poor Sisters of Nazareth.

The building, which forms a prominent landmark, may be visited daily between 2 and 5. In this part of the town are many pleasing residences and educational establishments, surrounded by large gardens and commanding excellent seaward views.

By walking in the westward direction from the Old Village we pass along High Street to **Belle Hill**, at the foot of which is the Church and Hall of the Good Shepherd. Passing under the railway bridge we reach –

The Down

A breezy, gorse-covered common, rather more than half a mile from the sea and 44 acres in extent. A large space has been cleared for cricket and other games, and there is also a pleasant riding-track, but the greater part of the expanse has wisely been left to Nature. In the season there are still purple patches of heather, and gorse flourishes amazingly. The road to **Little Common** skirts the Down on its southern side, and another road leads right across it to **St. Stephen's Church,** a picturesque red-brick building, which, with the neighbouring windmill, dominates the scene. On the adjoining Woodsgate Park estate are a number of chalybeate springs. A mile or so north-west of St. Stephen's are the links of the **Highwood Golf Club,** an inland course of considerable charm whether one visits it for golf or for scenery.

We can return to the sea-front by way of Sutherland Avenue, at the western end of the Down. In this neighbourhood, known as **West Bexhill,** there are many pleasant houses.

Bodiam Castle

Short Excursions from Bexhill

To Cooden. Cooden lies 2½ miles west of Bexhill and the intervening space has been completely developed with modern and attractive property. The beach, however, still remains popular for bathing and provides a pleasant route for those walking to Cooden.

On the inland side of the railway arch are the Links and club-house of the *Cooden Beach Golf Club*. The 18-hole course extends almost to Pevensey Sluice along the north side of the railway. Buses from Hastings, Bexhill, and Eastbourne pass the links and railway travellers may alight at Cooden Beach Station near the club-house.

The road inland leads in about a mile to **Little Common** (*see* below). The large house with the curious turret is *Cooden Mount*. Close at hand is the Convalescent Home, a striking building in Georgian style. The return to Bexhill from Little Common can be made by the main road (there is a fairly frequent bus service) or by Collington Lane, with its many charming houses.

If, instead of turning inland from Cooden, we keep along the shore for a mile and a half, we arrive at **Pevensey Sluice,** now also known as **Norman's Bay** (Pevensey Castle is another 3 miles). The hamlet once formed part of the ancient town of Northeye, which stood on land still spoken of as "Old Town Field." William the Conqueror landed in Pevensey Bay, but the configuration of the coast has so altered that it is impossible to indicate the spot with any precision.

The **Martello Towers** that girdle the shore were erected centuries afterwards to repel another invader, who, however, never arrived. Anglers frequently visit the Sluice for pike, perch, and other coarse fishing.

To Little Common. Whether Little Common is regarded as part of Bexhill or as a separate place will depend to some extent upon one's route of approach to the hamlet – there is no Common in the ordinary sense of the word. The house-lined Collington Lane or the bus route *via* Cooden will incline one to believe Little Common is just a suburb of Bexhill; but going by way of the Down and past the *Denbigh Hotel* a pleasant stretch of country intervenes until we descend the hill past the church of Little Common. *St. Mark's Church (Sunday services* 8, 11, *and* 6.30) is frequently attended by Bexhill visitors. The *Wheatsheaf Inn* overlooks a small green where meets of the Rivervale Beagles and the East Sussex Foxhounds take place.

To The High Woods and Hooe. The High Woods are about a mile north of Little Common. Perhaps the best route for walkers is *via* the Down to St. Stephen's Church, where take the Broadoak Lane (the Little Common Road). In about half a mile, beside **Broadoak Manor,** a path will be found on the right crossing open fields with views on the right of the Highwood Golf Course, part of which it subsequently crosses. On reaching Grinse's Farm follow the lane leftward into the Little Common–High Woods road, where turn right.

Another Route. Ascend Collington Rise and near top take the "short cut" path on the left. When this ends cross main road and pass through iron gate. On reaching the road, in about half a mile, turn right for the **High Woods.** For Hooe, however, take at the crest of the rise the path on the left labelled "High Peartree Avenue, to Whydown and Hooe." This cuts across the woods very charmingly and again leads into the road, where go straight forward. Descend for perhaps half a mile, then, just before the road swings to the right, leave it by a path on the left (by the wall of White Lodge) which leads across the rich fields to **Hooe.** It is a quaint little place of which much is situated off the road, and to some extent out of sight of it. It provides good views across to High Woods and Bexhill and has a small church with some ancient glass portraying King Edward III and his Queen Philippa.

A *return route*. About 200 yards south of the point where the path from Whydown enters Hooe another path returns eastward and southward to **Barnhorne,** whence the road runs eastward to Bexhill.

To Sidley and Crowhurst. Sidley, about a mile and a half from the sea-front, is a suburb of Bexhill but provides a pleasant short walk. The footpath route starts from the north end of Church Street and leads directly northward to Wrestwood Road where turn left. The road route is via Sea Road, Old Bexhill and Chantry Lane.

Crowhurst is famous for its old yew tree which stands propped up to the south of the church. It is believed to be over fourteen hundred years old.

The **Church,** embowered in trees, stands boldly out to view beside a crumbling pile of ruins. It consists of a chancel, nave, north aisle, and an embattled tower supported by buttresses of enormous size. It is in the Early English style; but, except the tower, little is left of the original edifice built by Sir John Pelham early in the fifteenth century.

Also to the south of the church are the ruins of the old Manor House, one of the most interesting examples of ancient domestic architecture in Sussex, and dating from the time of Henry III. For the village, the placid beauty of whose surroundings the visitor can hardly fail to admire, turn southward.

Crowhurst Park, to the north of the Hastings–Battle road, was formerly the property of the Papillo family. On the farther side of the same road is **Beauport Park,** a well-wooded estate of 900 acres. There are several caravan sites.

From the cross-roads at Crowhurst a pleasant road can be followed uphill to **Catsfield** ($2\frac{1}{2}$ miles). The ancient church (St. Lawrence), with its short square tower and shingled spire, looks very picturesque as it suddenly comes in view among the trees. In contrast the tall white spire of the Methodist church is a conspicuous land-mark.

Nearly 2 miles south-west of Catsfield lies **Ninfield,** and from here the return to Bexhill could be made by road.

Pevensey, Westham and Herstmonceux

Buses, etc. – There are hourly services by bus and coach.

Rail. – Pevensey and Westham Station is west of Pevensey village in the village of Westham, five minutes walk from the castle. Pevensey Bay Halt is midway between Pevensey village and the bay, about ten minutes walk from the castle. Both stations are served by trains from Eastbourne and Hastings.

Walk. – Those who prefer to approach Pevensey on foot from Eastbourne should first take bus along seaside. Turn left at second roundabout and then turn right (Priory Road). A footpath across the fields rejoins the main road about half a mile south of Westham. Pevensey village is then about a mile farther in a north-easterly direction. The return may well be made by way of Pevensey Bay reached by turning right at the east end of Pevensey village, and whence a road runs westward and joins the Seaside road at the roundabout mentioned above.

Pevensey (locally *Pemsie*) and Westham are twin villages on the great plain eastward of Eastbourne. The name of the first conjures up visions of the landing of the Normans, and the Bayeux Tapestry vividly illustrates what then took place. But the site which bears the name of Pevensey had acquired historic interest long before Norman William set foot upon it, and afterwards it was the scene of events in which all England had concern.

Westham has in its street some pretty cottages of the Elizabethan period. The large and scattered parish extends almost to Hailsham on one hand and to Eastbourne on the other.

St. Mary's Church (*Sunday Services at* 8, 11, 6.30), is a massive building and one of the most notable churches in the county. The fifteenth-century tower is especially fine. The south transept and south wall, with its three small round-headed windows, are part of the Norman church built towards the end of the eleventh century. The large Perpendicular window in the south wall was inserted at the Reformation. The north aisle and small turret date from about 1300. The chancel, in the Perpendicular style, was added about the time of Henry V (the glass in the small upper lights of the east window is of that date). The late fourteenth-century rood-screen has been restored and replaced in its original position and loft added. Notice the fine fifteenth-century carved oak screen and Norman arch of the south transept, or Lady Chapel. Raised on a massive oak table in this chapel is the stone of the original high altar. The font is fifteenth-century. From the tower are far-reaching views.

PEVENSEY

Pevensey Castle

Admission. – Daily, May–September 9.30–7, Sundays 9.30–7; October, March and April 9.30–5.30, Sundays, 2–5.30; November–February 9.30–4, Sundays 2–4. Admission charge.

Car Park in the Market Place, below the eastern gate of the castle.

The road turns off to the left and goes round the walls, but the public footpath leads at once through the gateway to a grassy area of about 10 acres, enclosed by great walls that are still in places from 20 to 30 feet high, and have stood the wear and tear of centuries in a manner almost miraculous. The walls of Pevensey are in fact one of the finest examples of Roman building in the country, and were built between A.D. 250 and 300 to form one of the Forts of the Saxon Shore. Within the walls is a smaller fortress, Norman in origin, so that we have here a castle within a castle, with an interval of about 800 years between the dates of building. Recently the remains have undergone very striking renovation. Tons of grass-grown earth have been removed, and the lower part of the walls again exposed; the Norman moat has been cleared, and all masonry carefully grouted with cement. In the course of the work a large number of stone "cannon balls" were unearthed, most of them lying on the spot to which they were projected by Roman catapults and the artillery of the Normans.

Historical Note. – The ground here has a history extending back for close on two thousand years. Nor was it devoid of human inhabitants in prehistoric days, for many Neolithic implements have been unearthed on the spot. In the words of Freeman, Pevensey is "a spot so memorable in the earliest English history that to one who muses there the landing even of William himself seems but of secondary interest."

The outer walls are of Roman construction and encompassed the city of Anderida, one of the nine great fortresses which guarded the southern shore. At that date, and until the thirteenth century, the sea washed the foot of the slight eminence occupied by the city, and ships could ride at anchor beneath the walls. In the fifth century the legions retired, and Britain became successively the prey of Picts and Scots and Saxons. Before the ravages of these sanguinary hordes the unfortunate inhabitants of the land fled from place to place, their numbers being thinned by repeated slaughters. Many sought refuge at Pevensey, and met with a dismal fate in A.D. 491.

It was here too, that the Norman fleet landed unopposed in 1066.

After Harold's defeat, Pevensey, together with other lands, came into the possession of William's half-brother, Robert, the powerful Earl of Mortain and Cornwall, who at once set about the erection of a fortress, the ruins of which stand in the south-east angle of ancient Anderida.

The Roman Walls. The Norman castle has a history of its own; but before dealing with that it will be more convenient to glance at the Roman ruins. Anderida has vanished, but its walls remain. They are of flint rubble, with facings of square green sandstone blocks. The mortar is of a ruddy hue, owing to the admixture of pounded tiles. The thin bonding courses are of brick and ironstone. The walls, nearly 200 yards long, are from 10 to 12 feet thick, and vary from 20 to 30 feet in height. The towers on each side of the entrance gate may possibly be Norman; it is certain that the Normans at one time or another repaired and altered the work of the Roman masons. The Decuman Gate stood here before these turrets, and part of it was probably embodied in the newer work. About two-thirds of the old wall still remain, and fifteen towers project from various parts of it. That at the north-east corner was raised to a height of 50 feet to serve as a watch-tower. The walls form an irregular oval, of which a good portion of the south side has decayed and fallen.

Among the objects unearthed here from time to time was a small piece of the original well rope, made of twisted strands of bark: "apparently the only piece of Roman cordage yet found in Britain."

The Norman Castle. As already stated, this stronghold was erected by the Earl of Mortain shortly after the Conquest. Pentagonal in form, it covers $1\frac{1}{2}$ acres, and is partly constructed of Roman material, the wall at the south-east side having been retained and used by the Norman builders. The difference between Roman and Norman building will readily be observed. The red-tinted mortar of the former disappears in the latter, the stones of which are larger and the walls higher, though not so thick. Five towers and a moat defended the fortress, which stood upon elevated ground. The irregular keep is unique in plan, and was built about 1100. The gate-house, and the walls and towers of the inner courtyard, are mid-thirteenth century. Excavation has revealed much masonry, and among other discoveries have been a dungeon, 15 feet deep, just inside the entrance gate, and the foundations of the chapel.

Pevensey

Returning to the road, we have on our left the **Mint House** (Open Mondays, Tuesdays, Thursdays, Fridays, 9-1 and 2.15-5.30. Wednesdays and Saturdays, 9-1 and 2.15-5. Closed Sundays.) This interesting old building is said to date from 1342, and the site of the present structure is reputed to have been used as a Norman Mint in A.D. 1076. The celebrated Andrew Brode considerably altered the interior about two centuries later.

The house, which is said to have been occupied by Edward VI, is used as an antique shop, its twenty-eight rooms being appropriately fitted up with antique furniture and ornaments. There are fine old carvings, and in a downstairs room is some good oak panelling found *c.* 1900 under the plaster. On the wall of a corridor on the first floor, and also in one of the bedrooms, some fifteenth-century frescoes have been brought to light, and on the walls of a bedroom which Edward VI is said to have occupied are traces of sixteenth-century frescoes. There is the traditional haunted room with its ghost, said to be that of the murdered mistress of a Thomas Dight in 1586. On the ground-floor is the minting chamber. This ancient apartment has no ceiling, and beneath the rafters of the roof can be seen openings into a series of seven dark rooms on the upper floor, once used by smugglers.

A little way down, on the the opposite side of the village street, is the old **Town Hall,** or court house, a survival of the days when Pevensey had its Mayor and Corporation. It is a small two-storey building with a projecting window. The upper storey was the court room, the lower the lock-up, containing two cells. The building now houses a **museum** *(open from June to September)*. Interesting exhibits include the municipal regalia of the defunct Corporation of the Liberty of Pevensey, including silver-gilt mace, beadle's cloak, hat and staff, and constable's truncheon. Also to be seen is the Corporation's iron seal, dating from the early years of Henry III and the oldest existing seal of any of the Cinque Ports, dated, *c.* 1230.

Pevensey Church, dedicated to St. Nicholas *(Sunday Services, 11 and 6.15)*, is an Early English structure of green sandstone erected in the reigns of King John and his son, Henry III. The chief characteristic is the very long chancel with a marked deflection to the north. In the north aisle is the elaborate monument of John Wheatley, a wealthy parishioner in the reign of Elizabeth. In the west wall of the aisle is a lancet window containing a representation of St. Nicolas (Archbishop of Myra), the patron saint of the church. A similar window in the south aisle contains a picture of St. Wilfred, the founder of the diocese of Selsey, afterwards Chichester, 681. At the other end of the south aisle are two mediaeval stone coffin lids of Sussex marble, found at the restoration of the church. In the south wall of the chancel are twin windows with deep mouldings, dating from about 1215, and good examples of Early English work.

Pevensey Bay

a mile south of Pevensey, is a popular little holiday resort. There are several shops and cafés and hotel, caravan, beach chalets and other accommodation, but on quieter parts of the beach still grow sea-asters, star thistles, sea-poppies and sea-kale. All this land has been gained from the sea, which formerly flowed right up to the castle walls.

PEVENSEY TO HERSTMONCEUX

Having crossed the old grey bridge over *Pevensey Haven* at the end of the village, turn to the left, and, disregarding a by-road on the left, continue due north for rather more than 3 miles. Except for modern innovations in the form of electric grids, the Marshes have changed but little since the time of Charles II.

Wartling *(Lamb Inn)* is entered by a pleasantly-shaded road, above which stands the quaint old Church (dedicated to St. Mary Magdalene), which has suffered much at the hands of "restorers."

Westward from the churchyard there is a fine view across the Marsh to Pevensey. Half-a-mile north of the village there is seen on the left the buildings of the Royal Greenwich Observatory in the grounds of Herstmonceux Castle.

Herstmonceux Castle

There is no public access to the Castle, but the grounds are open on Monday, Wednesday and Thursday afternoons from April to October from 2–5. The Isaac Newton Telescope is reached by a footpath from the car park in the Wartling Road. Open daily from 2 p.m.

The castle is occupied by the Royal Greenwich Observatory and part is used as the residence of the Astronomer Royal. Several buildings to house the various telescopes have been erected in the famous grounds.

Herstmonceux Castle, restored by the late Colonel Lowther and Sir Paul Latham, is a fine example of a mediaeval moated brick mansion. It is situated in a hollow in one of the prettiest spots in the county, some 9½ miles north-east of Eastbourne. The castle stands on the site of a Norman manor-house, long the seat of the family of De Monceux. The name is derived from the Old English *hyrst*, a wood, and the name of the family. Locally it is pronounced *Herstmonsoo*.

In the fourteenth century the property passed by marriage to the Fynes, or Fiennes, and it is to Sir Roger of that ilk that we owe the foundation of the present building in 1440. This knight was one of the heroes of Agincourt, and having gallantly served Henry V in war, he was now engaged in acting for Henry VI in the more peaceful capacity of treasurer. His descendants bore the title of Lord Dacre; and although the castle was several times carried into fresh families by marriage, the owners of Herstmonceux still retained the name.

Built in the days of the "last of the Barons," at a time when the old order was giving place to the new, the castle combined the old idea of a defensive fortress with that of a comfortable and luxurious mansion. Under Edward III, castles had expanded into an admixture of palace and fortress, with magnificent apartments. Windsor, Warwick, and Raglan had led the way; now Herstmonceux followed, exhibiting a still greater departure from the massive masonry of old. It was constructed of hard Flemish brick, with windows, door-cases and copings of stone. It is said that in its finished state it contained as many windows as there are days in the year, and fifty-two chimneys, one for each Sunday.

Herstmonceux long enjoyed the reputation of being the largest private house in the kingdom and the finest example of English domestic architecture of the fifteenth century. The shell remains much as Sir Roger built it, with its embattled turrets and magnificent southern gateway; but it would appear as if the mansion itself had received scant attention from most of its owners. The structure gradually fell into decay, the time-worn roofs became unsafe, and in 1777 its owner dismantled the building, and used much of the material in the construction of a new mansion at the northern extremity of the park.

Herstmonceux Church, dedicated to All Saints, crowns a slight eminence a quarter of a mile to the west. Of Early English and Perpendicular architecture, it consists of chancel, nave, and aisles, with a chantry chapel on the north side the newly converted Dacre chapel, and a tower at the north-west angle.

The monuments are of great interest. Adjoining the chantry is the lofty canopied tomb of the second Lord Dacre, d. 1533, and his son, d. 1528, with effigies in armour. On the chancel floor a fine brass bears the effigy of William Fiennes. The ancient square font is said to be that in which Sir Roger Fiennes, the builder of the Castle, was baptized, but a large portion of the basin of an older font was discovered in 1911 in the grounds of Cherry Croft Farm, about $\frac{1}{2}$ mile west.

Herstmonceux village lies some way north of the church and castle, on the main Hailsham-Bexhill road. **Windmill Hill** is a mile east of the village on the way to Bexhill. The huge derelict windmill is said to be the largest post mill in Sussex, or even in England.

Eastbourne

Banks. – Each of the big banks – *Barclays, National Westminster, Lloyds, Midland,* has a branch in Terminus Road and one or more subsidiary branches in and about Eastbourne. *Trustee Savings* in Cornfield Road.

Bathing. – All sea bathing arrangements are under the control of the Corporation. Tents, costumes, towels, caps, shoes, bathing floats and sunbathing bags may be hired. There is an authorized bathing station between the Wish Tower and the Bandstand.

The beach is of shingle, gradually sloping; flat sand as the tide recedes.

The **Devonshire Baths,** Carlisle Road, the property of the Corporation, include up-to-date private baths (hot or cold, sea or fresh water) and swimming baths filled with water direct from the sea at every tide and heated to a temperature of 74°.

Boating is favoured by the slight shelving of the beach. Boats and floats can be hired. Motor-boat trips are made daily in the season out to sea and to local places of interest and speed-boats operate from the pier.

The *Eastbourne Sailing Club* has headquarters at the Redoubt, and some club boats may be hired. Racing on Wednesdays, Saturdays, and Sundays from April to October. There is an annual Regatta. There is also children's and adults boating in Prince's Park.

Bowls. – Municipal bowling-greens in Prince's Park, Motcombe and Helen Gardens, Gildredge Park, Redoubt Pleasure Grounds and Hampden Park. There are open tournaments for men and ladies.

There are also greens at the Eastbourne Club on the Saffrons.

Bridge. – Devonshire Club, Hartington Place (Tel. 31341). Also the Whitehall Bridge Club, Whitehall Hotel, Howard Square (Tel. 30492).

Bus and Coach Services. – The Eastbourne Corporation maintain bus services through the principal thoroughfares.

Southdown Motor Services Ltd. run to and from Brighton, *via* Seaford and Newhaven; to Lewes, Uckfield, Alfriston, Pevensey, Hailsham, Herstmonceux, and Hastings, and connexions to other towns and districts. Long distance coaches operate along the coast to Margate and to the West Country. There are also through coaches to the Midlands and the North.

Cinemas. – *A.B.C.,* Pevensey Road; *Tivoli,* Seaside Road.

Cricket. – The *Eastbourne Cricket Club* plays on the Saffrons, one of the finest grounds in Sussex. It is the centre of the County Cricket Week. The ground adjoins the Town Hall. Cricket is also played in Hampden Park and in Prince's Park.

Croquet. – The *Compton Croquet Club* has courts at the Saffrons, Compton Place Road. Visitors are welcomed.

The annual *South of England Tournament* is held in October, in Devonshire Park.

Dancing. – Popular dances from time to time in the Floral Hall, Winter Gardens. Dances at several of the hotels are open to non-residents.

Early Closing Day. – Wednesday.

Entertainments. – Performances by the Eastbourne Theatre Company throughout the year at the Devonshire Park Theatre. Variety entertainments in the Royal Hippodrome, Seaside Road. The Congress Theatre, Carlisle Road, offers concerts, plays, opera, ballet and all kinds of stage productions. *See also* under Dancing, Music and Cinemas.

Fishing. – The fish chiefly caught in the shallow waters immediately fronting Eastbourne are pollack, bass, conger eel, codling, whiting, and dabs. Bass may be taken off Beachy Head, and bream and pollack off Langney Point. Many useful hints as to bait, grounds, etc., can be gleaned from the fishermen on the beach eastward of the Redoubt. Prawn fishing affords good sport at the foot of Beachy Head.

There are two local sea angling associations: *Eastbourne Angling Association* (headquarters, Royal Parade), and the *Nomads Angling Club* (Secretary, 4, Woodgate Road). Sea Angling Festivals are held.

For freshwater fishing there are several streams in the district, Pevensey Haven and the Cuckmere being the nearest. Both afford good sport. The local club is *The Compleat Angler,* headquarters Pevensey Road.

Golf. – The **Royal Eastbourne Golf Club** founded in 1887. The course provides considerable variety of play, and the surface of the green is, as a rule, excellent. There is a 9-hole course available.

Willingdon Golf Club. This course (18 holes) is situated at the foot of the Downs, 2 miles from Eastbourne. There is a large clubhouse.

The **Eastbourne Downs Golf Club** has an 18-hole course on the Downs above the Old Town. Pits, ponds, and gorse are natural hazards. Several challenge cup competitions are held.

Putting. There are greens near the Redoubt, in Gildredge Park, in Hampden Park, and Helen Gardens. There is a miniature golf course (18 holes) at Prince's Park.

Hotels. – *Alexandra*, Grand Parade; *Burlington*, Grand Parade; *Cavendish*, Grand Parade; *Chatsworth*, Grand Parade; *Clifton*, South Street; *Cumberland*, Grand Parade; *Grand*, King Edward's Parade; *Imperial*, Devonshire Place; *Lansdowne*, King Edward's Parade; *Lawns*, King Edward's Parade; *Mansion*, Grand Parade; *Norfolk*, Grand Parade; *Princes*, Lascelles Terrace; *Queen's*, Marine Parade; *Sandhurst*, Grand Parade; *Sussex*, Cronfield Terrace; *Vernon House*, Crompton Street; *Wish Tower*, King Edward's Parade; and a great many others of all grades.

Libraries. – **Central Public Library.** Grove Road. Branch libraries at Seaside, Hampden Park, Old Town, and Langney Village.

Museums. – Lifeboat Museum, adjoining the Wish Tower. *Open every day, admission free.* The Wish Tower Museum. *Open daily,*

Spring Bank Holiday to October, admission charge.

Music. – Famous Military bands play during the summer at the Band Arena. Orchestral concerts by popular orchestras are given in the Congress Theatre, Carlisle Road, and well-known dance bands are engaged.

Population. – The population of the County Borough is approximately 70,000, the area being 11,356 acres.

Postal. – Upperton Road (nearly opposite the railway station). There are several sub-offices.

Railway Station. – At the head of Terminus and Gildredge Roads. About half a mile from the sea-front by way of Terminus Road. Buses run between the station and all parts of the town.

Tennis. – Public grass courts at Manor Gardens, Hampden Park and Old Town. Hard courts at Manor Gardens, Redoubt, Old Town and Hampden Park. There are facilities for refreshments at Manor Gardens and Hampden Park.

The *Eastbourne Lawn Tennis Club* plays in Devonshire Park where there are numerous courts open to visitors.

The *South of England Lawn Tennis Championships* are held in Devonshire Park in June where also Inter-County, International and Professional matches are played.

Theatres. – *Congress Theatre*, Carlisle Road; *Devonshire Park Theatre*, Compton Street; *Winter Gardens*, Devonshire Park; *Royal Hippodrome*, Seaside Road, *Pier Theatre*. *See* under Entertainments.

Beautifully situated at the eastern foot of the South Downs, close to Beachy Head and within easy reach of some of the loveliest of Sussex scenery, Eastbourne is undoubtedly one of the finest and most healthful holiday resorts on the South Coast.

The county borough, which covers 11,000 acres, is built against the eastern slopes of the South Downs, bounded on the south by the waters of the English Channel and on the east by the lowlands of Pevensey, and is being developed to the north where it borders on some of the best of Sussex scenery. The town, which has grown rapidly during the past hundred years, owes its initial development to the Dukes of Devonshire, and a spirit of enterprise persists behind a general air of comfortable leisure.

There are few resorts that can rival Eastbourne in respect of its **Seafront.** From beyond the fishing quarter on the east to the slopes of Beachy Head on the west it extends for nearly 3 miles, carefully kept throughout, and beautified by shrubs and lawns and flower-beds. Broad-terraced drives and walks border the beach. Between the tiers slopes of neatly-trimmed shrubs or clinging ivy rise to the wide roadway on a level with the town. To the west is the lofty Beachy Head; eastward is the low-lying shore which between eight and nine centuries ago formed the landing-place of William of Normandy and his army. Throughout the whole length of the building line are hotels, luxury flats and boarding houses.

EASTBOURNE

The Pier and Pavilions. The Pier runs out some 1,000 feet into the sea, and is 60 feet in width. At the head are landing-stages often tenanted by hopeful and frequently successful anglers.

On the promenade decks are automatic machines, games saloons and amusement arcades.

Spacious balcony tea-rooms command extensive views of Beachy Head and the Parades. There are licensed buffets and a cafeteria.

That part of the Esplanade which lies immediately east of the Queen's Hotel is called the **Marine Parade,** the first to be built. In one of the older houses Charles Darwin wrote a portion of *The Origin of Species.*

The Marine Parade is continued eastward by –

The **Royal Parade,** originally carried out by the local authority as part of a scheme for reclaiming the foreshore as far as the Redoubt. Just beyond the Redoubt Gardens, is the **Great Redoubt,** a circular fort built in 1806, during the Napoleonic scare, comprising barracks, storehouses, and a magazine, the whole being surrounded by a deep entrenchment. Here is the large *Model Village* with several models of famous buildings, and the *Blue Temple Grotto* and *Aquarium.* Public bowling-greens are nearby as also is the Eastbourne Sailing Clubhouse. Further eastward are putting-greens and tennis courts.

Here, too, is the headquarters of the Eastbourne Angling Association and the **Fish Market.** This portion of the beach is favoured by local fishermen, whose boats, nets, and other gear make a scene of picturesque confusion.

The Lifeboat Station houses the R.N.L.I. lifeboat *Beryl Tollemache.* This boat was built in 1949 and was the first of the Beach type of lifeboat to be built with a cabin. The **Lifeboat Museum** at the Wish Tower was the first of its kind.

The Parade ends at **Princes Park,** which has been attractively laid out as a sports centre and has a large lake where model yacht racing is held at week-ends during the season. There is also a Children's Boating Pool. The Eastbourne United Football Club play at The Oval, and athletic and sports meetings are held from time to time. Near **Langney Fort** (now the property of the Corporation) is the first of the chain of Martello Towers lining Pevensey Bay; it overlooks the **Crumbles,** a curious expanse of pebbly common giving a good view of the Downs.

Westward from the Pier runs –

The Grande Parade, one of the finest of its kind in England, and the most imposing part of the sea-front.

When **Cavendish Place,** running inland from the Pier, was being built, the remains of a Roman bath and pavement were found. Attractive features of the Parade are the gorgeous **Flower Beds,** laid out in carpet patterns, the fine rockery above the bandstand and flower beds by the Wish Tower.

At the seaward end of **Devonshire Place,** one of the finest and widest avenues in the town, is Goscombe John's *Statue of the Seventh Duke of Devonshire,* the principal founder of Eastbourne, erected in 1901.

Eastern Esplanade, Eastbourne

Opposite Devonshire Place is the fine **Band Stand,** with seats for an audience of 3,000; teas can be obtained nearby. A little farther westward **Carlisle Road** runs inland. One of the longest and straightest of the many tree-lined roads of Eastbourne, it forms one of the approaches to the district of Meads, and is also a convenient approach to the Royal Eastbourne Golf Links and the Downs.

Near the lower end of Carlisle Road are the **Devonshire Baths,** and a short distance above them is the main entrance to –

Devonshire Park, Congress Theatre and Winter Garden. This popular and well-known entertainment centre caters for many and varied tastes. Grouped together on an island site are two theatres, concert hall, restaurant, twenty-three grass and four hard tennis courts, a squash rackets pavilion and, in summer, a children's corner. In the **Congress Theatre** first-class orchestral, celebrity, and popular concerts are given and during summer a top-line variety show is staged. Ballet, opera and plays are produced. Well-known dance bands visit from time to time and popular stage and screen stars appear. In the early and late parts of the year many conferences are held. Adjoining the **Congress Theatre** is the **Winter Garden,** scene of many social functions.

In the east corner of the grounds stands the **Theatre** (entrance at corner of Hardwick Road and Compton Street).

The **Park** is some 12 acres in extent, the principal entrance being in Carlisle Road, opposite Wilmington Gardens.

The Park proper comprises the oval and the middle and upper lawns, devoted to lawn tennis. During the season matches and tournaments are held, e.g., Rothman's Open Tournament and an Inter-county week in June. In July, the National Junior

161

Grass Court Championships take place, and in August, the championships of the Registered Coaches of Great Britain. Around the Park is a tree-shaded terrace, forming a delightful promenade. Two squash courts are available to the public. A novel and welcome feature is the well-equipped Children's Corner.

Devonshire Baths comprise two good swimming baths. There are also separate suites of private baths, comprising the usual hot and cold baths. Badminton is played here during winter months.

College Road, skirting the western side of Devonshire Park, is so named from **Eastbourne College,** a public school for day boys and boarders. The handsome Central Tower is a War Memorial.

Returning to the sea-front, we reach the Wish Tower Grounds. Adjoining the Parade is the first permanent **Lifeboat Museum** in the world, opened in 1937 in a boathouse built by public subscription 40 years before in memory of William Terriss, the nautical actor who was stabbed outside the Adelphi Theatre. The exhibits illustrate most vividly the progress made since the first lifeboat was launched at South Shields in 1789, and include parts of the vessels and moving models. *(Admission free, open daily.)*

Beyond the Lifeboat Museum is the **Wish Tower,** a Martello Tower such as may be seen all along this part of the coast and now open as a Museum. The name is derived from "wisc", an Old English word for a marsh, which once existed nearby. From the summit of the mound is an excellent view. Fronting the Wish Tower and overhanging the lower promenade is a modern sun lounge and café.

The Martello Towers

Seventy-four of these towers were built along the South Coast, from Folkestone to Seaford, and a vivid appreciation of the dimensions of the Napoleonic scare is conveyed by the long line of towers skirting Pevensey Bay. The towers were most numerous between Eastbourne and Hastings, the 16 miles being guarded by no fewer than thirty-one towers. The design was suggested by a fort at Cape Mortella, in Corsica, which had offered a prolonged resistance to a British force in 1794. It was thought they would prove a strong defence against the army of Napoleon. The Eastbourne one was used as a heavy gun position between 1939 and 1945 to repel another invasion which never came.

The height of the towers was 32 feet; the circumference at the base was 132 feet. The walls were from $5\frac{1}{4}$ to 6 feet thick. The magazine was placed at the bottom of the tower, over which were two rooms for the garrison of from six to twelve men. When necessary, the garrison could be increased to twenty-four. Most of the fortresses were surrounded by a fosse, about 37 feet wide, across which was a drawbridge. Access to those without a fosse was gained by means of ladders.

The westward slope of the Wish Tower mound has been cut away to screen the café and sunlounge. This sunny, wind-sheltered spot, with its pleasant view of Beachy Head, is one of the most attractive parts of the town.

The Western Lawns are a popular promenade. In the centre is a bronze *Statue of the Eighth Duke of Devonshire* (d. 1908), robed as Chancellor of the University of Cambridge, by *Alfred Drury, A.R.A.*

Continuing in the direction of Beachy Head, we find that for a considerable distance the Parade comprises four thoroughfares on as many levels, as they were constructed on the cliff face. The slopes between are clothed with shrubs and ivy, and in spring and summer are gay with daffodils and wallflowers. Rustic shelters have been erected at suitable places, and the lowest promenade has its westward termination in a picturesque horse-shoe-shaped dell known as –

Holywell

Here a former chalk quarry at the foot of the cliffs has been cunningly transformed into a sheltered retreat with pleasant lawns and shelters, rockeries and pergolas, screened from nearly every wind that blows and trapping nearly every available sunbeam.

On the lower lawn is a Tea Pavilion. Between the lawn and the beach runs a terrace of well-designed Chalets. A tablet on one records its occupation by King George V and Queen Mary.

Nearly opposite Holywell is a large bed of quicksand known as the **Falling Sands.** It is said that the hull of a ship, wrecked in 1872, lies beneath.

Just beyond is the beginning of the **Duke's Drive** and of the plainly marked footpath which leads upwards to Beachy Head.

By any of the roads running inland from this end of the seafront we may ramble through –

Meads

Meads Road, partly bordered by elms, leads back towards central East-bourne, passing Compton Place, the Saffrons Grounds and the Town Hall. **Compton Park,** now a Ladies College of English for Foreign Students, was a former home of the Duke of Devonshire. The grounds adjoin the links of the Royal Eastbourne Golf Club, along the western side of which is a fine semi-circular country road called **Paradise Drive,** taking its name from the wooded glen through which it passes.

On the opposite side of Meads Road from Compton Place is **St. Peter's Church,** a building with remarkable rows of lancet windows. A short distance southward in Carlisle Road is **All Saint's Church,** and **St. John's Church** in St. John's Road.

The **Saffrons** is the scene of cricket, football, and hockey matches, and is the centre of the Cricket Week held annually in July or August. North-ward is **Gildredge Park,** where there are bowling-greens, and northwards again, in Borough Lane, the **Manor Grounds** and the Towner Art Gallery. The grounds, which are charmingly laid out, were purchased by the Corporation in 1923. There are some excellent tennis courts, and a large rock garden.

The **Towner Art Gallery,** *daily, free.* The building was erected by a former Vicar of Eastbourne and later became the Manor House of the Gilbert family. It dates from about 1775 and was bought in 1923 with money left by Alderman Towner, for the purpose of acquiring an Art Gallery, together with twenty pictures from his private collection. The main part of the permanent collection consists of paintings by British artists of the nineteenth and twentieth centuries. There is an important collection of contemporary original prints, over 400 water colours, Georgian caricatures and original book illustrations. A series of temporary exhibitions of Fine Art, Industrial Art, and Crafts, as well as the work of local societies, is held each year.

Northward by Borough Lane, Gildredge Park is connected with the heart of the **Old Town** (*see* below). Southward, Meads Road, running eastward from the southern end of Compton Place Road, leads to the **Town Hall,** with its 130 feet high domed clock tower.

At the corner of Grange Road, opposite the Town Hall, is the **Roman Catholic Church of Our Lady of Ransom.**

South Street, connecting the Town Hall with the important junction of thoroughfares at the War Memorial, contains –

St. Saviour's Church, one of the largest of the nineteenth-century churches of Eastbourne. The building was erected in 1867, from designs by G. E. Street. The spire, 176 feet high, is the loftiest in the town. The chief feature of its interior decoration is the series of mosaic panels around the nave and apsidal chancel, illustrating the Parables of Christ. Street designed the font of Mexican Montezuma onyx, and also its oak cover. After war damage the apse was rebuilt, a magnificent reredos erected and a new organ installed.

Nearby is the bronze angel of the **War Memorial,** and **Holy Trinity Church,** leading to Terminus Road, the principal shopping street, extending from the sea-front back to the station.

THE OLD TOWN

From the Railway Station the easiest way to the Old Town is by bus along Upperton Road, taking the first turning on the left along **The Goffs,** which leads past Gildredge Park to the High Street and the old Church.

At the top of **High Street,** overlooking the churchyard, is the **Lamb Inn,** probably one of the oldest in the county.

The Parish Church is dedicated to St. Mary the Virgin. Dating from the twelfth century, it was erected to replace a Saxon church dedicated to St. Michael, probably a wooden structure. The present building consists of nave, chancel, clerestory, chapels and aisles, and has a low tower, with a fine peal of bells, recast in 1818.

Viewed from the west end, the interior is of great beauty. The chancel inclines slightly to the south. In a similar manner the chancels of two other churches in the district (Pevensey and Eastdean) deviate to the north. Another feature of the chancel is that the floor, instead of being, as usual, above the level of the nave, is a step below. The oak screens in the chancel and chapels date from the fourteenth century, and, though much restored, have been described as "the finest screenwork of the Decorated period in Sussex." That on the north wall of the sanctuary on either side of the Easter Sepulchre, is from the doors of the old rood-screen. Just below, on the left-hand side, is the oldest brass in the church, a small tablet commemorating John Kyng, Rector (d. 1445); near by is a brass to James Graves, Vicar (d. 1647). The reredos, sedilia, and piscina are good specimens of Perpendicular.

In the north chapel are memorials of the Davies Gilbert family, including one to Davies Gilbert, sometime President of the Royal Society (d. 1839). This is known as the Gildredge chapel. Note the Leper peep-holes, and the stonemasons' fish marks. The fine chancel arch and the arches of the chancel arcades are Transitional-Norman.

The pretty **Motcombe Gardens** lie to the north of the Parsonage and are reached in about three minutes by way of Ocklynge Road and to the left along Lawns Avenue. The circular flint building towards the western end of the gardens is the ancient manorial **Dovecote.** The square pond, now the home of a family of swans, is also an interesting relic, being fed by the *Bourne*, which issues from a spring near at hand and flows underground towards the railway station. In the early days of Eastbourne this was the reservoir from which the town was supplied. The lawn on the east side of the gardens has been laid out as a public bowling-green.

The square tower, 102 feet high, of **St. Michael and All Angels Church,** Ocklynge, is a prominent feature in the view northwards from the Parish churchyard and from the neighbouring Downs. It is reached by a few minutes' walk up Ocklynge Hill, and just beyond the church the higher ground falls away to open a fine prospect across the marshes to Pevensey and beyond, the line of Martello Towers being prominent along the shore. In Victoria Drive, beyond the cemetery, is the splendidly proportioned church of **St. Elisabeth,** consecrated in 1938. In the crypt is a large modern mural of Pilgrim's Progress by Hans Feibusch.

Hampden Park is a fine wooded tract of 82 acres to the north of the town, near Willingdon. From the sea-front it is about 2½ miles, the last part of the journey being by way of King's Drive. The Park has bowling-greens, tennis courts, putting green and a cafeteria.

Near the Park is **Martin's Field,** home ground of the Eastbourne Rugby Club.

Beachy Head

Cars must not be driven on to the Downlands. There are several parking places.

There is a good alternative to the usual walking route by the path which runs above Holywell, and the pumping station, and then skirts the *lower* edge of the cliff. After a mile or so, turn inland and up the hill. The last part involves some steeper climbing, but it is generally less crowded and has the advantage of being close to the sea.

Very few people remain long in Eastbourne without making a visit to the Head. On fine mornings especially it is the favourite walk of hundreds, and a popular drive with many more. There are buses along the Front to the foot of the Head and also to the top and on to Birling Gap.

Beachy Head is one of the boldest, most romantic, and highest points of the South Downs, of which it forms the eastern termination. Three miles from Eastbourne, with a gradual ascent, the way lies over short, springy grass, and among bushes of gorse and bramble. The views backward include the whole of Eastbourne and the low-lying coast of Pevensey Bay. The summit is 536 feet above sea-level, and provides one of the most varied and glorious views in the South of England.

Beachy Head, in addition to being the "lion" of Eastbourne, is indeed its greatest friend. Acting, as it does, like a wall between the town and the boisterous gales which ravage this part of the coast, it affords a friendly shelter in nearly all weathers and in nearly all winds. Through its good office, too, Eastbourne is more favoured with foliage than any other place on the south-east coast.

For those who go by road the route is by **The Duke's Drive,** which starts from the west end of King Edward's Parade. This fine drive, with its sweeping curves, crosses the ravine near Meads by a winding embankment, and avoids the steepness of a direct ascent, mounting by easy gradients to the crest of the Downs. The views *en route* include a magnificent expanse of sea and landscape, while the town nestling below looks like a vast and skilfully painted panorama.

The View from Beachy Head. Stand for a minute or two at the top of the Head and note each feature of the picture. Away eastward the farthest point in view is Dungeness. On the edge of the sweeping bay may be seen Hastings, Bexhill, and the ancient, once important town of Pevensey, while to the west on a clear day the Isle of Wight is discernible. Two miles westward of the summit a prominent feature on the lower cliff is the disused lighthouse of Belle Tout. The sea in front is full of shipping, though most vessels keep well out along this dangerous coast. Inshore a small boat occasionally crawls over the water's face like a swimming beetle. With the changing

Beachy Head

tints of green and blue, grey and indigo, lent by the overhead clouds, and the white curls of foam that top each wave, the sea itself is a panorama. Turning from seascape to landscape, there are the swelling Downs, whose hills rise and roll beyond each other, making a dry-land ocean, with cottages and farmhouses in the snug hollows instead of ships, and cattle and sheep, with following shepherd and dog, creeping over the close-cropped, everlasting sward; but, as Dr. Johnson once said of the Downs, with not a tree to hang yourself upon.

Warning. – Foolhardy attempts are made from time to time to climb the face of Beachy Head from the shore, or to descend, even a short way, from above; but so many accidents have occurred that such efforts should be sternly discouraged. The action of the weather, especially frost, has a marked and weakening effect upon these cliffs, and there is a heavy landslip against the Head itself.

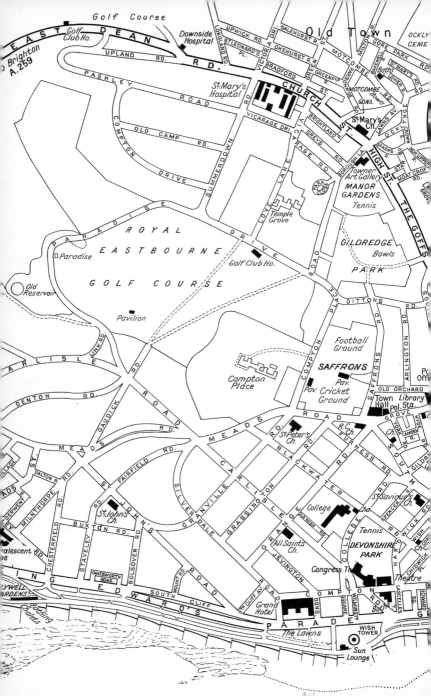

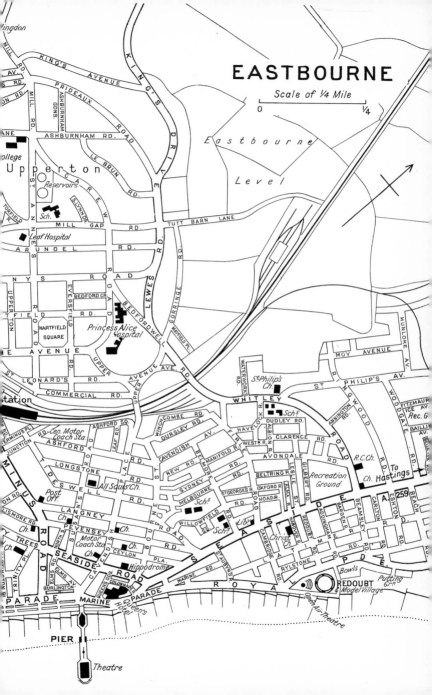

BIRLING GAP–SEVEN SISTERS

"Beachy" is derived from the old French *beau-chef*, "fair head or promontory." In the third year of Henry IV's reign the Commissioners of Sewers were directed to view the banks of Pevensey Marsh lying between Bixle (Bexhill) and Bechief (Beachy Head).

The Lighthouse on the rocks below Beachy Head was completed in 1902. The lighthouse is hyperbolic in form, of the same pattern as the famous Eddystone light, and is composed of great blocks of grey Cornish granite, each of from four to five tons' weight, the foundations being embedded 18 feet in the chalk. The tower is distinguished by a broad red band while the lantern and gallery are also painted red. The diameter at the base is 47 feet, and the lighthouse rises to a height of 142 feet. The structure contains in all 3,660 tons of granite, which was conveyed from the top of the cliff by a rope railway. The burner employed is a Hood petroleum vapour burner. Around this burner is a dioptric lenticular apparatus which gives two powerful white flashes every twenty seconds. A complete revolution is made in one minute. The intensity of the light is 510,000 candles, and is visible 16 miles. The fog explosive gives one report every five minutes.

The majority of visitors, having reached the headland, are content to turn back, but those with time to spare will find that an even more enjoyable walk is to descend by the cliff-path to –

Belle Tout, 2 miles west of Beachy Head. The old lighthouse, erected in 1828, is used as a private residence. The stone is said to have been drawn by ox teams from Maidstone.

Beneath the old lighthouse are two or three caves excavated by Trinity House for the purpose of providing shelter to shipwrecked seamen.

After skirting the old lighthouse the path turns slightly inward (there has been much cliff erosion of late) to –

Birling Gap

A remarkable dip between the lofty cliffs and once favourite with smugglers. There is a car park near the hotel, within a stone's throw of the sea, and a flight of steps gives access to the shingly beach. A submarine telegraph cable crosses the Channel from here to Dieppe, and there is a coastguard station.

A variation of the return to Eastbourne can be made by following the lane inland from the Gap to **Eastdean** on the Seaford-Eastbourne bus route.

The Seven Sisters

Good walkers will certainly be tempted to continue beyond Birling Gap over the brows of the famous Seven Sisters chalk cliffs. There is no more enjoyable walk on the coast than this. Much of the Downland and private agricultural land is protected from development.

The walk continues to the mouth of the *Cuckmere*, which is defended by a bar of sand and shingle. A path runs beside the river and the canalised portion to Exceat Bridge. From **Exceat Bridge** a bus can be taken back to Eastbourne via Friston and Eastdean.

Two miles west of Exceat Bridge lies Seaford.

Walks and Excursions from Eastbourne

Approximate Distances

	MILES		MILES		MILES
Alfriston (road)	10	Litlington (road)	10½	Pevensey	5½
Alfriston (footpath)	7	Litlington (footpath)	7	Seaford (road)	10
Battle (road)	16	Lullington (road)	9½	Seaford (rail)	25
Eastdean	4	Lullington (footpath)	6½	Wannock	4½
Friston	4½	Newhaven (rail)	23	Westdean	8
Hailsham	9½	Newhaven (road)	13	Westham	5
Jevington (road)	5			Willingdon	3
Jevington (footpath)	3¼			Wilmington	8

To Willingdon. In spite of its proximity to Eastbourne, only 3 miles from Devonshire Park and quickly reached by car or bus, Willington still remains a picturesque village. There are some beautiful old houses in Church Street while the nearby paths over the Downs are a delight. Lord Willingdon, the distinguished diplomat and one-time Viceroy of India lived in Ratton, the ancestral home of the Parkers. The house was destroyed by fire and much of the estate built over, but considerable woodlands remain with sheltered hillside walks.

The church is probably of Norman origin but the oldest parts of the existing building – the tower and south porch door – date from the early thirteenth century. Of special interest are the fourteenth-century north aisle, nave and chancel. The sanctuary contains a fifteenth century piscina, an old sedilia and aumbry. The font is late fourteenth century. The window glass is modern.

To Eastdean, Friston and Jevington. Eastdean is a pretty, secluded South Down village, about 3 miles west of Eastbourne on the Seaford road, and rather more than a mile inland from Birling Gap. It is a fine, bracing walk from Eastbourne either over Beachy Head, turning inland by the lane from Birling Gap or by way of the Old Town and Eastdean Road.

Eastdean church is a typical Sussex building consisting of nave, chancel and tower. The latter has walls about 3 feet thick, built about the beginning of the eleventh century, and is probably more than a hundred years older than the rest of the church. The nave roof is of fifteenth-century oak. There is a mid-fourteenth-century stoup near the door, and an aumbry in the south wall close by the beautiful carved oak

Wilmington Long Man

Jacobean pulpit. Above the elaborate panels of the pulpit are the date 1623 and the names of the churchwardens of that time. Near the tower entrance are fragments, pieced together, of a sepulchral cross slab bearing the arms of the ancient family of Bardolf, long lords of the manor of Birling. In a glass case are a lead chalice and paten of *c.* 1225, found buried with a priest by the chancel.

From the west end of the churchyard turn to the right along the lane, keeping the village green on the right. At the top of the green, where the lane turns off sharply, take the footpath leading straight up to Friston Church. This route avoids the steep and narrow main road with its heavy traffic and its awkward bends.

Friston is a tiny village at the top of a hill (373 feet) half a mile west of Eastdean. The village commands magnificent views. The nave of the church was built in 1060 and the chancel some two or three centuries later. There are interesting memorials to the Selwyn family who resided from 1500 to 1704 at *Friston Place*, a picturesque Tudor mansion in the valley half a mile north-west of the church.

The main road continuing westward from Friston leads to Exceat Bridge and Seaford, with glorious views over the Downs to the right. Two miles to the north of Friston is Jevington.

Jevington. This small village stands halfway along the Polegate to Friston road, the only route across this bulk of downland. It is today a pleasing place with its cottages set amid the rolling downland that stretches away on all sides – on the east to 636 feet at Combe Hill and 659 feet at Willingdon Hill. The Saxons, who founded the village, have left masonry in the church tower (but the window arches are of Roman masonry) and the fine tower arch is also Saxon. Of interest in the

172

building are the fourteenth-century font, the Tudor wagon roof and a fragment of sculpture of Saxon period showing Christ thrusting a staff into a serpent's mouth.

Just north of Jevington is *Filching Manor*, an old house with fine timberwork and farther on still is **Wannock,** a hamlet at the foot of the Downs with an old windmill and a beautiful sylvan glen as features of note.

To Litlington and Lullington. Litlington is a pretty little village about 10 miles north-west of Eastbourne, with several popular tea gardens. Good fishing may be had in the Cuckmere River, and another attraction is the small Church, dating from 1150, though the nave is fourteenth century and the chancel roof late fifteenth century. There is also an interesting old dovecote.

Lullington, about a mile north of Litlington, claims to possess the smallest church in England. The internal measurement of the tiny building is 16 feet square, but some ruins near the west end clearly show that the structure is only the chancel of a larger building.

The view from the churchyard is one of the best in Sussex. The parish contains only some half-dozen houses, in addition to *Lullington Church.*

To Wilmington. Wilmington is a village and parish 8 miles north-west of Eastbourne. The place is of great interest to the lover of the picturesque as well as to the antiquary. In 1925 the ninth Duke of Devonshire presented the Priory to the Sussex Archaeological Trust, and the ruins have been most carefully examined and cleared of modern additions, so that now one has a very fair indication of the original beauty of the place. *(Open daily except Friday, 10–6 p.m. and Sundays 2–5 p.m. in summer, charge.)* Wilmington Priory was the property of the Norman abbey of Grestain, but in 1413 Henry V gave it to the Dean and Chapter of Chichester, from which date it appears to have been a manor-house. Note the fourteenth-century vault, excellently preserved and the charming thirteenth-century doorway forming the main entrance to the hall.

Wilmington Church, dedicated to St. Mary and St. Peter adjoins the Priory. It retains much twelfth-century work. On the north wall of the chancel is a small Norman carving. The font is early fourteenth century, and the beautiful pulpit is Jacobean of 1610. In the churchyard there is a gigantic yew said to be 800 years old.

A very remarkable curiosity is the famous **Wilmington Giant,** or Long Man, a figure 80 yards in height, cut in the face of the Downs on **Windover Hill** (600 feet high). The arms are extended upwards, and in each hand is a long staff. This is the largest representation of the human figure in the world. Its origin is unknown.

To Hailsham, Polegate and Michelham Priory. The chief attraction of **Polegate** is its fine red-brick windmill beside the main road. It was built in 1817, and is one of the few tower mills in Sussex still turned by the wind.

Hailsham, 7 miles from Eastbourne, is a busy market town. The cattle market held every Wednesday is well known. The place forms a pleasant objective for a short run from Eastbourne or if preferred, a walk through country lanes via Stone Cross and Down Ash. There are several tea rooms.

The fine Perpendicular **Church of St. Mary** has an embattled and pinnacled chequer-work tower, and dates from the early part of the fifteenth century. The fine East window is modern.

MICHELHAM–ARLINGTON

Hailsham to Michelham Priory and Arlington

From the west end of the old railway bridge enter the Recreation Ground and cross to a stile on the farther side. Cross the succeeding field and go through a gap in the hedge. Bear left towards an over-grown hedge, cross a second stile and cross the sports ground to a third stile. Cross this and turn right along a lane and follow this round until the A22 is reached. Cross over A22 and walk northwards alongside the road for about 200 yards, where there is a signpost indicating footpath to Michelham Priory. Enter the field and follow the right-hand path, crossing stile at end. Cross a small field ahead and continue on across open ground towards a gap in the hedge visible in the distance. Here cross another stile and go through gates to another field and cross this left diagonally passing through gates leading to a farm. Keep to the right-hand path past the farmhouse and continue along this path until it meets a farm track running through the woods. Turn left along this and follow it through (uphill) until an open tract is reached (Milton Hide) leading to the road, on reaching which, turn right to where the road forks.

For Michelham Priory (about three-quarters of a mile distant) take the road to Upper Dicker on the right. Soon after crossing a bridge over the Cuckmere a lane on the right leads in a few yards to the Priory.

Michelham Priory is about 2½ miles west of Hailsham, and 9 miles north of Eastbourne. The Priory is owned by the Sussex Archaeological Society and is open Easter to mid-October, 2–5.30, (June to September, 11–5.30). There are restaurant facilities, and concerts, lectures and exhibitions take place in season.

The buildings consist of an Augustinian priory of canons founded in 1229 by Gilbert de Aquila, Lord of Pevensey; a Tudor wing and other additions of that period; a fine fourteenth-century gate-house in original state, and a large mediaeval barn, all in a beautiful natural setting of lawns, flower borders, trees, and one of the largest moats in England. The house is fully furnished with many rare and interesting exhibits.

Returning to the sign-post on Milton Hide, take the road to Arlington (about 2 miles south-west), passing on the left *Abbot's Wood*. (The wood is Forestry Commission property: there is public access.)

Arlington Church, dedicated to St. Pancras, contains much that is of interest and specimens of almost every style of architecture. Few churches have a history going so far back, for in a case in the chapel will be seen fragments of the burnt clay of a Roman building, which were found under the floor, also pieces of tiles and glass and a thirteenth-century storage urn. The chapel is Norman, and has two round-headed windows. On the north side is a corbel showing fine dog-tooth moulding, and on the wall of the north aisle some notable murals. From the outside can be seen, on the east side of the porch, a Saxon window built with Roman tiles.

Continuing southward down the main road, in a few yards a stile will be found on the right bank, and a path across the fields may be taken. Passing out of the second field, the path bears slightly to the left. On reaching the road at the end of the third field turn to the right for a short distance and immediately after crossing the river leave the road again by another path on the right leading up to a farm. Go through the farmyard and turn to the right for a few yards along a lane. Immediately on passing through a gate, turn to the left along the right-hand side of a hedge, and Berwick Station is quickly reached (about 1½ miles from Arlington).

Seaford

In Saxon times Seaford stood on a ford across the estuary of the *Ouse*, which then flowed parallel with the coast from the site of Newhaven to Seaford. It was a place of importance, and rose to considerable eminence as a "limb" of the Cinque Port of Hastings. During the great storm in 1579, the river burst through its right bank and made for itself a new channel, in which it flowed until the present artificial passage was cut a little farther to the west.

The town is comparatively sheltered from east winds by Seaford Head and the high land on the east. The River *Ouse*, terminating in Newhaven Harbour, on the west, and the River *Cuckmere* on the east, drain the surface water from the surrounding district, and the physical character of the land makes the town an ideal health-resort.

The beach of shingle affords pleasant bathing; there is a good supply of rowing boats; the sea-fishing is excellent, and the freshwater angler can obtain good sport in the neighbourhood. The Seaford golf links –

there are two courses – are known to nearly every golfer of experience; there are bowling-greens and tennis courts, miniature golf courses and a pleasant cricket ground.

The chief charm of Seaford, however, lies in its restful seclusion. The walker has in the Downs unlimited scope for his energy. Coaches and buses bring many places of interest within easy reach.

The Sea-Front, some 2¼ miles in extent, forms the shore of Seaford Bay, which is bounded on the east by Seaford Head and on the west by the picturesque Castle Hill, adjoining the entrance to Newhaven Harbour. The view seawards is delightful by reason of the number of steamers and sailing vessels entering or leaving Newhaven or passing up or down Channel.

From the east end of the promenade a good general view of the town may be obtained. An official-looking building of two floors, standing on a slight hill, is **Seaford College,** now used as a training college for teachers. Farther back are the **Crouch Public Gardens.**

Towards the eastern extremity of the sea-wall is a **Martello Tower,** the last of the series of seventy-four placed at short intervals along the coast from here to Folkestone.

Sheltering behind the sea-wall, the Recreation Ground has tennis courts, a putting-green, miniature golf, cricket and football grounds, children's playground and a municipal café.

The **Parish Church** is dedicated to St. Leonard and was built by the Normans *c*. 1080. It was originally a plain, solid, low-pitched building, adaptable as church or place of refuge and later enlarged. Of special interest are: the two 1120 arches and the two original nave windows just above them: and the varied carvings on the capitals of the Early English pillars.

In South Street, a turning on the left a short distance south of the church, is the little old **Town Hall.** On a level with the road is the small window of the chamber in which law-breakers were confined when Seaford had its own Quarter Sessions.

In Church Street facing South Street is a thirteenth-century **Crypt,** supposed to have been connected with the pre-Reformation Hospital of St. Leonard. It withstood the onslaught of enemy bombs when all the surrounding shops and buildings were demolished.

In the High Street is an interesting relic of old Seaford, known as **The Old House.** This was formerly the residence of the Town Bailiff and is now an antique shop. The Roman Catholic Church of St. Thomas More, Sutton Road, is a beautiful modern building.

Adjoining Seaford on the north is –

East Blatchington

A suburb noted for its church, its trim churchyard, and its picturesque houses. The Church is a flint and stone building mainly in the Norman and Early English styles and with some Decorated work. It has been much restored and the base of the tower made into a baptistery in 1968.

Excursions from Seaford

	MILES		MILES		MILES
Alfriston . .	4½	Eastbourne (road)	10	Newhaven . .	3½
Brighton (road, *via*		Eastbourne (rail).	25	Piddinghoe . .	6
Rottingdean) .	12½	Iford . . .	10½	Rodmell . .	9
Bishopstone (road)	3	Lewes . . .	10½	Southease . .	8
Bishopstone (foot-		Litlington . .	4½	Westdean . .	3½
path) . .	2	Lullington . .	5½	Wilmington . .	7
Denton . . .	4				

To Seaford Head. The Head is the site of a prehistoric Camp, probably constructed about 300 B.C. but mostly destroyed by the action of the sea. The magnificent view is sufficient attraction, however, the hill-top being nearly three hundred feet above sea-level. The camp was probably occupied by a Roman garrison guarding the mouths of the Ouse and Cuckmere, and a Roman cemetery lay on the links a little to the north. Eastward may be seen Beachy Head, and the remains of the Belle Tout Lighthouse on the cliff beyond Birling Gap. Westward are the harbour of Newhaven with the fortifications above; farther away the piers at Brighton; and, on a clear day, Selsey Bill, together, perhaps, with the high grounds of the Isle of Wight and those above Portsmouth.

The walk to the Head can be extended by continuing over the hill and descending to **Cuckmere Haven,** 2 miles from Seaford Church.

In Norman times the Chyngton estate, which consists of 1,026 acres, belonged to the powerful De Aquila family, whose badge – the eagle – figures on the Seaford coat of arms. At **Chyngton** there is a singular indent in the surface of the Downs, terminating in Hope Gap. This indent communicates with the beach and was very useful to smugglers. It is crossed in places by a terraced bank, composed for the most part of flints. Stone steps lead down to the beach.

To Bishopstone. About 2 miles to the west of Seaford, at the head of a valley open to the sea, is the pretty village of Bishopstone. It may be reached by following the Esplanade westward and turning inland through the railway arch from which point the church is clearly seen ahead. (The walk may be shortened by taking the bus as far as the Bishopstone turning.) The most direct way is by footpath leaving Belgrave Road *via* Carlton Road, a little west of the station. From the third field there is a magnificent view of the Castle Cliff and harbour mouth at Newhaven, and straight in front is Bishopstone.

The village is also easily reached by road or footpath from Bishopstone station. It lies about a mile north-west of the station.

Bishopstone owes its name to the fact that it belonged from early days to the bishops of Selsey. In Domesday Book it is counted among the possessions of the Bishop of Chichester. Many years later it came into the possession of the Pelhams, of whom Thomas Pelham Holles, the great political Duke of Newcastle, had a seat here, which was the centre of much hospitality. The mansion was pulled down in 1831; the rookery south of the churchyard was once part of its park.

To the right on entering the village is the former *Manor House*, a charming old building, since converted into maisonettes. On the front is a small stone slab with the Pelham buckle and the date 1688.

The **Church** is remarkable for its ancient architecture, which includes Saxon, Norman, and Early English work. The oldest portion is the Saxon south porch, over which is a decorated Saxon sundial on which is carved a small cross and the name EAD-RIC, in two lines. Note the restored Norman font, the chancel arch, and, on the south wall of the twelfth-century tower, a remarkably well preserved stone slab on which are inscribed in three cabled circles a cross, the *Agnus Dei*, and two doves drinking from a vase; the whole being emblematic of the Trinity. The work is Norman, and was found in 1885.

To Hindover. Hindover, or High-and-Over, 2 miles north-east of Seaford, is a favourite spot for picnics, with free car-parking facilities. It is nearly 300 feet high and commands a beautiful view over the valley of the Cuckmere and over Seaford Bay.

Leave Seaford by Eastbourne Road, and at the top of Exceat Hill turn left and thence along the ridge above the Cuckmere valley. The road route is via Sutton Road and Alfriston Road, where there is a long ascent.

To Westdean. Proceeding in an eastward direction into the Eastbourne Road, in a little over 2 miles we reach **Exceat Bridge.** (If preferred, the first 2 miles of the excursion may be covered by the Eastbourne bus.) Another way, more pleasant than the high road, but not quite so direct, is over the open Down on the cliffs, and bearing round to the left to Exceat Bridge. Continue eastward along the road past *Exceat Farm*, a picturesque and ancient place. Here turn off to the left by the path which starts between the farm and a pair of cottages on the right. After a short climb a steep descent leads to the pretty and sequestered little village of Westdean.

The beautiful little church of All Saints has a Norman nave and a fourteenth century chancel. The tower has a fine Norman arch, the upper part being decorated. There are several interesting memorials. The rectory, like the church, is of flint with stone dressings and dates from the thirteenth century.

To Alfriston. The direct road leaves the town at Sutton Corner, and passing High-and-Over descends and runs almost parallel with the west bank of the Cuckmere. An alternative is via Exceat Bridge, Litlington and Lullington, following the east bank of the river.

Alfriston is a picturesque old-world village just over 4 miles from Seaford on the west bank of the Cuckmere. It is a charming place amid quiet meadows between the river and the Downs. With its narrow streets of colour-washed houses and shops, the village has a great deal of beauty. The church on a riverside knoll, the stump of a market cross and a vast chestnut tree in the village centre, all give Alfriston a distinctive charm and appeal.

The fine old cruciform church, dedicated to St. Andrew, is often called the "Cathedral of the South Downs". It stands in an open space a little east of the main road, with the river behind. The whole building dates from the second part of the fourteenth century, and is one of the finest specimens of flint-work in the kingdom. It has a central tower and a graceful shingled spire, which has a considerable slope to the north-east.

In the top light of the north transept window is a small piece of ancient stained glass representing St. Alphege. The marriage register, which dates from 1504, is probably the oldest in England.

Close to the church is the Old Clergy House, one of the few remaining pre-Reformation clergy houses. It dates from about 1350. The rooms at the western end contain fourteenth-century fire openings; the doorway leading into these rooms is a fine example of the workmanship of those far-off days. The hall has a splendid carved roof. The house is now National Trust property and is open daily.

Another great attraction of the village is the **Star Inn**, which dates from the early fifteenth century. It is adorned both inside and out with curious old contemporary wood carvings. At the corner is a large red wooden lion supposed to have been the figurehead of a vessel wrecked on the neighbouring coast in the seventeenth century. The carving just above this, of a bear and another beast with a staff between them, is thought to represent the supporters of the Dudley arms – a bear and ragged staff.

Another interesting relic of by-gone days is the **Market Cross House**, an old inn taking its sign from the Market Cross opposite. It contains several hiding-places, and is said to have been a noted rendezvous of smugglers. The Market Cross was probably first erected in 1405, though the original top had disappeared by 1787. In 1955 a lorry collided with it, and the present cross was built of old stones similar to those formerly used. This cross and that at Chichester are the only two now remaining in Sussex. The *George Inn*, opposite the Star Inn, is late-fifteenth century and has a splendid stone fireplace.

When visiting Alfriston it is usual also to have a peep at the diminutive church at **Lullington** (see p. 173), one of the smallest in England. The distance is slight. Take the footpath skirting the north side of the churchyard, cross the river by the footbridge, and on reaching the road cross to a footpath opposite leading to the church (which is almost hidden by trees) in about a quarter of a mile.

To Firle Beacon and Glynde. The Beacon lies 5 miles south of Seaford and is a favourite objective for a tramp on the Downs via the Bletchington road and the golf links. The summit of Firle Beacon is 718 feet above sea-level and is the highest point of this length of the Downs. At the top is a small cairn. When the wind is not too high the spot is delightful for a picnic and there are wonderful views.

The return to Seaford can be varied and one interesting way is via **Glynde** which lies just below the Beacon and is reached by a path which descends by a plantation a little west of the summit. At the foot turn along the road to the left, skirting Firle Park and passing through the village of **West Firle**. Here is **Firle Place,** the seat of Lord Gage and home of the family since the fifteenth century. The Tudor mansion has a long panelled gallery and contains an outstanding collection of paintings, porcelain and furniture. *(Open Easter, then June to September, Wednesdays, Thursdays, Sundays and Bank Holiday afternoons, charge.)*

Close to Glynde village is **Mount Caburn** (490 feet) the site of a hill-city occupied by Celtic people in the Early Iron Age.

Glynde Place *(open Easter, then May–September, Thursdays, Saturdays, Sundays and Bank Holidays, charge)* is a fine example of early Elizabethan architecture with collections of bronzes, needlework and pottery. There is a small aviary.

Newhaven

The river Ouse reaches the sea at one of the finest stretches of unspoiled coastline in the county and here is the busy port of Newhaven. Formerly known as Meeching, the town owes its present name to the change in the course of the river Ouse caused by a great storm in 1579; the river having previously entered the sea a little way to the east of Seaford.

The **harbour** entrance is dominated by a high chalk cliff and the harbour is protected by a breakwater on the western side. This breakwater, extending 2,400 feet out to sea, gives shelter from the south-westerly gales and affords an easy access to the harbour. The breakwater, together with the lighthouse at the end, is an interesting feature. From the end of the breakwater visitors get an excellent view of the harbour, the coastline and the surrounding downland country. The lighthouse is 46 feet high and has a double occulting light having a visibility of 12 miles. On the eastern side of the harbour is the East Pier which extends seawards 1,400 feet and at the end has a lighthouse which shows a fixed light.

It is from this fine harbour that the Newhaven-Dieppe Cross Channel Service operates daily and approximately 100,000 cars and half a million passengers are carried annually on the modern drive on/off carriers. The crossing to Dieppe takes about 3¾ hours and is 64 nautical or 72 land miles. The shortest and most direct route from London to Paris is *via* Newhaven and Dieppe. The total distance is 256 as compared with 288 miles *via* Dover and Calais. In addition to accompanied cars and passengers, the car ferries convey commercial vehicles with perishable and general traffic, also many new cars in both directions. The Port has a flourishing import trade of perishable traffic brought in large ships from the U.S.A., Portugal and Mediterranean area. The coastwise trade is concerned chiefly with sand ballast. For anglers there is good fishing from the breakwater and the East Pier; boats are available for hire for those who prefer deep-sea angling.

During the summer months the harbour is popular with yachtsmen and many different types of craft can be seen.

The Newhaven Lifeboat Station was established in 1803 and is one of the oldest in the country. Visitors to the boathouse are always welcome, and are gladly shown over the lifeboat.

The Parish **Church of St. Michael** is on Church Hill, which leads to Meeching Down from which there is a magnificent view up the Ouse Valley towards Lewes. The church was built on high ground overlooking the harbour by the Normans. It first dates from about the year 1120. The church register dates from 1553. A feature which is unique is that the chancel is formed in the lower stage of the tower. This feature is very rare in England but, being of Norman origin, it is probably a copy of an ancient church which still exists at Yainville, on the bank of the Seine in Normandy. The interior of the chancel and apse are well worth seeing.

Near the lychgate, a tall obelisk in the churchyard is in memory of the crew of 106 of the war sloop H.M.S. *Brazen*, who with one exception were drowned when their ship was wrecked close to the cliffs of Newhaven in 1800.

At the west end of the churchyard is a quaint epitaph on the gravestone of Thomas Tipper, the original brewer of "Tipper ale," a popular beverage of George IV at Brighton. Brackish water was used in its manufacture. Near the bus terminus is the Bridge Hotel, built in 1623 and visited by Louis Phillipe in 1848.

Newhaven to Lewes

The route lies along the west side of the Ouse via Piddinghoe. **Piddinghoe** is less secluded than other villages of the Ouse, but it is still as picturesque as its name.

Its church stands on a miniature cliff above the river and the windvane made famous by Kipling may be seen sparkling among the trees from Bishopstone almost to Lewes. The tower is one of the three Sussex round towers and is of Norman date. The arcade is also Norman, and the chancel, with its beautiful arch, is thirteenth century.

Two miles beyond Piddinghoe the road runs above **Southease,** with a little twelfth-century church, also famous for its round tower

The tower possibly served as a beacon to the ships which, before the Ouse valley was reclaimed, passed by on their way to Lewes, the quaint shingled spire being added later. Items of interest are the Norman font, mural paintings and a window believed to date from 1100. An old round chalice with a beaten silver cover is one of three remaining in the country. The original date is unknown, but it was remodelled in 1568.

North of Southease the Lewes road comes to **Rodmell.** The name of this village is derived from its Saxon name of Ramelle, which became changed to Rademald, Rademele, and eventually Rodmell.

Some of the first mulberry trees in England were planted here in the reign of James I, and for a time the village was famous for its silk industry. There are some picturesque old thatched cottages at the northern end, and recently many buildings have been delightfully restored and several flint barns converted into houses.

The ancient **Church** is one of the most beautiful in Sussex, and has many rare features, notably the elaborately-carved rebuilt Norman chancel arch, with the three little windows above. The single pillar between the nave and south aisle has an unusual arrangement of four pendent corbels supporting the square capital. A fragment of ancient glass is in the window next to the pulpit; and a portion of the fourteenth-century rood-screen and a palimpsest brass (dating from 1433) in the south chancel chapel.

Between Rodmell and Lewes are the pretty villages of **Iford** and **Kingston,** nestling among trees just off the main road. Iford consists of a collection of farms clustered around a Norman church. Kingston, half a mile distant, has a fourteenth-century church (much restored). There are fine views from the top of its nearby hill.

Lewes

Access. – Buses connect Brighton and Lewes; Brighton, Newhaven and Seaford and Lewes, Newhaven and Seaford. The railway runs via Lewes, where it is sometimes necessary to change trains for Newhaven and Seaford.

Car Parking. – Southover Road, Mountfield Road, Albion Street, Rotten Row.

Cattle Market. – Monday.

Distances. – Brighton, 8 miles; Newhaven, 7; London, 51.

Early Closing. – Wednesday.

Hotels. – *White Hart*, High Street; *Downside*, *Tatler*, High Street.

Population. – 14,160.

Lewes, the county town of Sussex, is an ancient town picturesquely situated on a hill on the banks of the river *Ouse*, 8 miles as the crow flies north-east of Brighton.

From the earliest times it has been a place of importance, for in bygone ages the mouth of the Ouse was a wide estuary, narrowing as it approached Lewes, where all travellers from east to west, or *vice versa*, had to cross.

In Saxon times there were two mints and a fortress here. Remains still exist of a Norman castle of the motte and bailey type.

The **Battle of Lewes,** in which Henry III was defeated by the confederated barons led by Simon de Montfort, is one of the most famous in English history and had results as important and far-reaching as those of any battle fought on English soil. The scene of the encounter was the ridge of hills to the north-west of the town, one of which is known as Mount Harry.

The street plan of Lewes may be likened to a three-pronged fork, of which the handle and the centre prong is the Eastbourne-Brighton road, running east and west. Rising from the river, passing under the railway and climbing the hill, it passes through Lewes as its High Street and continues to Brighton. The right-hand branch at the foot of the hill becomes the London Road; the left-hand branch passes the station and then bears right to Southover High Street and the road to Newhaven and Seaford.

Reached by a short turning from the High Street is –

The Castle

Open weekdays, 10 a.m. to 6 p.m. and Sundays (Easter to Michaelmas) 2–5.30. Admission charge (apply at Barbican House, opposite).

The Museum in Barbican House is open weekdays only, 10 a.m.–6 p.m. Admission charge.

Lewes came into the hands of Earl de Warenne after the Norman Conquest. Recognizing the strategical importance of the place, this powerful noble at once set to work to repair the fortifications, and erected what must have been in its time one of the finest and strongest castles in the kingdom. It had two keeps, an eastern and a western, a feature which no other castle in the country is known to have possessed. In 1922 the Castle was acquired by the Sussex Archaeological Society to be held in trust for the nation.

The **Barbican** is the latest part of the structure and was built early in the fourteenth century. Passing through this solid erection the public roadway then goes through the original Norman entrance, of which only the front wall remains.

The public entrance to the grounds, however, is by the iron gate on the left, opposite Barbican House. The south keep dominates Lewes, and from the top of the tower magnificent views are to be had, extending as far as the Reigate hills.

Barbican House at the corner of High Street and Castlegate is the headquarters of the Sussex Archaeological Society. The **Museum** contains a good collection of querns, flint implements, Roman remains, and Saxon grave goods.

Those with interest in archaeology should follow the lane passing under the Barbican and descend to the right. At first opportunity turn to left; then left again, and then on the right will soon be seen the unprepossessing **Church of St. John-sub-Castro,** built in 1839 on the site of the original Saxon Church. The chief items of interest are the celebrated Magnus memorial and the Saxon doorway of the south porch of the original building, which is inserted in the eastern wall of the north aisle. The date (1635) on a stone above it has reference to a restoration of the church. The **Magnus Memorial,** an archaeological puzzle which has been the subject of much controversy, will be seen on the outside of the south wall of the chancel.

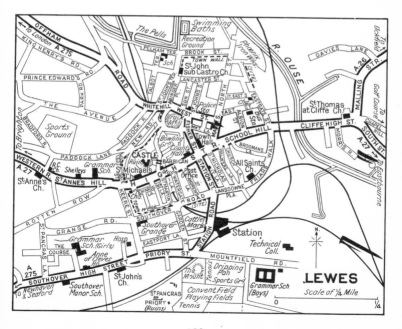

183

Passing down High Street from Barbican House, on the right notice the picturesque sixteenth-century **Church House of St. Michael and St. Andrew.** On the left a little lower down is the **Town Hall.**

From the steep School Hill, a prominent object on the Downs is the **Obelisk** erected in 1901 in memory of the Lewes Martyrs, who were burnt at the stake, 1555–1557.

Crossing the hump-backed bridge over the river, we are now in the **Cliffe High Street,** the Cliffe being the name given to this part of the town. Just at the end of the street is the fifteenth-century **Church of St. Thomas à Becket-at-Cliffe,** parts of which date back to the early twelfth century.

Return under the railway and turn to the left along **Friar's Walk,** passing **All Saints' Church,** a most extraordinary building. The tower is that of the church of St. Peter-the-Lesser, which formerly stood on this site.

A hundred yards beyond the railway station bear to the right, down Priory Street. This reaches Southover High Street almost opposite **Southover Church** (dedicated to St. John the Baptist), where now lie the remains – transferred from the neighbouring Priory – of the Conqueror's daughter and her warrior husband. The church contains some interesting Norman work in the short massive columns and arches between the nave and south aisle. Extensive alterations and renovations were made in 1846 and the **Gundrada Chapel** *(fee)* at the south-east corner was erected in the Norman style, to receive the remains of the famous Earl and his wife, who are depicted in the stained-glass windows.

The **Priory of St. Pancras.** To the south-east of St. John's Church lay the great Priory founded by Earl de Warenne and his wife for twelve Cluniac monks, on the site of a small Saxon church dedicated to St. Pancras. Until its destruction under Henry VIII the Priory covered 30 acres, but now the only remains above ground are those south of the railway line. Parties may visit the ruins accompanied by a guide if appointments are made through the Borough Treasurer, Lewes 6151.

A little farther westward along Southover High Street, an ancient building will be noticed on the right. In olden times it was the Manor-House. Tradition says that this was –

The **House of Anne of Cleves** *(open weekdays, fee)* after her divorce from Henry VIII but although the manor of Southover was granted to her in 1541, there is no proof that she actually lived here. On view in the ten rooms is a large display of old English furniture, tapestries and bygones including the Every Collection of Ironwork.

Returning past the Church, we turn to the left at the *King's Head Inn*, passing on the right (at the foot of the hill) **Southover Grange,** one of the finest old stone-built houses in Lewes. Here Southover High Street ends and we continue up Keere Street, a steep and narrow thoroughfare in the upper half of which it will be noticed that the gutter, as in olden days, is in the middle of the road. At the top of the hill we are back in **High Street,** the main street of Lewes.

A short distance westward is the **Old Grammar School,** founded by

Dame Agnes Morley in 1512, and rebuilt in 1851. Shelley's Hotel, next to the school, bears on its porch the date 1577, and was formerly, as Shelley House, the seat of one branch of the Shelleys, an eminent Sussex family.

At the top of the hill on the left is –

St. Anne's Church, the most interesting church in the town, for although Lewes has many ancient churches, all except this have been much altered.

Formerly known as the church of St. Mary Westout (as it was outside the West Gate of the town), its dedication was changed in the sixteenth century to that of St. Anne. The building, in the Transitional-Norman style, dates from the end of the twelfth century. One of the first things noticed on entering is the barrel-shaped Norman font, with basket-work carving. Another interesting feature is to be seen in the arcade dividing the south aisle from the nave, the capitals of each pillar having four pendent corbels. This is quite a local peculiarity of style, the churches of Rodmell, Telscombe and Beddingham containing similar work. Notice also the round chancel arch, the altar-tomb on the north side of the chancel, and the Jacobean carved oak pulpit, much restored.

Unless the walk is to include Mount Harry, at the end of the street, we now return towards the centre of the town. The fifteenth-century **Bull House** at the corner of **Bull Lane,** just past Keere Street, was once the Bull Inn. It now bears a tablet recording that –

"Thomas Paine B. 1737, D. 1809, Author of *Common Sense, Rights of Man* and *The Age of Reason*, a founder of American Independence with pen and sword, lived in this house as Exciseman and Tobacconist, 1768–1774."

The next building to claim attention is –

St. Michael's Church with its circular tower and tapering shingled spire. On the north wall to the left of the organ, is a monument with kneeling effigies of *Sir Nicholas Pelham* (d. 1559) and his wife Dame Anne, below which are small figures representing their six sons and four daughters, and a punning poetical epitaph. At the west end of the north wall are two stones, inlaid with ancient brasses (1457), removed from the nave at the restoration in 1878.

Brighton and Hove

Angling. – Good sea fishing for sea bream, pollack, whiting, conger, codling and tope.

Bathing. – Good bathing from pebble beach with sand at low tide.

Baths. – Freshwater swimming baths at North Road. Seawater baths (King Alfred Baths), Hove. Open-air pools at Black Rock, Rottingdean and Saltdean Lido.

Boating. – Boating of all kinds is available. The *Brighton Cruising Club* and the *Brighton Sailing Club* encourage yacht racing and hold races at week-ends between the piers. The *Sussex Motor Yacht Club* is well known and the *Model Yacht Club* has members of all ages who throng the Hove Lagoon for races each Sunday. A very popular *Regatta* is organized annually and there is a host of sporting and motoring events and other attractions throughout the season.

Bowls. – Excellent public greens in Preston Park, Vicarage Lawn, Queen's Park, Hollingbury Park, Dyke Road Park, Mackie Gardens, Moulsecomb Sports Ground, on the Western Lawns, Hove, in Hove Park, Knoll Recreation Ground and in St. Ann's Well Gardens.

    Indoor bowls is played during winter at the King Alfred, Hove. 10 *Pin Bowls* at the King Alfred and Top Rank Hove Bowl, Denmark Villas.

Bus and Coach Services. – The district is well served by the Brighton and Hove transport system and by the Southdown Bus Company. Bus service runs at frequent intervals between various parts of Brighton, one terminus for the town service being at Old Steine. The usual starting place for many of the long-distance buses is at Pool Valley, behind the Cinema, Old Steine, from where journeys may be made to Portsmouth, Hastings, or to the country towns and villages of mid-Sussex. In addition there are motor-coach excursions to the many beautiful and historic places in Sussex and beyond, and to the various racecourses and sports meetings.

Camping. – A Municipal Camping Ground is available from March to October close to the sea and shops in the Sheepcote Valley, Black Rock.

Casino. – At the Hotel Metropole.

Cinemas. – *Academy*, West Street; *Astoria*, Gloucester Place; *Classic*, Western Road; *Continental*, Sudeley Place; *Duke of York's*, Preston Circus; *Vogue*, Lewes Road; *Regent*, Queens Road; *A.B.C.*, East Street; *Odeon*, West Street, Hove; *A.B.C.*, Portland Road; *Embassy*, Western Road; *Brighton Film Theatre*, North Street.

Cricket. – The main interest centres in the County Cricket Ground at Hove, where the *Sussex County Cricket Club* play. The *Brighton and Hove Cricket Club* have their headquarters at the Sports Arena, Tongdean Lane.

Croquet. – The local headquarters of the game is the *Sussex County Croquet and Lawn Tennis Club* at Victoria Road, Southwick. There are nine excellent croquet lawns where the National Championships are held, and a public lawn at the Western Lawns, Hove.

Distances by Road. – Arundel, 21; Bognor Regis, 28; Chichester, 31; Devil's Dyke, 5½; Eastbourne, 22; London, 53; Lewes, 8¼; Newhaven, 9; Ovingdean, 3; Peacehaven, 7; Steyning, 12; Worthing, 11.

Early Closing. – Wednesday, Thursday or Saturday.

Golf. – Six excellent courses within 3 miles of Brighton. They are the *Dyke Golf Club* (18 holes); *Brighton and Hove* (18 holes) at Hangleton; *East Brighton*, Black Rock; *Brighton Municipal* (18 holes) at Hollingbury Park; *West Hove* (18 holes) near Portslade station; and *Waterhall* (18 holes), Dyke Road.

Hotels. – *Bidford*, Kings Road; *Brighton Touring*, Preston Road; *Clarges*, Marine Parade; *Cook's*, Old Steine; *Courtlands*, The Drive, Hove; *Crest*, Marine Parade; *Curzon*, Cavendish Place; *Dudley*, Lansdowne Place; *Grand*, Kings Road; *Imperial Centre*, First Avenue, Hove; *Langfords*, Third Avenue, Hove; *Lawns*, First Avenue, Hove; *Metropole*, Kings Road; *Nevill House*, Marine Parade; *Norfolk Continental*, Kings Road; *Old Ship*, Kings Road; *Queens*, Kings Road; *Royal Albion*, Old Steine; *Royal Crescent*, Marine Parade; *Snekville*, Kingsway House; *St. Catherine's Lodge*, Kingsway, Hove; *Seven*, Fourth Avenue, Hove; and many others of all grades.

Ice Skating takes place at the Top Rank Centre.

Population. – Brighton, approx. 164,680; Hove, 72,140.

Postal. – Head Office in Ship Street. Hove Post Office is at 107 Church Road.

Races. – The "Sussex Fortnight", the busiest period of the Brighton season, is comprised of the closing week of July and the opening week of August, when horse-racing is held at Goodwood and Brighton. The Brighton race-week follows the Goodwood week. There are six other meetings during the year and also at Plumpton and Fontwell.

The Downs around Brighton have a great reputation among horse trainers; there are training stables at Findon, Lewes, etc.

Greyhound Racing takes place at the Stadium at Nevill Road, Hove.

International Motor Speed Trials are held annually in September on the Madeira Drive.

Tennis. – There are at least 100 public courts, most of them maintained by the Corporations and situated on the Western Lawns at Hove and in the parks.

Theatres. – *Theatre Royal*, New Road; *Palace Pier* (summer); Concerts at the *Dome*, *Western Bandstand*, *Western Lawns*, Music festival in March. Brighton Festival in May.

The borough covers a vast area. With Hove, it has a population of over 236,800 and also attracts many thousands of holiday visitors by its high sunshine records, and invigorating air. The beauty of the surrounding downs and the splendour of the Regency architecture, classical terraces and fine squares and streets combine to make the twin towns one of the most splendid resorts in Europe.

The Sea Front

The Sea Front extends eastward from Hove five miles to Black Rock, and the Undercliff Walk carries on for nearly four miles farther to Saltdean.

The **Brighton Beach** is interesting at all seasons. But it is in July and August that it is in its most characteristic mood, when from end to end it is crowded with happy folk paddling, bathing, boating, or just finding a vicarious satisfaction in the activities of others. There are rowing-boats, canoes and speed-boats; and at the back of the beach, the arches below the promenade house a highly miscellaneous collection of clubs and shops.

The central part of this promenade is known as **King's Road,** in honour of King George IV. The scene at any season of the year is full of interest, especially at the point where West Street runs down from the Railway Station – one of the busiest corners in Brighton. Westward are promenade shelters, putting greens and a children's paddling pool.

The **West Pier,** built in 1866, is 1,150 feet long. At the head is a Games Pavilion, bars and cafés, a games arcade and a "Kiddies Corner". There is a concert hall and speedboat trips are available.

Just west of the Pier, a stretch of the foreshore has been very attractively laid out with a Boating Lake on which children can navigate a miniature motor-boat. The adjacent lawns are laid out as Putting Greens.

The Hove Esplanade

Westward of the King Edward Memorial statue the sea-front becomes more spacious, with a long stretch of wide lawns between the Esplanade and Kingsway. The broad, well-planned avenues and drives of Hove are very admirable and provide a good example of how a seaside town should be laid out and developed.

Mid-way along Kingsway on the seaward side is the famous **"King Alfred",** the indoor sports and social centre of Hove. The building includes two swimming pools; there is a restaurant, Sauna, underground car park, indoor bowls, tenpin bowling centre, cricket, badminton and other sporting facilities.

West Hove

At one time the sea flowed right up to the roadway and at times threatened further invasion; hence the stout sea-wall and the ground on which the lawns were laid out. A similar plan was carried out westward of the baths, but here the reclaimed land has been made into tennis courts, bowling-greens and a large **Lagoon** for boating. Many visitors consider that this is the most attractive part of the twin boroughs. Certainly bathing is popular; and the grounds on the inner side of the Esplanade have the additional advantage of being sunk at a lower level, so that on days when a fresh breeze blows in from the sea one can play tennis or bowls.

The **Palace Pier.** A peculiar interest attaches to the Palace Pier since it is the modern representative of the Old Chain Pier – the first pleasure pier ever built. Brighton Palace Pier, reputed the finest in the world, was opened in 1901. It is a third of a mile in length, and well to the fore in having the latest devices of the entertainment world. The Theatre, which has a large stage and excellent seating accommodation, stages Summer shows. Other amenities include cafés, bars, shops, open-air dancing and the "Palace of Fun".

At the pierhead there is a landing stage from which speedboats operate in summer months.

When the pier is illuminated at night and every turret and pillar is outlined by all forms of lighting, the effect is exceedingly attractive.

Opposite the broad opening to the Old Steine, and at the foot of the Palace Pier, the road divides, the upper portion, or **Marine Parade,** running along the high ground at the edge of the cliff, the lower, or **Madeira Drive,** continuing its course nearly on a level with the beach. In the angle formed by the two roads is –

The **Aquarium** *(daily, fee)*. Opened in 1872, the old Aquarium has had a varied career, but today it contains a world-famous collection of living marine specimens, including seals and sea-lions and in recent years a Dolphinarium.

The very fine sun Terrace provides deck chairs, children's playground, amusement arcade, and restaurants and convenient access from Madeira Drive to Marine Parade.

Volks Electric Railway is a modest little line running along the beach from the Palace Pier to Black Rock ($1\frac{1}{2}$ miles), with an intermediate station at the Children's Playground.

The **Madeira Drive** runs from the Aquarium to King's Cliff, Kemp Town, the sea-wall rising from it to the Marine Parade. An Arcade, about half a mile long, running eastward from a point near the Aquarium, with a terrace walk on the top, affords cover in wet weather. A **Lift** communicates with the Marine Parade above.

At the eastern end of the Madeira Drive is –

Black Rock Bathing Pool, a sea-water pool 165 feet long by 60 feet wide, with a space of 2,000 square yards available for sunbathers. There are aquatic sports and water polo during the season. Around the pool are promenades and terraces, a fully licensed bar and buffet surmounted by a sun-lounge and there are also deck games and a children's pool.

Rottingdean Pool is situated on the sea-front in a sheltered spot below the Rottingdean cliffs. It is a sea-water pool, and measures 100 feet by 35 feet (open from May to September).

The **Undercliff Walk.** This is a further extension of the sea-wall and extends from Black Rock to Saltdean, where is a fine lido with Children's Pool, Reasturant and Car Park.

Public Buildings in Brighton and Hove

Most prominent and distinctive among the public buildings is that Oriental structure, rich in cupolas and minarets, the once laughing-stock of the witty and now the admired of the many, that fantastic edifice which grew up, as we have already noted, at the bidding of the fourth of the Georges, and rejoices in the name of –

The Royal Pavilion

Admission. – Open daily (including Sundays) October to June 10 a.m.–5 p.m., July to September 10 a.m.–8 p.m. *Fee.*

After having been partly dismantled, on the disuse of the building as a royal residence, the Pavilion was in 1850 acquired by the Brighton Commissioners as town property for the sum of £50,000. The Pavilion has, in recent years, been re-furnished and its original interior decorations restored, as it is now open to the public as a past Royal residence. It is also used to some extent for social functions, concerts and lectures, chiefly for civic purposes.

In 1950 a systematic programme of restoration was begun, and the State and Private Apartments are now rapidly assuming the appearance they had in the days of King George IV, after many years of the dinginess and gloom of Victorian and Edwardian overpainting and decoration. The Pavilion now has its own permanent collection of furniture, carpets, silver and other works of art of the late 18th and early 19th century. During July, August and September each year all the apartments are fully arranged with period furniture and works of art, and a great banqueting display of silver, porcelain and glass in the Banqueting Room. This forms the famous "Regency Exhibition" which is one of the principal summer attractions of Brighton every year.

The **Entrance Hall** has a ceiling painted as a sky, and dragons and other Eastern decorations figure on the walls.

The **Corridor** has recently been restored to its original decorative scheme of a Chinese design of bamboos, peonies, palms and pagodas, in blue and pink, in place of the dark Victorian decoration which had existed for many years.

The **Banqueting Room** is one of the two principal State Apartments added by John Nash in 1815. The great domed ceiling is painted to represent a palm tree, and in its cascades a silver dragon holds an immense chandelier like a cascade of diamonds, out of which rise five smaller dragons carrying lotus-shaped lights. The wall paintings on the wall opposite the window are original, the others painted in 1856. All the decorations in this room have recently been restored to

Brighton and the Piers

their original brilliant colour scheme of gold, silver, scarlet, yellow and blue, after being obscured under dark varnish for many years.

The **Saloon,** with the two adjoining Drawing Rooms, formed the principal part of the first Pavilion built by Henry Holland in 1787. The ceiling is painted as a sky and the wall panels are filled with yellow Chinese wall-papers of about 1800.

The **Music Room** is the second of the two new State Apartments added by Nash, and is one of the most magnificent rooms in England. It represents the culmination of the "Chinese taste" in decoration, with its wonderful wall paintings of red and yellow lacquer and gold, its lotus-shaped chandeliers, and domed ceilings of innumerable gilded scallop-shells.

On the first floor are the Private Apartments.

The **North Gallery** contains prints and pictures of the history of the Pavilion and a model of Brighton as it was in 1805. "Mrs. Fitzherbert's Drawing Room" has been furnished in the simple style of about 1780 to 1805, "Princess Charlotte's Bedroom" is decorated in Chinese style as originally, with furniture probably used by the Princess Charlotte, daughter of the Prince Regent, during her stay at the Pavilion at Christmas and the New Year, 1816 and 1817, when her engagement to the Prince Leopold was announced.

On the ground floor are the **King's Private Apartments,** consisting of an Anteroom, Library and Bedroom, overlooking the Western Lawn. These rooms have been completely restored to their original appearance, with wall decorations of dragons, birds and stars in white upon green. The rooms are fully furnished, a number of the articles originally belonging to the Rooms.

The Dome

Brighton's Dome is included in with the Royal Pavilion Estate, and was built as a stable to serve the Royal Pavilion when it was the seaside palace of King George IV.

It was built from designs by William Porden between 1803 and 1805 in the style of the Moghul architecture of India. Round the outer walls of the building were stables for forty-four horses, and on the upper floor were harness and saddle rooms and accommodation for grooms and other servants. In the centre was a drinking fountain for horses. To illuminate the building a great glass dome surmounted the roof and from the top of this dome to the floor was a height of about 65 feet.

In 1850 the Brighton Corporation purchased the Royal Pavilion Estate from Queen Victoria, and the interior of the Dome was rebuilt as a concert hall, the work being finished in 1867.

In 1935 the interior of the Dome was again remodelled to convert it into a great theatre with a fully raked floor and permanent fixed seating. The present seating capacity is 2,096, and during orchestral and choral concerts it is possible for about 250 performers to appear on the stage at one time.

Another very important feature of the Dome is the magnificent theatre organ. Music from this organ is frequently broadcast. Productions featured at the Dome include orchestral and choral concerts, opera, ballet, jazz and variety performances. The Dome is also used as a conference hall and as a ballroom.

Adjoining the Dome is the **Corn Exchange,** formerly the Riding School. This has now been reconstructed and is used for exhibitions and social functions. The **Pavilion Theatre** forms an annexe and is available for concerts and theatrical productions.

Adjoining the Dome in Church Street are –

The Public Library, Museum, and Art Gallery

Open. – *Library*, 10 a.m.–7 p.m. Saturdays 10 a.m.–4 p.m. *Museum and Art Gallery*, 10 a.m.–7 p.m. Saturdays 10 a.m.–5 p.m. Sundays 2 p.m.–6 p.m.

The **Library** comprises reference and lending departments, newspaper and magazine rooms. The Reference Department is available to all readers, and contains 100,000 volumes. There is also a valuable collection of works relating to the history and topography of the town and county.

The **Art Gallery** contains paintings by old masters. There are fine collections of Early English water-colours, modern water-colours, modern paintings, drawings, prints and engravings. Temporary art exhibitions are frequently held, and free concerts of gramophone music take place every Tuesday in the Annexe from 2 to 3 p.m.

The **Museum.** The Sussex Archaeological Collection consists of objects from early Stone Age to Mediaeval times. There are displayed large aerial photographs of the principal pre-historic sites in Sussex and a collection illustrating the past agricultural, social and domestic life of Sussex.

The Willett Collection of Pottery is one of the finest collections of its kind in the country. There are also fine collections of Worcester porcelain, English and European glass, ancient Roman glass, furniture and silver. The Spencer Collection of Musical Instruments possesses an extensive range of exhibits illustrating their development from the early eighteenth century.

There are also large Natural History collections, an aquarium, and special exhibits for children.

The **Booth Museum of British Birds** *(daily, fee)* can easily be reached by the Dyke Road buses, which pass the door. Mr. Booth died in 1890, and by his will gave the Museum and collection to the Corporation of Brighton. Several other collections have been purchased in recent years, and the Museum contains many rarities. In the Museum there are 534 separate cases showing birds in natural surroundings.

At Preston Manor, in Preston Road, is the **Thomas-Stanford Museum,** where eighteenth-century period furniture and silver are exhibited. *Open daily,* 10–1 *and* 2–7 *(5 in winter); Sundays* 2.30–5.

Brighton **Town Hall** between Market and East Streets was originally erected in 1828–30. The visitor who likes exploring in old book and curio shops should take a stroll through the narrow lanes or "Twittens" between the Post Office in Ship Street and the vicinity of the Town Hall.

The **Hove Public Library.** The Library consists of Reference, Lending and Children's Departments; a Music Library and newspaper and magazine room. The reference library has an extensive collection of trades and telephone directories, timetables, holiday guides, transparencies, maps and plans, and a very interesting selection of photographs of Sussex, many of which have been taken from the air. Its special feature is a collection of valuable books. The Library also functions as a Tourist Information Centre.

There is a branch library near the Grenadier Hotel, in West Way, Hove, 4. It is planned on Scandinavian lines and has a stock of 15,000 books.

Art Exhibitions are held at **Hangleton Branch Library** and at **Langfords Art Gallery** in Third Avenue, Hove.

Some Interesting Churches

There are in Brighton something like a hundred and twenty places of worship, of which rather more than a third belong to the Church of England. By far the most interesting historically is –

St. Nicolas Church at the top of Church Street, to the right of Queen's Road coming from the Station.

Before the Reformation the seamen of Brighthelmstone used to celebrate St. Nicolas Day (December 6) with great enthusiasm, St. Nicolas being the patron saint of sailors and children. The church appears to have been partially destroyed and rebuilt on various occasions, as it exhibits several dissimilar styles, although some later fourteenth-century pillars and the original arch of the chancel have survived. The main body is of cut flints and grouting of lime and coarse sand, with stone coigns, and is surmounted by a low embattled tower, containing a peal of ten bells. The church was largely reconstructed in 1853 in memory of the Duke of Wellington, who as a boy was for some time a pupil at the Vicarage. Near the west door is a memorial to the Duke. The Early Norman font has sculptures representing the Lord's Supper; the Baptism of our Lord; a panel of doubtful significance; and a fourth panel depicting "St. Nicolas admonishing pilgrims to throw into the water a vessel of oil received from the Devil."

The churchyard, now an open space, is as interesting as the church itself. It contains the stump and steps of the ancient churchyard cross, mutilated, probably, by sixteenth-century iconoclasts and now restored, and interesting headstones.

Of the modern churches, **St. Paul's** is noteworthy for its paintings by Burne-

Jones and William Morris; **St. Peter's** for its fine peal of bells, and **Holy Trinity** Church for its connection with the famous preacher, the Rev. F. E. Robertson.

All Saints' Church, Hove. The Parish Church of Hove is in The Drive, on the corner of Eaton Road. The nave was built in 1890–1, J. L. Pearson, R.A. being the architect, and the choir and narthex have been added since. The church is in the Early Decorated style, and is generally conceded to be the finest ecclesiastical structure in the two boroughs. Features include a fine stone reredos, good carved woodwork and Willis organ.

St. Andrew's (Old Church), Hove, the former Parish Church of Hove, is in Church Road. It is interesting as one of the few relics of the time when the town of to-day was simply a picturesque and isolated village. For many years the church was almost a ruin, only the nave standing as the remains of what had undoubtedly been a fine building. In 1836 restoration was begun, care being taken to retain some of the ancient features.

Parks and Open Spaces

The central area of Brighton has approximately 30 acres of gardens, squares and enclosures including a large children's playground at the Level. The main floral display, magnificent in its colour, is centred around the Victoria Gardens, the Old Steine Gardens, Royal Pavilion Grounds, and the Sunken Gardens on the sea-front. This is the culminating point of display, extending some four miles to Patcham, consisting of 350,000 bedding plants set in a framework of carefully tended lawns. The Gardens are flood-lit at night by concealed lighting which also illuminates large fountains in colour.

The largest park is –

Stanmer Park, part of a 5,000 acre estate purchased in 1947. This beautiful park lies on the outskirts of Brighton. Some 200 acres with footpaths to the Downs is set aside for public use. Of the remainder, 500 acres are run as commercial woodland, 36 acres as the Parks Department's Nursery and the rest leased as farm land. Sports facilities include football, rugby and cricket. On the north are the grounds and buildings of the University of Sussex.

Largest of the central parks is –

Preston Park, the main portion of which is on the east side of Preston Road (the main thoroughfare to London). Buses bring this green and shady park of 66 acres within a few minutes of the sea-front. Provision for sport includes 8 bowling greens, 20 tennis courts, 5 football pitches, cricket ground surrounded by a cycle track, and pitches for netball, rounders and stoolball.

Ornamental features include a formal rose garden with thousands of roses of all varieties, a large rock garden with waterfall and pool, a scented garden for the blind, borders with formal bedding running parallel with the main London Road.

Preston Manor-House. Preston Park was formerly part of the Manor of Preston, which extends as far as Crawley. The Bishop of Chichester had a large house here in Domesday times. This was superseded by another in 1250. The present house was built on these foundations in 1738. The site became Crown property in the sixteenth century and was then let. Anne of Cleves' coat of arms is on the porch to the south side, but there is no evidence that she lived here. On the walls of the Cleves Room hangs leather which formed part of the dowry of Catherine of Aragon. The ivy-covered dovecote near the Tennis Club is Elizabethan and served to cover the village well.

The House now forms a **Museum** having been bequeathed to the Brighton Corporation by the late Sir J. C. Thomas-Stanford.

A few yards from the house is the old **Preston Church,** a typical Sussex building of flint with a square, tile-capped tower and original doorway and wall paintings of religious events.

BRIGHTON AND HOVE

Brighton Sports Arena is at Tongdean Lane, just off the main London–Brighton road. Several buses, with frequent services stop at Tongdean Lane, one minute's walk from the Arena and bus No. 112 stops outside the Arena.

Brighton Sports Arena covers 14 acres and is the finest sports centre in the South. It is the headquarters of many athletic associations and clubs, and attractive meetings, events, shows and displays are frequently presented. The squash rackets courts are open to the public daily.

Withdean Park, a natural park of 38 acres is situated at the east side of the London Road (A23) almost opposite the Sports Arena.

Queen's Park lies between Queen's Park Road and Freshfield Road. It is best reached from the Marine Parade by way of Rock Gardens and Egremont Place. Within the large park are tennis courts, bowling greens and a small lake.

The Victoria Gardens were formerly known as the North Steine, or North Enclosures. **The Level,** the farthest inland of this series of gardens, is an open space of about ten acres north of St. Peter's Church, girdled by trees.

Hollingbury Park is a tract of downland comprising 180 acres, on the northern outskirts of the borough, adjoining the Ditchling road. Here are the **Municipal Golf Links** and the site of the prehistoric hill-fort called **Hollingbury Camp.**

Other parks totalling several hundred acres in Brighton include Patcham Place, Moulsecomb Wild Park, East Brighton Park and Dyke Road Park. At all are splendid facilities for sports.

Hove Park, a tract of 40 acres on the Old Shoreham Road, at the west end of Hove, is attractively laid out, and provision is made for games.

Facing Hove Park in Nevill Road is the **Brighton and Hove Stadium,** where sporting meetings are held. Opposite the park, in Old Shoreham Road, is the Goldstone Ground, the headquarters of **Brighton and Hove Albion F.C.**

A little to the east of the Park is Hove's oldest **Recreation Ground,** an area of 20 acres acquired in 1887. It has a border of fine trees and football and cricket pitches. Both these open spaces are within easy walking distance of Hove Railway Station and are served by bus.

St. Ann's Well Gardens, Hove, are on the slope of Furze Hill, adjoining Lansdowne Road, near the top of Brunswick Place. The Gardens took their name from a chalybeate spring which did so much to spread the fame of the locality as a health resort. The beautiful grounds of about 13 acres are wooded with chestnut and fir trees and afford a pleasant air of seclusion. There are sheltered seats, a bowling green, tennis courts and a lily pond and a scented garden for the blind.

Palmeira Lawn, Hove. This small, formal garden in the centre of the town has as its main feature a **two-dialled Floral Clock** commemorating the coronation of Queen Elizabeth II. One of the four sides is laid out with the borough of Hove coat of arms, while the remaining sides are used from time to time to celebrate various national and local events.

The Race-course, vested in the Brighton Corporation, is on the highest part of White Hawk Hill, not far from White Hawk Bottom and Down, east of the town. The **Grandstand** probably commands finer views than any similar structure in the country, its height above sea-level being over 400 ft. Buses run frequently from Old Steine and from the station and during race meetings special buses run to and from the course to various points in the town. The Brighton Race Club was established in 1849.

Walks from Brighton and Hove

To Patcham and the Downs. The real Patcham – as distinct from the modern settlement – is only revealed to those who climb the narrow lane striking up to the east of the busy London Road beside the *Black Lion Hotel*. Low-roofed cottages border the ascent and at the top extensive barns and farm buildings including the mediaeval Tithe Barn and Dovecote and the church, recall the Patcham known to John of Patcham who rose from poverty to be Archbishop of Canterbury and the first Sussex author to appear in print.

Much of the **Church** is modern but visitors are always interested in the "Doom" painting on the wall above the Norman arch; 1170 is given as the date of its execution, one of the oldest in the country. Note the blocked-up "Devil's Doorway" in the North wall. Near the door is the tombstone of Daniel Scales, the notorious smuggler, shot on the Downs nearby.

Leaving Patcham Church and continuing uphill, go straight ahead at the cross-roads, and take the road leading out on to the Downs. When the brow of the rise is reached there will be seen ahead, about a mile from Patcham, the solitary but beautiful memorial known as –

The Chattri. It was erected by the India Office and the Brighton Corporation in memory of the Indian soldiers who gave their lives during the 1914–18 War. Its impressiveness is heightened by the fact that the monument stands on the site of the burning ghat on which were cremated the bodies of Hindu and Sikh soldiers who died at Brighton. The Chattri (the traditional form of memorial to the dead in India) is borne on a broad platform approached by steps, at the head of which are granite slabs indicating the exact site of the crematory slabs. Beyond rises a white Sicilian marble dome, supported on eight pillars, the whole memorial being of true Indian design.

Those who desire a longer walk than the return from Patcham should continue along the track above the Chattri as far as the hollow holding the picturesque collection of farmsteads comprising **Upper Standean.** A good tramp of two miles north-eastward would land one on **Ditchling Beacon** whence a very fine walk along the grassy track to the right leads one to **Lewes,** with fine views to left and right as the track follows the ridge. Lewes comes in sight as we near the race-course.

An alternative is to turn down to the right at Standean, through farmyards, to the floor of the valley and follow the rough road as far as a lane turning sharply back on the left. Follow this up past more barns and so eventually to the Ditchling road. Here turn right as far as the twin cottages guarding the upper gates of **Stanmer Park,** the wall of which borders the road on the left (fine views on right). A few yards along the road in Stanmer Park open up a splendid picture of sheltered woods and bare downland. Immediately in front Stanmer and its trees shimmer in the sun; beyond roll the Downs, terminating in the sharp escarpment of Firle Beacon (to the right), Mount Caburn, equally precipitous, holding the Glynde gap on the left. This is one of the finest "surprise" views in the neighbourhood.

The drive leads down to **Stanmer** village, beautifully situated.

The light and handsome interior of the **Church** is in marked contrast to the plain exterior and contains notable monuments. In the Churchyard is a sixteenth-century Donkey Wheel once drawing the communal water supply for the village. Confronting the church is **Stanmer House** at the side of which is an eighteenth-century "horse gin". The house is now part of the University of Sussex.

To The Devil's Dyke (5½ miles). Buses run from the Pool Valley, and there is a licensed hotel on the crest of the Dyke. The gradual ascent makes the journey very interesting. Magnificent views are to be had all the way – first of the sea and of Hove, then of Kingston, Shoreham and the mouth of the Adur, and finally, of the great expanse of the Downs.

Hangleton Church, on the hillside, has many features of interest; an early thirteenth-century tower, Norman windows, mediaeval wall paintings. The nave is probably late eleventh century and the chancel was erected about 1300. There are early windows, a stoup and a fourteenth-century piscina. An unusual feature is the sloping floor of the nave which follows the natural fall of the ground.

Some distance up are the links and club-house of the *Brighton and Hove Golf Club.* Beyond are the *Waterhall* links and the breezy links of the *Dyke Golf Club.*

The feature which originally called forth the diabolic name is a large earthen rampart raised in early times to isolate from the main line of Downs the tongue of land on which the present modern appurtenances now stand. But the name to-day is usually applied to the great V-shaped cleft in the downs seen on the right as one approaches.

In 1928 the Dyke and surrounding Downland were bought for the public, and the stone seat commemorates that event. Beside it is a useful indication of the chief points of the view.

Before exploring the declivity of the Dyke proper, it is well to pass out on to the projecting tongue of Down and gaze at the majestic panorama here unfolded. The prospect is, beyond question, one of the finest in the South of England.

The View. – Westward the northern escarpment of the Downs is traced past tree-crowned Chanctonbury (783 ft.) to Duncton (837 ft.) and the hills above Bignor. Slightly to the north (right) of these are the heights around Haslemere and Hindhead. Almost due north from the Dyke is the line of Downs above Dorking and Guildford, Leith Hill prominent towards the eastern end. Between these heights and the Dyke lies the Weald, peaceful farmland now, but once a dense forest and later the scene of the activities of ironworkers. Slight, dark mounds in the midst of the Weals indicate the whereabouts of St. Leonards Forest (North) and Ashdown Forest (N.E.). Eastward the line of Downs culminates in the sharp escarpment of Firle Beacon.

At our feet, 600 feet below, the little village of **Poynings** nestles peacefully and cosily under the protection of the Downs.

From **Fulking Hill,** equally fine views may be obtained, heightened by peace and isolation.

Looking seaward on a clear day nearly the whole coast of Sussex, with its seaside towns, and Beachy Head on the extreme east, can be traced. Beyond is the ocean, and far away in the west, on a clear day, may be seen the Isle of Wight. The whole prospect along the shore, over the undulating Downs and across the far-stretching plain, is alluring in its grace.

View from Devil's Dyke

The rift popularly known as –

The Dyke slopes at an angle of about 45 degrees; quite enough to tire the pedestrian who attempts to walk up it from the lowest point. There is a legend that the Devil, being greatly alarmed at the increase in the number of churches in this part of Sussex, determined to dig a trench from this point to the sea, and so inundate the district; but an old woman, hearing a noise, held up a candle at the window of her cottage in order to see what was going on. The Devil was stupid enough to be frightened by the candle (thinking it was the rising sun), and decamped.

Having inspected the Dyke and its views, many visitors make their way down to pretty little **Poynings,** and after visiting the beautiful Church, walk to Pyecombe, on the main road, and so home by bus. (*Newtimber Down,* between Poynings and Pyecombe, was given to the National Trust in 1935). Not every day can one reach the altitude of 697 feet with so little effort, however, and those who wish to make the most of this easy arrival on the summit of the Downs should walk westward over Fulking Hill, and by the solitary Paythorne Barn to **Beeding,** in the Adur valley. On **Truleigh Hill** are earthworks of considerable interest to archaeologists, while running to the sea from Paythorne Barn is **Thundersbarrow Hill,** the site of a busy village nearly 2,000 years ago. The return from Beeding to Brighton can be made by bus. To Beeding from the Dyke takes about two hours' easy walking.

ROTTINGDEAN – SALTDEAN

To Rottingdean (4 miles). Rottingdean is situated in a *dene* or valley of the Downs on the seashore, about four miles east of Brighton. Buses run at frequent intervals from the Old Steine, or one may walk along the cliff or use the Undercliff Walk from Black Rock. As already mentioned, the top of the sea-wall forms the Undercliff Walk. The wall extends beyond Rottingdean to Saltdean.

Soon after the road reaches the cliff-top level there come into view the striking buildings of **Roedean School**, for girls. Then the road falls to the Ovingdean valley, to rise and fall again to Rottingdean.

On the landward side of the coast road by Ovingdean Gap is the large modern building of St. Dunstan's, where many blinded service men receive training.

Rottingdean and its neighbour, Ovingdean, can also be reached by a charming walk over the Downs from Elm Grove and the Race Hill.

Another attractive route for walkers is by the lane running behind Roedean School. This leads over the Downs to Ovingdean, whence a path continues the route south-eastward to Rottingdean.

Almost midway between Kemp Town and Rottingdean, and lying in the hollow of the Downs, is the village of –

Ovingdean, the scene of Harrison Ainsworth's *Ovingdean Grange*. The **Church,** which has been described as an almost perfect specimen of Saxon architecture, was probably built between 1042 and 1066. It is dedicated to the seventh-century Archbishop St. Wulfram – a dedication shared in this country only with the parish church of Grantham.

Rottingdean has developed rapidly in recent years but still retains much of its old-world flavour.

St. Margaret's Church is chiefly Early English, but can show some Saxon work and a Norman chancel. The South side was added by Sir George G. Scott. Note the Norman corbel stone at the west end of the south aisle, also the curious alms-box and the old font bowl, found some years ago buried in the vicarage garden. At the east end of the church is a beautiful window designed by Sir E. Burne-Jones, containing figures of the three archangels, Gabriel, Michael and Raphael. There are other examples of Burne-Jones in the chancel. The church is notable for the double flight of steps from the nave into the choir and thence to the chancel. In the north wall of the nave (exterior) the remains of a Saxon doorway may be seen.

Opposite the church is the house where Rudyard Kipling lived, and Sir Edward Burne-Jones occupied *North End House*, also on the green.

Near the pond is "Whipping Post House" said to date from the time of Henry II, beside which used to stand the village stocks, pound, whipping post and probably a ducking stool.

Near the Church is **The Grange,** an early Georgian house, remodelled in recent times by Sir Edwin Lutyens. It was for a time the home of Sir William Nicholson, the artist, and it is now used as a Public Library.

Saltdean is now a rising township, with a population of over 8,000. The modern church, dedicated in 1965, was designed by Sir Edward Maufe, R.A. Between it and the sea is an extensive recreation area with facilities for tennis, putting, etc. Next to the coast road is a **Lido** open in summer. Small settlements have arisen at **Telscombe Cliffs,** a mile short of Peacehaven.

Peacehaven has become a popular residential area. On the cliff here a concrete monument marks the point where the prime meridian of Greenwich leaves these shores. On the north side a bronze plaque is marked with the names, spherical distances and azimuths of many places in the Commonwealth.

Telscombe has been described as the most remote of Downland villages. It consists of a church and perhaps a dozen houses and cottages clustered together in a bowl-like valley of the Downs, and from almost any point provides a good walk for those who wish to get away from houses and main roads. From Rottingdean a lane leads up the hill in an easterly direction from near the church and behind Saltdean to a point on the Downs from which one looks down on Telscombe.

The shortest walk is by the rough track leaving the coast road (*bus route*) at the top of hill beyond Saltdean. Motorists will find a good approach by the lane opposite Southease, on the Lewes-Newhaven road.

The major part of the village including the Manor House, its gardens, areas of downland, etc., was purchased and improved by Mr. Ernest Thornton-Smith in 1934. In 1960 he presented his property to the National Trust.

The Manor House has the original Tudor cellars or Priest Holes, where priests hid in the reign of Elizabeth, and which were subsequently used by smugglers. The jewel of the village is the church, dedicated to St. Lawrence, which has been in use for nearly a thousand years. The church of Telscombe or Tittelscombe was given by King Edgar to the Abbey of Hyde, Winchester, in 966. It has been restored and is in perfect condition, with Norman chancel, twelfth-century tower and Lady Chapel, fourteenth-century font and fourteenth- and fifteenth-century windows.

To Ditchling Beacon and Lewes. Of the ridge walks in the vicinity of Brighton, the best is undoubtedly that from Pyecombe to Lewes, 8 or 9 miles. Either walk from Patcham *via* Standean, or take the bus to **Pyecombe**, with a picturesque smithy and a curious churchyard gate. The church has a Roman font and chancel arch. Follow the Clayton road for a short distance and then strike up a lane on the right towards the twin **Clayton Mills**. With ever-widening views of the Weald, continue to ascend in an easterly direction, and in about three miles from Pyecombe **Ditchling Beacon** will be gained, 813 feet above the sea. Four acres on the north-east slope of the Beacon were bequeathed to the National Trust in 1952 by the late Sir Stephen Demetriadi as a memorial to his son, killed in action in 1940.

From Ditchling the walk eastward to Mount Harry is less arduous than the earlier portion of the ramble and one has ample opportunity to revel in the magnificent views on either hand. On and about **Mount Harry** was fought the Battle of Lewes, and from the mount a steep descent past the Racecourse leads to Lewes town, which has for some time been in view, backed by Mount Caburn – the pointed Firle Beacon beyond – which blocks the entrance to the Ouse Valley.

Shoreham by Sea and the Adur Valley

Access. – Shoreham by Sea, midway between Brighton and Worthing, is easily reached from both centres, by rail or bus. The station is in the town centre.

For Walkers. – The walk along the main road is not to be recommended, but a visit to the twin Shorehams may very well be linked with a trip to the Devil's Dyke by walking westward along the Downs from the Dyke to Beeding whence either bus or walk down the valley.

Post Office. – Brunswick Road.

Shoreham by Sea, midway between Brighton and Worthing, appeals especially to lovers of old churches and to all who are fond of those quaint and picturesque scenes which a seafaring town never fails to present. The air is bracing and Buckingham Park is a particularly beautiful natural park of 38 acres with facilities for tennis, cricket, football, bowls, putting and hockey. The beach is two miles long and one may swim, sunbathe, row, yacht or fish.

Shoreham lost much of its old-time importance as the principal port for Normandy, especially with the development of Newhaven. Now, however, the harbour has been greatly enlarged and it is the largest commercial harbour between Southampton and Dover. There is a considerable trade in coals, oil, corn, timber and wine, and there are still several small ship-building yards. Many vessels entering Shoreham harbour turn east into the Canal which extends from the harbour mouth eastward to Aldrington, a distance of two miles. The Prince George Lock was opened in 1933 and the larger Duke of Edinburgh Lock in 1958.

Shoreham Church is a cruciform structure, part Norman and Early English in style, equalled in all the South Down country only by Chichester Cathedral, Boxgrove Priory and the churches at Steyning and Winchelsea. It dates back to within half a century of the Conquest, and its dedication – to St. Mary de Haura (St. Mary of the Harbour) – is unusual. The lofty and stately central tower has some fine Norman windows and massive supporting arches. The thirteenth-century chancel (now serving as the nave) replaced an earlier Norman chancel and side chapels. It is divided into five bays by Transitional-Norman arches; those on the north side are supported on columns which are alternatively round and octagonal and have foliated capitals; those on the south side are carried on composite or "engaged" columns with foliated capitals. The triforium and clerestory belong to the Transitional period, but the arcading along the north and south walls is Norman. Mounted on the south aisle wall are some brasses including figures in costume of the period of Henry VI.

Going southward from the churchyard by either East Street or Church Street, we come to High Street. To the right is the **Town Hall,** formerly the Custom House, and opposite an old building of flint and stone, known as **Marlipins.** It dates from the twelfth century, having probably been erected for the purpose of collecting the tolls paid by all ships entering the port. About 1500 it was acquired by the then Prior of Lewes. A few years ago it was developed as a local museum embracing some valuable water-colours and oils, ship models and objects of antiquarian interest. (*Admission free. Open during summer months.*)

At the farther (west) end of High Street, opposite the entrance to the bridge, the road bears right and then left and leads in a mile to Old Shore-ham. The road follows the course of the Adur. At low tide the Adur is a mere streamlet; but at other times it provides a prospect of rare beauty. The view of Old Shoreham Church, seen behind some picturesque old cottages as we approach it from New Shoreham, and the river scenery, with the quaint timber bridge, the chapel of Lancing College soaring on the height beyond, is especially fine. Perhaps the best view of Old Shoreham is gained from the river bank a few yards below the farther end of the timber bridge.

The Church, dedicated to St. Nicolas, stands in the angle of the roads leading to Brighton and Bramber. It is a cruciform Norman building. The tie-beam in the chancel displays tooth-moulding, which is rare in wood. Notice also the chevron carving round the four arches of the tower, in the north transept, and in the nave. At the west end of the nave is rough work from part of a Saxon church.

That delight of artists, **Old Shoreham Bridge,** is a picturesque timber structure first built in 1781. Modern traffic, however, now uses the new fly-over bridge and by-pass.

Shoreham Airport. The airport lies immediately west of the Adur. Some of the earliest flights in Great Britain were made at Shoreham. Considerably enlarged since those early days, the present Airport belongs to the municipalities of Brighton, Hove and Worthing, and includes a fine Terminal Building with public restaurant and bar. There is a flying club.

On a slope of the Downs overlooking the Adur is –

Lancing College. *The College Chapel is open to visitors from* 11 *a.m. until* 5 *p.m. every day. Apply at the Porter's Lodge. The public are admitted to all services.* The college is a conspicuous landmark to all passing across the flat lands bordering the last two miles of the Adur. By train it is best approached from Shoreham station; by road, from the A27 and the new Adur bridge. Shoreham Bridge is most convenient. From the *Sussex Pad,* turn north and almost immediately bear left up the drive.

The College was founded in 1848 by the late Canon Woodard, and stands in its own grounds of 550 acres. The buildings include chapel, great school library, dining hall, seven boarding houses, science laboratories, a music school, a gymnasium and covered swimming bath; and a detached sanatorium. Below the College lie the playing fields of 24 acres, and a rifle range up to 500 yards.

Eastward from Ditchling Beacon

The Chapel, dedicated to St. Mary and St. Nicolas, is in geometrical Gothic and was designed on exceptionally magnificent lines. It has been described by a great architect as "the finest piece of pure Gothic put up in England since the Reformation". Its exterior height is 150 feet.

Bramber

Bramber (from the Saxon Brymmburh – fortified hill) is much visited both from Brighton and Worthing, and generally has a quota of staying visitors, who find it a convenient centre for Downland rambles. It is also a favourite with artists. With its near neighbours, Steyning and Upper Beeding, it really forms a considerable township, modern houses and delightful old timber-framed cottages lining the main road with but a few gaps for nearly two miles. The village is unspoilt and maintains the reputation of being one of the prettiest spots in Sussex.

The dominating feature of the village is the ruined **Castle,** perched high on a tree-clothed mound. It is the property of the National Trust and is open free daily. The view all round through the trees is very fine, the Downs stretching away east and west, while to northward, on a clear day the monuments on Leith Hill can be seen. The height to the north-west, with its prominent clump of trees, is Chanctonbury Ring.

Close to the path leading up to the Castle is the **Church of St. Nicholas,** a small Norman building. It is only a fragment of the original cruciform structure but retains some unique carvings on the capitals of the tower arch.

The Castle is not the only attraction of Bramber. Many visitors, especially the children, display equal if not greater interest in the little **Potter Museum,** in the High Street *(Admission fee, closed Sundays. Cafeteria adjoining)*. Only part is a museum in the ordinary sense of the word, and the establishment would be better described as a kind of bird and animal Madam Tussaud's. The founder, a self-taught taxidermist of more than ordinary skill, conceived the idea of arranging his specimens in groups to illustrate well-known nursery rhymes and fables.

Also in Bramber is **St. Mary's House,** a fifteenth-century timbered building of great historic interest. It has a quaint flagged courtyard with two ancient elms. The present owner has restored the house, and made it into a fascinating museum of English social history. *Open Easter to end of October daily (except Mondays) 11–6 p.m., Sunday 2–6 p.m., fee.*

To the east of Bramber, and practically joined to it, though the Adur runs between, is the picturesque village of **Upper Beeding** (Lower Beeding is about sixteen miles to the north, between Cowfold and Horsham, near one of the sources of the Adur). The **Church** (St. Peter's), a 1,000 year-old Monk's Church, stands on rising ground north of the village.

About a mile to the north-west of Bramber, and connected with it by a pleasant road, is the old-world town of –

Steyning

Steyning (pronounced to rhyme with "penning") has a population six times that of Bramber, but it is almost as quiet and reposeful in aspect, consisting of a long main street, with several old inns, a Grammar School founded in 1614, and some picturesque half-timbered houses.

The main road leads to cross-roads in the highest part of the town. Turn right along Church Street, with a range of picturesque old houses and on the right the prominent gable of **Brotherhood Hall,** a building dating from the sixteenth century. Originally the home of a religious Order, it became in 1614 the **Grammar School.** At the Chantry House at the end of the street, W. B. Yeats wrote the draft of his last play.

The **Church,** founded in 1110, and one of the most beautiful examples of pure Norman architecture to be seen in England, stands a little back on the north side of Church Street, amid prettily wooded surroundings. The splendour of the interior will surprise the visitor who enters what he expects to be an ordinary country church. The magnificent Norman nave, almost cathedral-like in appearance, with its massive round pillars and semi-circular, richly ornamented arches and clerestories, and especially the lofty Norman arch between the nave and the chancel, all show that the Benedictine monks who built the Norman work that we can see, constructed a priory church of far larger proportions than a parish church.

Returning to the main street, notice the quaint little **Market Hall,** almost extinguished by its clock tower.

The walk over the hills from Steyning to Amberley (12 miles) is one of the finest in all the South Down country. Even better is that onward from Amberley to Goodwood – not characteristic scenery according to those who know only the treeless expanses of the eastern Downs; but almost unmatched in its combination of turf-covered slopes and lovely woods.

Steyning is one of the best points from which to ascend to **Chanctonbury Ring** (783 feet). Anyone will point out a path leading straight up to the Downs, from the point where Church Street joins the main road, or the road can be followed to Wiston (1½ miles) and the ascent made by the track from there.

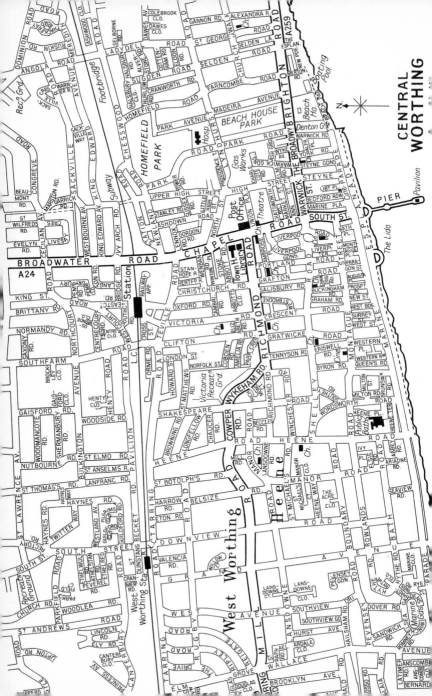

CENTRAL WORTHING

Worthing

Angling. – There is sea-fishing from boats and from the Pier for bream, bass, conger and whiting.

Bathing. – The upper part of the beach is shingle, but except at high tide an extensive stretch of gently-shelving sand is exposed. Chalets and huts are available for hire. Indoor swimming (freshwater) at the Aquarena, Brighton Road. *The Lido*, west of pier, has an open-air pool with purified heated sea-water (mid-May to the end of September).

Boating. – Boat trips available from beach east of pier. *Worthing Amateur Boat Club* at Splash Point, Marine Parade and *Worthing Sailing Club* at Sea Place, Goring. Regatta held annually in summer.

Bowls. – Public greens at Beach House Park; Marine Gardens; Field Place, Durrington; Beach House Grounds, West Tarring. Indoor greens in Pavilion Road and Field Place, Durrington. Open tournament during August–September, and Ladies' tournament in July.

Buses start from the pier and connect with neighbouring centres.

Car Parks. – Numerous car-parks (3 multi-storey).

Cinemas. – *Dome*, Marine Parade; *Odeon*, Liverpool Garden.

Cricket. – *Worthing Cricket Club* matches are played at the Manor Sports Ground. The *Broadwater Cricket Club* plays at Broadwater Green.

Dancing. – Dances are held at the Pavilion in winter, at Assembly Hall on Saturday evenings throughout the year.

Early Closing. – Wednesday. Some shops close all day.

Golf. – There are three very fine 18-hole courses within easy reach of the town. The *Hill Barn Municipal Links* cover 130 acres on the flank of Cissbury. Adjoining are the two 18-hole courses of the *Worthing Golf Club*.

Hotels. – *Beach*, Marine Parade; *Berkeley*, Marine Parade; *Burlington*, Marine Parade; *Chatsworth*, The Steyne; *Cumberland*, Marine Parade; *Eastley*, Marine Parade; *George*, Goring Road; *Kingsway*, Marine Parade; *Spaniard*, Portland Road; *Warnes*, Marine Parade; *Whitehall*, Marine Parade; and many others.

Library and Museum. – Public Library in Chapel Road. Museum and Art Gallery.

Information Bureau. – East of the Pier.

Parks, etc. – There are 21 parks and recreation grounds within the borough. The chief of these are Beach House Park, Homefield Park, Marine Gardens, Denton Gardens, Steyne Gardens.

Population. – 83,080.

Postal. – The chief office is in Chapel Road, nearly opposite the Library.

Putting. – Greens in the Marine Gardens, Brooklands (Brighton Road), Field Place, Denton Gardens, and Alinora Open Space. There is also a practice putting course at Hill Barn.

Riding. – Horses may be hired from numerous stables and riding schools. The downland bridle paths are within easy reach.

Tennis. – Public tennis courts in Homefield Park, Beach House Park, Denton Gardens, Field Place (Durrington), Church House Grounds, at Tarring. Visitors are welcomed at the *Arcadian Lawn Tennis Club*, Cecilian Avenue.

Theatres. – The *Connaught Theatre*, in Union Place, near the Post Office is the home of an excellent Repertory Company. At the *Pavilion* the municipal orchestra plays for afternoon tea. Concerts on Sunday afternoons, and on weekdays there are all types of entertainment.

Worthing's chief attractions to the summer holiday-makers are good bathing, boating and fishing, a long sea-frontage, a splendid variety of countryside and Downland rambles, coach trips, and good golf, tennis and bowls. For those of a studious turn there are the architectural delights of Shoreham, Sompting and Arundel, to name but three places; the archaeological problems enshrined in the immense camp at Cissbury, in Park Brow, and in a chain of smaller earthworks; while the chalk of the

Downs has entertainment ad infinitum for geologist, entomologist and botanist.

The residential advantages of Worthing are considerable. It is only 75 minutes from Victoria by through electric train, and is therefore in favour with City men, who find the journey up and down but little more tiring than a journey from one of the suburbs.

Situated in the most favoured part of the Sunny South Coast, Worthing has been shown, ever since records were kept, to enjoy an average of over 500 hours more bright sunshine a year than London.

In and About Worthing

The **West Parade,** connecting with the coastal road at West Worthing, joins the **Marine Parade,** which extends to the Denton Gardens on the east, and then on again to the fast-developing quarter where the Brighton Road comes down at a tangent to the shore. The seafront is 4¾ miles in length. The greater part of the promenade is raised, the beach shelving gently down on one side, and a long series of garden slopes, gay in summer with flowering plants and ferns on the other. These pretty embankment strips are, indeed, the most attractive feature of the Front, and redeem it from the monotony and dullness of the usual Parade.

The Sands. The higher portion of the beach is of shingle, but this soon gives place to a stretch of sand upon which children may paddle and play to their hearts' content. At low water a strip half a mile in breadth is uncovered, extending westward for nearly ten miles to Littlehampton and eastward for another four miles to the mouth of the Adur. The receding tide also uncovers many rocks, the pools in which present alluring possibilities to youthful crab and anemone-hunters. Boats may be hired at various points along the Sea-Front, and beach cabins and chalets may be rented from the Town Hall. Sea bathing is best at, or near, high tide.

The **Pier,** opened in 1862, was one of the first of the kind on the coast. In March, 1913, it was practically demolished by a storm but it was immediately rebuilt. In 1919 the Corporation of Worthing purchased the Pier and in 1924–5 set about building at the shore end the commodious Pavilion where good entertainment is offered. At the end of the Pier is the Southern Pavilion, with vita-glass sun lounges, and a café and a good dance floor. The view from the Pier in clear weather is very fine.

Walking westward from the Pier we pass the **Lido** which is open for swimming throughout the summer. The facilities include a purified heated sea-water pool, sheltered sun-bathing and refreshment facilities.

West Worthing and Goring

Bear the same relationship to Worthing as Hove to Brighton, except that they are incorporated in the borough, and do not, like Hove, maintain a separate municipal existence. Some of the most attractive residences are in this part of the town.

The Marine Parade has been extended under the name of the **West**

Parade, and at this end of the Parade are tastefully laid out **Marine Gardens.** They contain a café, bowling and putting-greens.

Eastward from the Pier

The Parade immediately eastward of the Pier is the usual starting-point of the buses and coaches and is consequently one of Worthing's busiest spots.

A few hundred yards from the Pier are the secluded –

Steyne Gardens. On a hot afternoon this elm-shaded spot, away from the glare of the sea, forms a delightful lounge. The Gardens may be entered either from the sea-front or from the Brighton road.

The Marine Parade proper terminates at the Boat-house of the *Worthing Rowing and Canoe Club*, a popular local institution, welcoming members.

At the Boat-house the roadway turns inland, but the promenade continues eastward beside the Beach chalets and so by the **New Parade** and the Esplanade meets the Brighton road. When a strong breeze is blowing, some very fine rough sea effects may be witnessed at the end of the Parade. Hence the name, **Splash Point.** Adjoining the Boat-house are the **Denton Gardens,** charmingly laid out with green lawns (used for putting), tennis courts and a sunken rose garden.

The northern end of the Gardens opens on to the **Brighton Road,** on reaching which we may note, at the corner of Park Road, the **Friends' Convalescent Home,** built and endowed by the late John Horniman for the benefit of handicapped children. Not far ahead the Brighton road widens. On the left of this happily named **Broadway** is the **Steyne Gardens Methodist Chapel,** a building of considerable architectural merit.

Following the Brighton road to the Borough's eastern boundary, we come to **Brooklands,** a recently developed site just off the sea front. Attractions here are the Pitch and Putt Golf Course, a large boating lake and, for the smaller children, paddling pools constructed in animal shapes.

By crossing the Brighton road from Denton Gardens we may enter –

Beach House Park and so become acquainted with the second link of the chain of gardens which, with but small breaks, extends from the sea to the northern confines of Worthing.

Beach House Park, with its ten acres of lawns, flower-beds, tree-shaded paths, its tennis courts and bowling greens, has been laid out with excellent taste. Beach House grounds adjoining the park are especially popular with children, for here are a paddling and model yacht pool of purified water, and a boating lake with rowing and motor-boats. Though close to the heart of the town, the Park commands a fine distant view of the Downs and is a favourite resort of those desiring rest and recreation away from the sea. There is an attractive sports pavilion and modern cafe.

Adjoining Beach House on the east is the Aquarena (opened in 1968) with swimming pools and café.

Park Road leads northward to –

Homefield Park, one of Worthing's largest open spaces, the enclosure comprising seventeen acres. The principal entrance is in Park Road, but there are several others. Part of the ground is reserved for bowls, tennis and a children's recreation ground.

South of the Park is the **Worthing Hospital,** a large building, with entrance in Lyndhurst Road.

For those who have wandered inland through the parks and desire to vary their return to the Pier, **Chapel Road,** Worthing's chief business thoroughfare, provides an interesting but often crowded route. The upper part of Chapel Road has in fact become one of the most important parts of Worthing, as is evidenced by its public buildings, chief of which is the –

Town Hall, a dignified building of brick and stone. The main features of the Chapel Road frontage are the pillars upholding the portico on which is inscribed the town motto: "Ex terra Copiam: e mari salutem." (From the earth abundance, from the sea health.)

The **Assembly Hall** adjoining the Town Hall is entered from Stoke Abbott Road. With seating accommodation for over 1,000 people, and a splendid dance floor, the building is utilized as a reception hall for various conferences, for civic functions and balls, public meetings, concerts, etc.

In front of the Town Hall is the local **War Memorial.**

Adjoining the Town Hall another imposing building in the Georgian style contains –

The Central Public Library, Art Gallery and Museum

The Central Lending Library (open 10 to 7 except Wednesday and Saturday, 9.30 to 5.30) contains more than 50,000 volumes and may be used by visitors producing current membership tickets of other public libraries, or on payment of a deposit of 50p.

The Junior section of the Lending Library contains 6,500 volumes.

The Reference Library with a stock of 12,000 volumes is open daily from 10 to 7 as is the Sussex Room which contains about 5,000 books as well as large numbers of prints, maps, newspaper cuttings, pamphlets and photographs relating to the county of Sussex.

Adjoining the Central Library is the **Museum and Art Gallery** *(open daily* 10 *to* 7, *closed* 5 *p.m. October to March).* The excellent archaeological collections contain important material from Cissbury, Highdown, Harrow Hill and Blackpatch. There are also collections of local history material and costume; naval and military exhibits are housed in the Hargood Room. On the first floor is the Art Gallery which contains an attractive collection of paintings and a Foyer containing displays of glass, ceramics, ivories and needlework.

In Union Place, opposite the portentous Church of St. Paul, is the **Connaught Theatre,** seating 700.

Continuing down Chapel Road and South Street we reach the sea front.

Sompting Church

Walks from Worthing

To Broadwater. Broadwater Church, the mother church of Worthing, is a mile north of the Town Hall. Buses run at frequent intervals, the route being via the busy Chapel Road and over the bridge to the east of Worthing Central Station.

A pleasant alternative approach to Broadwater is by way of South Farm Road, which starts at the railway immediately west of Worthing Central Station and brings one to the western side of the spacious green of Broadwater. Here turn right for the church.

Broadwater village is now included in the boundaries of Worthing.

The **Church** is a cruciform building of stone, with a massive central embattled tower. Extensive restoration took place in 1936–39 when an ancient Saxon doorway was discovered. The style is chiefly Early English, the chancel being a striking example, but parts are Norman. Before entering, note the "lepers' hole" in the west wall of the north porch. The chancel arch is particularly fine. Notice the beakheads and the grotesque birds and palm branches on the capitals of the piers supporting the tower, also the brackets which formerly supported the rood beam. On the north wall of the unusually long chancel is the richly carved canopied tomb of the eighth Lord de la Warr (*d.* 1525). The south transept contains another canopied Renaissance monument to the Earl's son and successor, Thomas West, Lord de la Warr (*d.* 1554). Notice also the fine old brass (nearly 6 feet long) to John Mapilton (1432) (centre of chancel floor), and the cross to Richard Tooner (1445), with inscription below to John Corby (rector 1415) (at junction of aisle from north door with middle aisle). Both brasses are covered with matting for protection.

Broadwater formerly consisted of a long, straggling street, with a few old houses and many commonplace modern ones, but has rapidly increased in size, and with its shops is a centre for the more northerly parts of the borough.

A little south of the Green is the *Broadwater and Worthing Cemetery*, about ten acres in extent, and where two great naturalists are buried – *Richard Jefferies and W. H. Hudson*.

Less than a mile along the main London road are entrances to the *Hill Barn Municipal Course* and *Worthing Golf Links*.

If instead of proceeding westward from Broadwater Green we take the eastward (Arundel-Brighton) road we shortly come to the **Sompting By-pass,** skirting on the south the pleasant little village of –

Sompting at the base of the Downs, two miles north-east of Worthing Pier and included in the Rural District area. It is, however, more conveniently reached by bus from Worthing.

The **Church** (*open all day*) is visited by antiquaries from all parts on account of its remarkable late-Saxon tower. Rickman includes this among the twenty buildings in the country of which alone it can be said with certainty that they date from the tenth-century. The four high-pitched gables are surmounted by a steep shingled roof. The interior of the church shows some Norman work. The tower displays Saxon sculpture. On the east wall of the south transept is the fragment of a twelfth-century carving of a bishop. Standing as it does on a slope of the Downs, the tree-surrounded church with its quaint tower is seen far and wide.

The adjoining estate of **Sompting Abbots** (now a boys' school) recalls by its name that it formerly belonged to the Abbey of Fécamp in Normandy. It was the granting of certain lands in Sussex to this Abbey by Edward the Confessor which established that connection between England and Normandy of which the Conqueror took such keen advantage when he sailed from St. Valéry to win the English crown.

The lane passing Sompting Church continues up and over the Downs, providing a pleasant walk to Steyning and from which return to Worthing may be made by bus or train *via* Shoreham.

To Tarring and Salvington. The former village of West Tarring is now, like Broadwater, included in the borough of Worthing. Few of those passing along the main road northward realize that within a few yards there may still be seen many of the features of a truly old-world village. It includes picturesque old cottages, remains of an ancient palace, delightful gardens and a park, and a thirteenth-century church in a green setting that even the adjacent rows of modern villas can do little to mar.

The mediaeval building known as the **Old Palace,** dates from the thirteenth century. It was restored in 1958 and is in use as the parish hall. The manor of Tarring, mentioned in Domesday as Terringes, was granted by Athelstan to the See of Canterbury, and was held by the Archbishops until after the Norman conquest.

Continuing along the main street, which now branches obliquely rightward as High Street, we see on the right three picturesque **Old Cottages,** forming part of what was once Parsonage Row. They were acquired in 1927 by the Sussex Archaeological Trust (the centre hall and top floors of each cottage are open Tuesdays to Saturdays, 2.15–5 p.m. April to October, *fee*). Though much alteration and restoration had to be undertaken, the interior is interesting as showing clearly the construction of timber-framed houses of the fifteenth and sixteenth centuries.

St. Andrew's Church, well worth inspection, has a buttressed Perpendicular tower and tall spire. The lofty clerestial nave with zigzag rafters, and the aisles are Early English. The church was restored in 1854, and forty years later the walls of the nave were decorated with full-length figures of the Apostles. Notice the fifteenth-century carved oak screen, surmounted by iron spikes, the old stalls with quaint carved miserere seats, and the Jacobean altar table.

Between Tarring and Offington Corner lies the village of **Salvington.** From the *John Selden Inn*, Half Moon Lane leads up to the Arundel road. Turn up the main road and at the top of the hill Mill Lane will be seen on the right. This leads steeply up to –

High Salvington which can be more easily reached by bus all the way from Worthing, or by car from the Findon By-pass by way of Bost Hill. The most prominent feature of High Salvington is the **Windmill,** (owned by the Corporation) standing on a summit of the Downs. It is a favourite starting point for the fine elevated walk northward along the Downland spur towards Long Furlong with some glorious views. A descent can be made to Findon village, or the walk continued eastward above Long Furlong towards Clapham and Patching, or northwards in the direction of Storrington.

From the mill one can descend Bost Hill to the Findon Valley road (bus route), about half a mile short of Findon village.

To Goring and Highdown Hill. Goring-by-Sea is now the western flank of the Borough of Worthing, and in place of the former fields and lanes we find a prosperous township. One may continue westward along the sea edge, or turn slightly inland and follow the Littlehampton road, now broad, concreted and deprived of much of its former beauty.

Goring Church, rebuilt 1837 and designed by Decimus Burton, has an exceptionally light interior. The chancel contains some old brasses in memory of the Cook family, the tomb of John Cook, dated *c.* 1500, and a number of memorials of Hentys, Ollivers and other local families. The copper covering of the tower has been replaced by oak shingles.

Adjoining Goring on the west is **Ferring-on-Sea,** another resort which began by adopting the name of an ancient village and has since almost engulfed it.

Highdown Hill. Rather more than a mile north of Ferring on the other side of the Littlehampton road is Highdown Hill, an outlying spur of the South Down range, 269 feet high. The Littlehampton buses pass the two most direct paths to the summit – which are opposite the lanes from Ferring.

The **Miller's Tomb** is beneath a clump of trees near the top on the east side of the low wall. The worthy here interred, John Olliver by name, was a local eccentric who owned a mill close by.

A prehistoric earthwork crowns the hill and was in occupation from Bronze Age to Saxon times. The extensive Saxon burial-ground was unearthed in 1893. Among the bones were swords, a Frankish spear-head, a glass vase with Greek inscription, knives, cups and Roman coins. A small bath-house of late Roman date has been excavated on the western slope of the hill. Fifty acres of the hill are now vested in the National Trust.

Castle Goring, with its woodlands lies between Highdown Hill and the Arundel road. It was built by Sir Bysshe Shelley, grandfather of the poet, and has the peculiarity of being Grecian on one side and Gothic on the other.

To Clapham and Patching. Many are content to make Highdown Hill the sole objective of an excursion. Others, again, are drawn by the woods of Clapham to descend the north side of the hill, and as buses pass along the Arundel road this alternative descent may be used as part of a modest circular tour. To the east of the earthworks mentioned above there is a hollow, just behind which is the entrance to the path through the woods, a glorious walk to the Arundel road.

Those with time and inclination, however, should go as far as **Clapham.** Unlike the London district of that name, Clapham in Sussex is just a sleepy row of cottages, within hail of a farm or two and a secluded country church.

To Lancing. There are two road routes from Worthing: (*a*) by the lower Brighton road along the shore, turning inland at South Street for South Lancing; (*b*) by the upper road, *via* Broadwater or Offington Corner, the Sompting by-pass and North Lancing. There is a frequent bus service. It is also a pleasant stroll from Worthing to South Lancing by the sands at low water.

Lancing, the "sunbright Lancing" of Swinburne's poem, is two and a half miles east of Worthing. It is believed to owe its name to Wlencing, one of the sons of Ella, the founder of the South Saxon kingdom. His brother Cissa certainly gave his name to Chichester and to Cissbury. The discovery in 1825, near Lancing Ring, of the remains of Roman buildings, with coins from the reign of Claudius to that of Gallienus, leads to the inference that an important Roman station existed here.

There is a good sand and shingle beach and various recreational amenities which, complete with a warm and breezy climate, attract many visitors. Population is 14,250.

The Parish **Church** (St. James's), in North Lancing, is built of flint in the Early English style, though parts are Norman.

To the north is the imposing Lancing College, *see* page 201.

To Cissbury Ring. Cissbury Ring (603 feet), like Chanctonbury Ring, is a prehistoric hill-fort. Footpaths ascend from all directions including various parts of the Findon Valley Estate. Walkers using the bus as far as Findon should turn up Nepcote Lane, opposite the *Gun Inn,* and turn to the left past the village Post Office. The lane continues uphill, and after passing through woods comes out on the Downs, with the huge bulk of Cissbury Ring on the right. If the ascent is made from Offington Corner the route is by the lane about 100 yards east of the entrance to the Worthing Golf Club. This is, though longer, a more gradual ascent.

The return is usually made *via* Findon, but fine extensions can be made to Chanctonbury and Steyning, or over Steep Down, with its earthworks, to North Lancing.

Cissbury Ring is the largest and most impressive of the South Down earthworks. A great oval series of embankments in marvellous preservation, despite two thousand years' exposure to weather, man – and rabbits. In days when high-explosives were unknown the place must have been of immense strength. Six hundred feet above the sea, and with over a mile of ditch and rampart enclosing its eighty acres, it is still a wonderfully imposing relic. In 1925 the Ring passed into the care of the National Trust, having been bought by public subscription.

In 1930 excavations carried out by the Worthing Archaeological Society proved that the ramparts were constructed about 300 B.C., and that the hill was occupied as a walled hill-city until about 50 B.C., when it was deserted and the interior ploughed up. Later, probably as a defence against Saxon pirates, the native Britons repaired the fortifications and re-fortified the hill, whose history ceases with the Saxon conquest about A.D. 500.

About a mile north-east of Cissbury is **Park Brow,** another spot of great archaeological importance and interest.

To Findon and Washington. The roads from Worthing and West Worthing meet at the busy Offington Corner roundabout, whence walkers ascend the ridge of High Salvington and continue along the Downs and Findon soon comes in sight below on the right.

Findon is a picturesque little place, restored to its former charm now that the by-pass takes the greater part of the London-Worthing traffic. It stands in a narrow valley in the very heart of the Downs, almost under the shadow of Cissbury.

The Early English **Church** of St. John the Baptist, which is on a Saxon foundation, stands a little west of the village and retains many interesting features. The roof construction is probably unique. It has one span across a width of some 45 feet and a central plate which measures some 20 inches in width. The old sanctus bell under the roof above the pulpit is one of the few remaining in Sussex. In the floor of the chancel is a worn brass to Gilbert French, a Rector of Findon who died in 1374.

Findon has long been famous in connection with the training of racehorses and a number of stables provide hacks and hunters. The Downs provide magnificent opportunities for lovers of riding.

A height with a curtain of trees, known as **Church Hill,** shelters the Church and dominates the village from the west. The view towards Chanctonbury and Cissbury is unusually fine.

Two and a half miles north of Findon is **Washington,** the road thither steadily mounting (323 feet) and then abruptly descending. A half-hourly bus service (reliefs during holidays), makes Washington fairly easily accessible from Worthing.

The place has no connection with the famous hero of American independence. The name of the village is derived from *Wasa-inga-tun*, the settlement of the sons of Wasa. The village forms an attractive centre from which to make excursions over the Downs, and especially for the ascent of Chanctonbury. The **Church** with the exception of the Perpendicular tower, was rebuilt in 1866.

On Upper Chancton Farm, close at hand, a remarkable find of Saxon coins was made in 1866 and some of them are to be seen in Worthing Museum.

From Washington the road continues in a north-easterly direction to Horsham and London, but the buses turn off in half a mile for **Storrington,** a beautiful and secluded South Down village, with delightful country all about it.

Chanctonbury Ring

Parham House lies two miles westward of Storrington. It was built in 1577, and although alterations have been made at various times, it is still "one of the glories of Sussex", perhaps more so now than in 1593, when Queen Elizabeth visited it. *(The House is open Easter to September, Sunday, Wednesday, Thursday, Bank Holiday afternoons.)* Visitors are shown the Great Hall and panelled Long Gallery, among other principal rooms, which contain much beautiful furniture and needle-work and a notable collection of paintings. There is a walled garden and some pleasure grounds.

The Park contains a herd of fallow deer and a heronry. There is a footpath right-of-way from Rackham to Cootham. In the park stands the Church, an uninteresting structure, except for the fact that it contains a remarkable leaden font of the four-teenth century. Among the trees are some magnificent oaks. One is known as "Betsy's Oak", because it is said Queen Elizabeth sat under it.

To Chanctonbury Ring, 814 feet above sea-level. Seven miles from Worthing. There are four principal routes from Worthing to Chanctonbury, any two of which may be combined with excellent results.

(1) The most direct. Bus to top of Washington "Bostal", whence climb by obvious tracks – about 1½ miles from road to Ring.

(2) Bus to Findon. In the village turn up Nepcote Lane (on right) and almost immediately leave it by a lane on left ascending past training stables. Near crest of Down, where paths to Cissbury go off on right, bear left, skirt the edge of "No Man's Land" and continue towards the now prominent clump of trees.

(2*a*) From the well on the main road about a mile beyond Findon the way is obvious.

(3) *Via* Cissbury. The way is clear, across the "saddle" north of Cissbury and thence alongside "No Man's Land".

(4) From Steyning. Leave the village by Newnham Lane (the continuation of Church Street). Climb Steyning Round Hill and then follow the edge of the Downs, with wonderful views of the Weald.

Chanctonbury Ring is an ancient camp more or less oval. Within its area the remains of Roman buildings were disclosed by excavations in 1909. The principal remains appeared to be those of a small temple or hillside shrine. Roman coins and recent finds are displayed at the Potter Museum at Bramber.

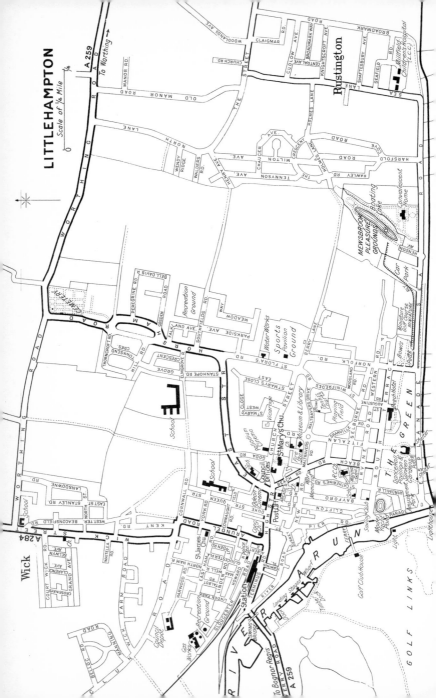

Littlehampton

Banks. – *Barclays, Midland, National Westminster* in High Street, *Lloyds, National Westminster* in Beach Road.

Bathing. – The higher part of the beach is of shingle, and gently sloping from that is an extensive tract of sand, on which there is safe and pleasant bathing. Alongside a portion of the Parade are bathing huts.

Boating. – There is boating on the sea and on the river. Boats, motor-launches, etc., can be hired in Pier Road or at the Ferry.

Motor-launches run daily up the river to Arundel, to the *Black Rabbit*, and to Amberley, Southwood and Houghton.

Visitors can become members of the *Littlehampton Sailing and Motor-Boat Club* (headquarters, 90–91 South Terrace) and the *Arun Yacht Club* (headquarters on west bank of river). They are then eligible to compete in the races that are held during the season, which extends from May to October. There is also an annual regatta.

At Mewsbrook Pleasure Grounds is an attractive boating lake.

Bowls. – Maltravers Road and Norfolk Grounds, *Maltravers* and *Norfolk Bowling Clubs.*

Buses and Coaches. – Good bus services link with nearby resorts. The Bus and Coach Station is in East Street. Coach trips daily through pleasant scenery to Arundel, Bognor Regis, Worthing, Goodwood, Petworth, Brighton, etc.

Car Parks. – Cars may be left on the Green at Mewsbrook. All car parks in the Town Centre are free.

Cinemas. – High Street and Church Street.

Cricket. – Club at the Sports Field, St. Flora's Road, on eastern side of town.

Croquet. – The *Littlehampton Croquet Club* has three full-sized courts in the Sports Field. Visitors may join for day, week or month.

Dancing. – Frequent dances are held at the Beach Hotel, and at the Badminton Club.

Early Closing. – Wednesday.

Entertainments. – There is a variety of amusements to be had on The Green throughout the season. The Western Pavilion presents various shows. There is a large Amusement Park at the western end of the Parade, with miniature motor cars and numerous attractions.

Fishing. – The facilities for angling, both in sea and river, are equalled in few other places. The stream below Pulborough and Amberley is noted for bream, dace, perch, pike and roach.

Golf. – 18-hole course on the western side of the Arun; a ferry crosses to the clubhouse from Pier Road.

The *Ham Manor Club* at Angmering and the Worthing course are within easy reach.

There is an interesting miniature golf course of 18 holes on Sea Road.

Hotels. – *Beach*, Sea Front; *Burbridge*; *Clarewood*, South Terrace; *Dolphin*, High Street; *Georgian House*; *New Inn*, Norfolk Road; *Stetson*, St. Catherine's Road; and many others.

Information Bureau. – On Sea Front.

Libraries. – Public Library at junction of Fitzalan Road and Maltravers Road.

Miniature Railway. – A miniature railway, with half-mile long track, runs from Norfolk Road corner of The Green to the Public Pleasure Grounds and Boating Lake at Mewsbrook.

Museum. – At 12A, River Road; contains items of maritime interest, and paintings of the locality.

Pleasure Grounds. – At Mewsbrook, 6½ acres of ground, and large Boating Lake. Sports field in St. Flora's Road. Caffyn's Field and Marina Gardens between Beach Road and St. Catherine's Road.

Population. – Urban district 18,200.

Postal. – The Chief Post Office is in the Arcade, near the junction of High Street and Beach Road. Branch offices in Norfolk Road, Horsham Road, and Wick.

Putting Greens. – 18-hole greens near the Beach adjoining Sea Road, on the Green adjoining the Esplanade and at Maltravers pleasure grounds.

Tennis. – Public courts in the Pleasure Grounds and on the Green.

Littlehampton is situated at the mouth of the Arun, about midway between Brighton and Portsmouth, and 59 miles from London. For the holiday-maker its chief charm is the combination of sea, river and wooded Downland close at hand.

LITTLEHAMPTON

The immediate coast is flat, but to the north lie the wooded slopes of Arundel Park, in the chain of enchanting Downs, and there is the perpetual beauty of the Arun.

The **Arun** is the largest of the rivers of Sussex. Rising in St. Leonard's Forest, in the neighbourhood of Horsham, it receives, near Pulborough, the *Western Rother*, the most beautiful river of Sussex, and farther on the *Western Arun*. It then passes Hardham and Arundel, and flows into the sea at Littlehampton.

Of the many features which distinguish Littlehampton from what may be called the stereotyped holiday resort, by no means the least important is –

The Green, a large, open space stretching between the town and the sands. Not only is the Green a splendid playground for young and old, but it serves to keep the town at a respectful distance from the Promenade, along which one may walk unworried by cars and other vehicles and fully exposed to the breeze from whatever quarter it may blow. At the northwest corner is a small artificial **Lake,** one of the attractions of Littlehampton from the children's point of view, for upon it they can sail their toy yachts in safety, while miniature yacht racing under the auspices of the local sailing club occupies many of more mature age. Close at hand is a thriving **Amusement Park.**

The **Sands** and the Green together fully entitle the town to be called the "Children's Paradise". There are no cliffs down which the little ones might tumble. The upper part of the beach is of shingle, but following that is sand – hard and clean, and sloping gradually to offer the best and safest bathing on the South Coast.

The pleasanter end is the east with its Regency houses and away from the blare of the Amusement Park. The latter, however, proves a haven in wet weather for day visitors and children.

The **Pier,** although not a promenade pier as usually understood by the term, is a pleasant resort when the tide is high, and is at all times a spot of some interest. The pier is the property of the Harbour Board charged with the maintenance of the Harbour and waterway. At the shore end is a **Lighthouse** (1947).

The **Harbour** is a never-failing source of interest to a large proportion of Littlehampton's visitors. A map drawn in 1671–2 shows the outlet 200 yards eastward of the present opening, which dates from 1733, when Parliament established a Board of Commissioners with authority to cut a new channel for the river through the shingle, to erect a pier, and to carry out other improvements. The Harbour affords good accommodation for yachts, and for all vessels up to 215 feet in length.

On the west side of the river are the *Golf Links*, and here is the **Western Beach,** fringed by sand dunes. The river may be crossed by a Ferry opposite the Golf House, or by The Bridge. Built in 1908, the latter can be opened to allow the passage of vessels. The road on the west side of the bridge is part of the direct route between Portsmouth and Chichester on one side, and Worthing and Brighton on the other.

The Town

Terminus Road connects the Bridge with the **Railway Station,** and then becomes **High Street.** On the left at the beginning of High Street is the **Congregational Church,** and another noteworthy building, **St. James's Church,** stands a short way up Arundel Road, on the left. It is a modern building, but contains the Norman or pre-Norman font of the old Parish Church.

For many years the town belonged to the Duke of Norfolk, and a considerable number of the roads are named after members of the Ducal family. **Fitzalan Road,** for example, runs inland from the Green to join **Maltravers Road** near the **Library and Museum,** the **Baptist Church** and the local headquarters of the British Legion.

The **Museum,** now in River Road, is interesting and contains a good collection of local archaeological specimens. Maps and charts of Littlehampton and the River Arun are a special feature.

A few yards eastward along Maltravers Drive are the **Pleasure Grounds,** with tennis courts and bowling greens, and by continuing eastward we should reach the **Sports Field** commanding a splendid view of the South Downs.

Berry Lane leads very pleasantly from the end of Church Street to the Mewsbrook Pleasure Ground and Boating Lake, where the way leads to Sea Road *via* Hendon Avenue and so to Rustington.

From the west end of Maltravers Road it is but a few steps to the **Parish Church,** rebuilt in 1935, and dedicated to St. Mary the Virgin.

A few yards westward of the church is the old Manor-House, now used as the **Council Offices** and beyond that point we come to **High Street** and the busiest part of the town. **Beach Road,** however, leads back to the Green by way of the *War Memorial* and the **Roman Catholic Church,** dedicated to St. Catherine. On the south of the church are the **Marina Gardens,** laid out with lawns and flower beds and with a tree planted to commemorate the Jubilee of King George V.

Walks from Littlehampton

To Rustington and East Preston. Rustington, though so closely linked with Little-hampton as almost to form a part of it, may be made the objective of a pleasant circular walk of barely 4 miles, or bus may be used.

From the Green, follow the Sea Road past the Mewsbrook Pleasure Grounds. The road turns inland at the end of the promenade and the way then lies straight ahead.

Rustington is developing into a pleasant suburb of Littlehampton and has a population of 9,000.

The **Church** shows various styles of architecture, and was built originally about 1100. The west porch is very attractive, its oak arch and barge-board especially claiming attention. The north porch (by which the visitor enters the church) is restored ancient work. The tower and south arcade are Transitional-Norman. The *One-handed Clock* was formerly in a church at Great Bedwyn, in Wiltshire. It was not until about 1670 that two-handed clocks were introduced into England. The chancel is Early English.

The foreshore at Rustington is of shingle, safe and unspoiled. A large expanse of sand is exposed at low tide.

East Preston village adjoins Rustington and is 2½ miles east of Littlehampton. It may be reached by following the main road eastward from Rustington Church.

The **Church** stands at the western extremity of the parish, at a bend in the main road. It is a long, narrow building, dedicated to the Virgin Mary. The oldest feature is the north doorway, Norman work in Caen stone and chalk, dating from about 1130. The chancel and nave (with the exception of the south aisle, which is modern) are Early English, with Perpendicular insertions. The tower dates from about 1550.

To Toddington. This is one of the most popular short excursions from Little-hampton. **Toddington** is a small village about a mile north of the town, in the midst of orchards and market gardens. Of interest is the Saxon chimney, the only one of its kind in Sussex, on Toddington House.

The direct route is by a field-path from East Street, but the village can be included in a circular walk of about 3 miles. Taking the high road portion first, the route is along Arundel Road, through **Wick,** and over the railway crossing. Beyond that take the first turn on the right, Mill Lane, which merges into Tod-dington Lane. At the end of about half a mile again turn to the right, and shortly afterwards re-cross the line and go southward to the spot where three roads meet; thence a footpath runs straight ahead to East Street.

To Lyminster. Lyminster is a village about 1½ miles north of the heart of Littlehampton. The route lies through Wick. The village dates from Saxon times. The manor was one of the possessions of King Alfred.

The **Church** which has a history of over a thousand years, was originally the chapel of a small nunnery that was probably founded in the time to Athelstan (925–940). Towards the end of the twelfth century, when a north aisle and a chapel to the north of the choir were added, the walls of the nave were raised 5 feet. The tower belongs to two periods. Its two lower stages date from 1200, while the uppermost stage was built about 1420. The roof of the aisle is upheld by roughly dressed timbers supported by timber pillars resting against the stone pillars – a highly unusual arrangement. The nave is very dark and appears unusually lofty. Note, in the south wall, the two lancet windows and the curious circular window, all dating from about 1260. On the north wall of the nave, over the most westerly pillar, is the head of a Saxon window. The long narrow chancel is unusual. Note the twelfth-century piscina in the south wall of the Sanctuary. The view from the Churchyard, looking towards Arundel Castle, is very beautiful.

To Angmering. Angmering, mentioned in Domesday Book as East Angmare, is an old-world village, about 4 miles north-east of Littlehampton. For walkers the route is along Church Street, or Norfolk Road, to the footpath to Rustington. From Rustington Church follow the street as far as Woodlands Avenue (on the left), at the far end of which is the main road near a railway bridge. Crossing this, turn left at the foot of the slope and take the footpath across the golf course to Angmering.

Angmering Church, dedicated to St. Margaret, is mainly a neo-Gothic structure. The tower was built by the Nunnery of Sion, whose arms are on the tower, which also bears the date of its erection, 1507, over the doorway. The tower is a fine specimen of chequered stone and flint work. There are some finely embroidered hassocks and seat cushions.

The **Golf Links** are laid out on the Ham Manor Estate, a little way north of the railway line. The beautiful old mansion now forms the clubhouse.

On the north-west border of the parish is **New Place,** formerly the seat of the Palmer family, but used as cottages for the last hundred years and more. Between Angmering and Poling, about half a mile due west from Angmering Church, excavations have uncovered the very extensive baths, hypocausts and drains of one of the largest **Roman Villas** in Sussex. Some of the chief finds are in the Museum at Littlehampton.

Angmering lies just over a mile north of the railway. About an equal distance south of the line, and on the edge of the sea, has arisen the modern extension of East Preston, sometimes known as "Angmering on Sea".

To Climping. Climping on the west side of the Arun, is most conveniently reached by the Bognor Regis bus to Church Lane, Climping. **Climping** appears in Domesday Book as Clepinges. It was part of the extensive possessions of Earl Godwin, father of Harold, the "Last of the Saxons."

The **Church** is a few minutes walk northward from the A.259 bus route. It is notable for the perfection of its design. The church was not the first to occupy the site, for one was built here by the Prioress of Leominster (Lyminster) before the Norman Conquest. To that building the nuns from Almanesches added the present tower, and the rest of the church that we see was erected by John de Climping, a native of the parish, who in 1253 became Bishop of Chichester. The tower occupies an unusual position at the end of the south transept. Its walls of Caen stone are four feet thick and on each side of the doorway may be seen recesses as if for the ends of a drawbridge.

TORTINGTON–FORD

Hardly less interesting than the Norman tower is the Early English Church. The font and pulpit are of the fourteenth-century. The front pews of the nave bear twelve old seat-ends, and in the north transept is an ancient chest with a slit for receiving offerings to enable poor knights to go on crusades to the Holy Land. Restoration work was carried out in 1875.

To Tortington, Yapton and Climping. This is a pleasant circular excursion on the west side of the Arun, involving a walk of about 6½ miles, if the train is taken to Ford. A couple of miles may be saved on the homeward journey by taking the bus from Climping to Littlehampton.

Tortington Church is picturesquely situated about 4 miles north-west of Little-hampton. This small but interesting building is nearly hidden by trees and farm buildings. It dates from about 1140, and is in the late Norman style, but the arches between the nave and the aisle are Early English. A remarkable feature of the building is the extent to which chalk has been used in the interior. It forms the chief part of the material of the remarkable chancel arch carved in the Scandinavian style. The large font is Norman; the pulpit is Jacobean; and at the foot of the chancel steps is a brass (restored) dated 1596, commemorative of one Roger Gratwik.

Adjoining the Church is **Tortington House.** A barn at Priory Farm, to the north, incorporates remains of the twelfth-century Tortington Priory. The woods in this parish are themselves worth a visit.

From Tortington a field-path (not always easy to follow) leads to **Yapton,** a more modern village, about 1½ miles west of Ford. Through it runs the disused Chichester and Arundel Canal. In the village is an inn displaying the remarkable sign of *The Shoulder of Mutton and Cucumbers.*

The **Church,** of which portions of the eaves are but five feet from the ground, has some features of interest. The nave and aisles are Transitional-Norman, as is also the tower, a picturesque structure much out of perpendicular, and propped up by a huge ancient buttress on the south side. The rim of the early Norman font is orna-mented with arrow-headed carving.

From Yapton churchyard a path leads in about a mile to Wicks Farm, on the outskirts of –

Ford, a small village which plainly owes it name to its site, and doubtless represents a very ancient settlement. The walls of the church are believed to be of Saxon times.

Irregularities of the surface of the ground near the church mark the site of a castle that is supposed to have been erected in the twelfth century. Some of its foundations were laid bare during the construction of the now disused Chichester and Arundel Canal, alongside which is a public footpath. The visitor crosses the Canal in passing northwards from the church to Ford Junction, from which one may return to Littlehampton by train. Or one may turn southward from Ford to **Climping,** about half a mile beyond which the bus route is joined.

A pleasant variation of this walk may be had by starting at Ford, walking thence to Yapton, crossing to Marsh Farm and going northward up a pleasant lane to remote little **Binstead.** This little detour introduces the visitor almost suddenly to a wooded country of hill and dell in striking contrast to the flat pastures around Yapton. Hence one may make one's way through the woods and back to Tortington or, omitting Tortington, Arundel is easily reached in about 3 miles (buses pass along main road).

To Burpham and Poling. Either or both of these places can be included in the excursion to Lyminster, or each can be made the object of a walk from Arundel.

Burpham, the more remote of the two, is almost due north of Littlehampton, from which it is distant some 6 miles, by way of Wick and Lyminster. It is very pleasantly situated near the Arun, across which there are fine views of Arundel's beautiful park and stately castle. The village is probably mentioned in Domesday under the heading "Wepeham," and was probably even then an ancient place, for in a creek near it was found, in 1885 an ancient canoe, 13 feet 9 inches long, formed from a single oak, hollowed out by some ancient Briton. A curious wooden anchor belonging to the craft was also found. Both treasures were transferred to the museum at Lewes.

The **Church,** dedicated to St. Mary the Virgin, is mainly in the late Norman and Early English styles. The most ancient portion is the north wall of the nave. The chancel is a beautiful specimen of Early English, its recessed lancets and plain vaulted roof being particularly admired. The piscina and double aumbry are other features worthy of note. There is also a so-called "leper window" containing fragments of seventeenth-century Flemish glass, and in this connection it is interesting to note that there was a leper settlement on the Downs near-by, while a path which leads up to the Downs from the village is still known as the Leper's Path.

In a hollow of the Downs beside the river, some two miles north of Burpham, is pleasant little **North Stoke,** with a church showing some interesting features. To the east of Burpham is **Wepham Down.**

Poling is about a mile and a half to the east of Lyminster. Apart from the scenery, the visitor's interest centres in the **Church,** which appears to have been erected near the close of the twelfth century, and to have been partly rebuilt about the beginning of the fifteenth century. It has, like the old Priory of St. John in the village, associations with the Knights Templars.

To Amberley, Bury and Bognor. The road route from Littlehampton is by way of Arundel, thence climbing through the woods to Whiteways Lodge. From this point it is a steep drop to the little hamlet of Houghton, beyond which is **Houghton Bridge,** where boats can be hired for excursions on the Arun, and teas and refreshments can be had.

Amberley village is rather more than a mile to the north of the station which bears its name, and 5 miles north of Arundel by road.

Amberley is a peaceful old-world village beloved by artists. Seen from any spot that shows the Downs behind and the River Arun in front, it has a picturesque appearance, but the best view is that from the Arundel road. To anglers especially Amberley is well known and was long famous for its trout.

The village is situated on a ridge, which descends precipitously on the north to the "Wild Brooks". At the western end of the ridge stand the remains of Amberley Castle, and between it and the village is the **Church,** an interesting structure, dedicated to St. Michael.

It is partly Norman, partly Early English. Originally, the church probably consisted only of a nave and chancel, erected about 1100. The present very long chancel, south aisle and tower were probably built about 1230. The south doorway, however, is in the Decorated style, and is one of the finest specimens of that period in Sussex. As specimens of Norman work, the visitor should look at the fine window at the west end, at the windows in the north wall, at the beautiful chancel arch, richly chevroned, and at the font. Also worthy of note is the brass to John Wantele, dated 1424.

BIGNOR

Amberley Castle *(not open)* was once the official residence of the Bishops of Chichester.

For **Bury** the road route is via Houghton Bridge and Houghton, where turn sharp to right just after passing the church on the left. Bury is a prettily placed little village, where John Galsworthy resided at Bury House. The fifteenth-century rood-screen in the Church has over it a thirteenth-century beam. A finely carved rood was replaced on the Rood-beam as a war memorial.

Bignor, famed for the remains of its Roman villa, is some four miles from Amberley station and two miles from the main road at Bury *via* quaint, little **West Burton,** or from Sutton.

For the greater part of the two miles that have to be traversed, the road is on the slope of elevated ground, and is parallel to the Downs, which are separated from its southern side only by a comparatively narrow valley. Crossing the Downs is **Stane Street,** the old Roman road between London and Chichester. Upon it is **Bignor,** the *Ad-Decimum* of the Roman itineraries – that is to say, "at the tenth milestone" from Regnum (Chichester). The remains of the Roman Villa form the principal attraction of the village.

The Roman Villa

Admission. – The Villa is on the West Burton side of Bignor. Open Tuesdays to Sundays from March 1st. to October 31st., 10 a.m. to 6.30 p.m. or one hour before sunset; also Bank Holidays and every Monday in August. Admission charge; party rates. Free car park.

In 1811 the ruins were accidentally discovered during the ploughing of a field. Excavations disclosed the foundations of a residence which had covered about five acres, and probably comprised not fewer than fifty rooms. The pavement of some of the apartments was well preserved. Over this, sheds were erected as protection from the weather, while the soil was replaced over the rest of the remains. In the subdued light which falls on the floors the mosaic work appears like a rich carpet.

The Villa must have been "a welcome and imposing site as one descended Bignor Hill by Stane Street, with its white walls and columns rising from the dark weald".

The rooms were arranged around an inner court, some 150 feet long by 120 feet wide. Round this enclosure was a covered gallery, 10 feet wide, with a tessellated pavement. The mosaic decorations of the floors consist of representations of various personages and scenes, enclosed with coloured borders of elegant designs. The rooms were heated by hot air; the pipes are still to be seen. The Villa is believed to date from the time of Titus, A.D. 79–81.

Instead of returning to the West Burton road, follow a cart-track running into Bignor from near the Villa. At the corner where this meets the village street is a fine old timbered cottage dating from the fifteenth century. By continuing straight ahead, the pretty lych-gate giving access to **Bignor Church** will be reached in a few yards. The most noted feature of the church is its chancel arch, of roughly-dressed stones of unknown but possibly Saxon date. The font is also Saxon and the Chancel screen fourteenth-century, though partly restored.

About a mile from Bignor is **Sutton,** an ancient and attractive village with an interesting old church showing Saxon herringbone masonry on part of the north wall.

From Bignor, the majority of visitors return to the main road at Bury, but those who are loth to return at once to the tarred highway should climb the Downs and endeavour to trace the route of **Stane Street,** descending to Eartham and Westergate, on the Arundel-Chichester road. From this point the return may be made by bus *via* Arundel.

An alternative route is to cross the Downs from Bignor to **Slindon** and so to the main road near Binstead.

Slindon was described by E. V. Lucas as "a Sussex backwater". It lies about half a mile off the main road, amid woods of great loveliness and variety, the beeches being particularly fine. Situated on the slopes of the Downs, Slindon commands fine views, including here and there among the trees glorious peeps of the coast between Littlehampton and Selsey, and even of the Isle of Wight.

Worth a visit is the building adjoining the church. It is 300 years old with small Gothic windows set in flint walls thought to have been outer walls of an ancient chapel or refectory and connected with Slindon House.

Slindon House has much Elizabethan work, and traces even of thirteenth-century building. It also has a priests hiding-hole; the house was the headquarters of local Catholics during the period following the Reformation, when Arundel Castle lay practically in ruins. It is now a boarding school for boys.

Slindon woods merge into those of **Rewell,** which clothe the crest above Fair-mile Bottom right up to Whiteways Lodge.

Splendid rambles westward along the Downs may be started from the vicinity of the Lodge.

It would be difficult to overpraise this beautiful piece of country. Kipling's "whale-backed Downs" are here replaced by wooded hills from which glorious and unexpected views are obtained through the trees.

The Arun and the Castle, Arundel

Arundel

Buses run from Littlehampton, Worthing, Bognor Regis, Chichester, etc.
Car Park. – Mill Road, between the Castle and the river (turn right after crossing bridge in approaching town).

Mediaeval Arundel, nestling around the foot of the famous Castle, owned by England's premier Duke, is one of the most idyllic spots in England. Looking at it from afar one sees houses rising one above another on the slope of a hill; a huge castle; a cathedral church towering high above the house-tops; trees here and there, among the buildings and on the outskirts of the town, hinting at more beyond; green fields spreading out at the foot of the hill, and holding a wide stream. Over and around all an air of restfulness and security.

The town consists of three parallel streets and an intercepting thoroughfare. This, the **High Street,** runs from the foot to the crown of the hill. Except during the holiday season, the current of life in the town flows as placidly as the neighbouring river. The industries, of which the chief are timber work and printing, cause no stir, and even the bustle and commotion of the market-place are as much things of the past as are the comings and goings of knights and men-at-arms.

It is fitting that Arundel should have an appearance of association with the past, for it really is an ancient place. Although at the time of the Conquest the Castle and the mill were almost the only buildings, yet after the Norman invasion the town grew rapidly under the fostering care of Roger Montgomery, first Earl of Arundel, who held it as a feudal appanage of the Castle.

Visitors arriving by rail or by the road that crosses the Bridge may begin their sight-seeing near the railway station, for adjacent to that is the **Priory Farm.** The central portion of the small farmhouse was the chapel tower of a Priory founded by Queen Adeliza (widow of Henry I), who entrusted it with the superintendence of the causeway across the marshes to the bridge over the Arun.

The Bridge, rebuilt in 1933–5, provides the most characteristic view of Arundel, the Castle rising grandly above the old town. The ruins by the Bridge are those of the Maison Dieu (1395). Beyond the bridge, on the right, is **Mill Road,** which leads to the spot where stood the old mill made famous by Constable's paintings. Mid-way along Mill Road, opposite the Lower Lodge entrance to the Castle is the large town **car park.** At the farther end are the Dairy and Swanbourne Lake, and the picturesquely situated *Black Rabbit Inn*.

Arundel Castle

Admission. – The Park is open daily, but cars, motor-cycles and dogs are not admitted. The Castle, including the Keep, Grounds, Fitzalan Chapel, and the principal apartments are open to visitors on Mondays, Tuesdays, Wednesdays and Thursdays from Easter Monday to late June, 1–4.30 p.m. Then from late June to end of September, Mondays to Fridays inclusive, 12 noon to 4.30 p.m., additionally Sundays in August. There is a charge.
The only entrance is by the "Lower Lodge" in Mill Road at the bottom of the hill.

Before the Conquest, the Castle belonged to the Kings of England. Of the forty-nine castles mentioned in Domesday, that of Arundel is the only one recorded as having been in existence in the reign of the Confessor. A documentary notice of the manor is found a hundred years earlier, in the will of King Alfred, who bequeathed it to his nephew, but there is no reference to the Castle.

When the Conqueror awarded it to Montgomery, the Castle consisted only of a keep, which he strengthened and repaired. Subsequent owners greatly enlarged the fortress and made it a lordly habitation.

The Montgomery family lost the Castle by the treason of their head to the Conqueror's son, Henry I. That monarch gave it to his wife, Adeliza, who, by her second marriage, carried it to the Albini family. When the last of the Albinis died, his possessions were divided among his four sisters, and Arundel was the share of the lady who was married to one John Fitzalan. In 1580 there were two co-heiresses to receive the property which the Fitzalans had held. One was the wife of Thomas Howard, Duke of Norfolk. To her fell Arundel, and from her it passed to her son.

Possession of the Castle of Arundel carried with it the title of Earl of Arundel and the office of Chief Butler of England.

The Castle has stood three great sieges. The first, due to the rebellion of the Earl in 1102, was conducted by Henry I in person. The second occurred during Matilda's contest with Stephen, who appeared before it, as the Empress had been received within its walls by her stepmother Adeliza. The third great siege took place during the Civil War, when the Castle after having been surrendered on several occasions alternately to the Royalists and the Parliamentarians, was finally laid in ruins by a Parliamentary force.

Extensive restoration was carried out at the end of the eighteenth-century and again at the end of the last century.

The Castle Gateway. The walls and gateway were built in 1851. Above the archway is a figure of the Howard lion.

The **Keep** is one of the oldest portions of the castle. It is of Saxon origin. Roger de Montgomery encased the walls with Caen Stone, and to him it probably owes the Norman doorways, St. Martin's Oratory, and inner Gateway at the base of the Keep, which stands on an artificial mound, 70 feet high. In shape it is nearly circular, the diameter varying from 59 feet to 67 feet. The walls are 27 feet in height and 8 to 10 feet thick. From the battlements, which are reached by a narrow circular staircase, an extensive view is gained. The long flight of steps to the entrance replaced a portcullis that defended the oblong tower flanking the Keep. Adjoining the Keep is a **Well,** 76 feet deep, supposed to have been dug in 1300 for the garrison. After the siege of the Civil War it was gradually filled in.

The oldest parts of the Castle are in the east towers and the adjacent south-east front. Next in point of age was the west wing, which was erected in the middle of the fourteenth century. The east wing is thought to have been built in the reign of Henry VIII. But not one of these is now seen in its original form.

The Fitzalan Chapel, actually part of the building housing the Parish Church, is the Collegiate Church of the Holy Trinity. Founded by the Earl of Arundel in

1380, it was occupied by various religious orders until the Dissolution of Monasteries, when it was granted back to the then Earl. Much has since been done to restore the chapel, which is used as the burial-place of the Howards, as for centuries it was that of the Fitzalans. There are some fine monuments. One of the most noteworthy is the tomb of *John, ninth Earl of Arundel.*

In the centre of the Chapel is the richly-carved alabaster tomb of *Earl Thomas Fitzalan*, son of the founder (d. 1415), and Beatrice his wife (d. 1439). On the north side is the tomb of Thomas, the twelfth Earl (1524) and his son. On the south side is the chantry of *William Fitzalan*, eleventh Earl, and his Countess, Joan, sister of the "King-maker" Earl of Warwick. It is a very elaborate structure of Sussex marble. Southward of this are the chantry and tomb, with effigies, of the fourteenth Duke of Norfolk, who died in 1860, and the Duchess, who died in 1886. In the Lady Chapel a black marble altar-tomb, sculptured in Paris, commemorates *Lord Henry Howard*, who died in 1824. The most recent memorial is that of the fifteenth Duke (d. 1917).

The **Park** can be entered by following Mill Road from the bridge, or by way of the Main Lodge at the top of High Street, turning to the right almost opposite the schools. A pleasant walk connects one entrance with the other. The Park comprises 1,100 acres. Cars, cycles and dogs are not admitted; otherwise it is freely open to the public. In the Park is the Duke's new residence, built 1961.

The carriage road through the Park is two miles in length. Near the Arundel Lodge it lies between high banks, and is in the midst of a thick wood. Farther on it rises to the level of the surrounding ground and, as this is approached, the marginal trees give way to the greenest sward, dotted with clumps of trees and single specimens. **Hiorne Tower** also comes into view, and a Grecian altar, taken from the museum at Sebastopol, on the capture of that fortress in 1855. The tower bears the name of the architect who designed it, in 1790.

Swanbourne Lake is one of the most beautiful features of the Park, and has formed the subject of more than one Academy picture. Those who wish to reach the lake directly from Arundel should follow Mill Road from the foot of High Street. The water turned a mill which stood by the lake from Saxon times until recent years. The site of the mill is now occupied by the Arundel Waterworks.

A favourite stroll is to the pleasure-grounds of the *Black Rabbit*, a riverside inn, about half a mile farther along the road. The inn is also a favourite objective for boating parties up the Arun from Littlehampton.

The **Parish Church** of Arundel is in the London Road and dedicated to St. Nicholas. It dates from 1380, when it replaced an earlier church. On the fine massive tower the soldiers of the Parliament planted the cannon which wrought the chief injury to the Castle during the siege. The font is of Sussex marble, and dates from the fourteenth-century. The ancient stone pulpit, which for a time was fitted as a pew, is another feature worthy of notice. The eastern portion – commonly called the Fitzalan Chapel can now be seen from within the Church.

The **Roman Catholic Cathedral Church.** The Church of Our Lady and St. Philip Neri is the most imposing public building in the town and one of the finest modern buildings of its kind in England. The architect was that J. A. Hansom who gave his name to the "hansom cab." The best general view of this beautiful edifice is obtained from the river-bank. Its large proportions are realized when seen from a distance.

Bognor Regis

Angling. – Good fishing in the Arun and from boats or from the Pier. Flatfish, shore bass and bream are common. Fishing Festival in June and frequent competitions during the season.

Banks. – *Lloyds, Barclays, Midland, National Westminster* all in High Street; *Trustee Savings*, London Road. The first four have branches in the west end of the town also.

Bathing. – Safe bathing from firm, extensive sands.

Boating. – Rowing boats, speed and motor-boats for hire. Children's Boating Pool in Hotham Park and Princess Elizabeth model yacht pond, Pavilion Gardens. Motor-launch trips are made along the coast and up the Arun.

Bowls. – Two excellent greens in Waterloo Square. Open tournament each year.

Bus and Coach Services. – Circular bus route through the town. Surrounding districts are well served. Frequent coach trips to all neighbouring places of interest.

Car Parks. – Fitzleet, East Esplanade, Colebrooke, Marine Drive West, Hothampton, Belmont Street.

Cinemas. – *Picturedrome, Odeon* and *Theatre Royal.*

Cricket. – In Nyewood Lane, West Bognor, there is a Sports Ground, covering about 16 acres, laid out for cricket, football and tennic. The *Bognor Regis Cricket Club* has matches throughout the season and a Cricket Week in August.

Early Closing. – Wednesday.

Entertainments. – In addition to cinemas and theatre, there is a resident concert party at the Esplanade Theatre. Orchestral Concerts at the Music Marquee or Esplanade Theatre.

Golf. – The 18-hole course of the *Bognor Regis Club* is on the outskirts of Felpham. There are Putting Greens in Marine Park Gardens and Hotham Park.

Hotels. – *Black Mill House*, Princess Avenue; *Clarehaven*, Wessex Avenue; *Marlborough*, Marine Drive West; *Royal*, Esplanade; *Royal Norfolk*, Esplanade; *Sussex*, High Street; *Victoria*, Aldwick Road; and many others.

Library. – London Road.

Population. – 31,220.

Post Office. – The Head Office is in High Street, a hundred yards or so east of the arcade.

Riding. – Excellent facilities for riding on the foreshore or on the South Downs.

Tennis. – Hard courts in Swansea Place, West Street, and at Blakes Road, Felpham. The *Bognor Regis Tennis Club*, with courts at the Sports Ground, in Nyewood Lane, admits visitors to play by the day, week or month. The West Sussex Championships are held here in August.

Bognor Regis has been known as a health resort for over a century, but it still retains a quiet individuality. All the usual entertainments are here for those who desire them, but they do not dominate the town. The climate is mild and dry and it is not surprising that many business people have taken up residence in the town.

For holiday purposes the "hub" of Bognor Regis is Waterloo Square, reached from the railway station by way of Canada Grove, Steyne Street and West Street, and only a few yards from the principal terminus of the bus services.

The Square has an excellent bowling green, a putting green and some tasteful rock gardens.

Inland are the Waterloo Square Gardens. At its seaward end the Square is almost closed by the buildings forming the approach to the pier.

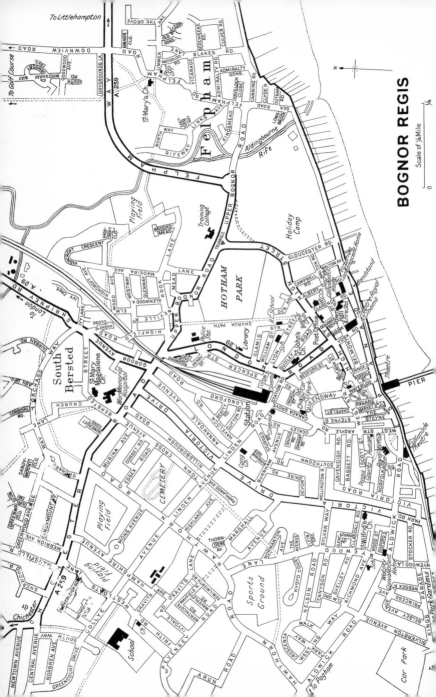

BOGNOR REGIS

Scale of ¼ Mile

The Pier runs seaward from the Parade for 800 feet. At the shore end are shops, tea and refreshment-rooms, and a Roof-garden Lounge Bar. Some good sea-fishing may be enjoyed off the pierhead.

The Sea-Front. Bognor Regis regards its sands and its beach as among the most valuable of its assets. This part of Sussex has been favoured by the formation of a hard and dry sand, where children can sport for the greater part of a summer day without danger. At low water one can walk eastward to Littlehampton or far westward with perfect safety. The sands are the pride of the place, and are cleansed daily by the incoming tide. It goes without saying that such a beach is excellent for bathing.

From the vicinity of the Pier we may pass eastward or westward along –

The Esplanade, or the **Parade,** as it is more generally called, a well-made walk 1¼ miles in length, raised a few feet above the sand collected on the groined beach. It is well furnished with seats and shelters, and forms an agreeable promenade. To the east it stretches as far as Felpham.

Westward of the Pier is **The Steyne,** with a number of boarding-houses, and farther west we arrive in a few yards at the **Esplanade Theatre.** Thence, after passing a number of well-situated hotels and boarding-houses, we come to a long row of bathing huts. At the rear of the beach is a large Car Park.

Eastward from the Pier is the large block of buildings containing the **Theatre Royal Cinema** and the **Rex Ballroom and Banqueting Hall.** A few yards farther is the **Eastern Bandstand.**

The buildings overlooking the Parade hereabouts include the **Victorian Convalescent Home,** for Surrey women. In Clarence Road, just off the Parade, is the fine Town Hall.

Inland from the Parade by Gloucester Road and the east end of High Street, is the tree-shaded –

Upper Bognor Road, among the most pleasant thoroughfares in the town. Here are some of the historic houses of Bognor Regis, and other fine mansions. The former Bognor Lodge, built by Sir Richard Hotham for himself, was the residence, for several years, of the princess who became Queen Victoria and of her mother, the Duchess of Kent.

Hotham House (formerly Bersted Lodge, and later, Aldwick Manor), was built by Sir Richard. The estate now belongs to the town and is open to the public. The Park, with its acres of woodland, has a serene and natural beauty, and is well known to horticulturists for its varieties of tulip tree, azaleas, camelias, rhododendrons, palms and willows. There are peaceful glades, children's zoo and miniature railway, beautiful lawns, a fine Georgian mansion and a Clock Tower whose clock, dated 1794, still chimes the hours.

Dome House, which we may reach by following the road to the left, was erected in the hope that George III would consent to occupy it, but the enterprising builder had to be content with the Princess Charlotte as the royal tenant. It is now a Teacher's Training College.

At the **High Street** the rural character changes to something more bustling.

On the left, in Clarence Road, is the **Roman Catholic Church.**

It is an imposing building in the nineteenth-century Gothic style of architecture. It is served by the priests of the Order of Servants of Mary, commonly known as Servites, who reside in the adjoining Priory.

Above the High Altar on the east wall is enshrined a most striking and life-sized statue of Our Lady of Seven Sorrows, to whom the Church is dedicated.

Just beyond the Church, on the right, is the **Town Hall** and the **War Memorial.**

In Sudley Road is the **Bognor Club,** and then on the left, in High Street, the **General Post Office.** In the vicinity of **The Arcade** are some of the best shops, and at its southern end the Arcade provides access to the Theatre Royal Cinema.

A number of good shops have been erected in London Road, which also contains an entrance to **St. John's Church,** a handsome flint and brick building in the Early English style. It was opened in 1882, but the spire – visible for many miles around – was not erected until 1895.

Returning to High Street and continuing westward we pass again the Methodist Church, and into West Street and, near the sea-front, Aldwick Road.

West Bognor Regis

Aldwick Road leads out to the West End from the Esplanade Theatre. It crosses **Victoria Drive,** a fine road containing many large detached residences and **St. Wilfrid's Church,** a chapel-of-ease to St. John's. St. Wilfrid's, in the Late Perpendicular style of architecture, was dedicated in 1910 but still remains to be finished.

Beyond Victoria Drive is the West End shopping quarter and Post Office, and a short distance farther is the **Watney Convalescent Home,** in connection with the East London Hospital for Children. Aldwick Road here meets Nyewood Lane South, which connects it with the shore, and Nyewood Lane proper, which runs inland to the Sports Ground. To the west of Nyewood Lane are the **Marine Park Gardens** with putting greens and recreation ground.

A little beyond is **Ashley House** belonging to the Shaftesbury Society and providing a home for severely handicapped boys.

Nyewood Lane runs northward to the **Sports Ground,** used by the local cricket, tennis, and football clubs. From the Sports Ground, Town Cross Avenue or Hawthorn Road runs to the right to Chichester Road. The Victoria Drive also leads into the latter. By following Chichester Road to the right and its continuation – Upper Bognor Road – we should be led again to the eastern end of High Street, and so should complete the circuit of the town. In Chichester Road (South Bersted) is the **War Memorial Hospital.**

Aldwick

The path continuing Bognor Parade in a westerly direction past the Marine Gardens and the **Car Park** soon bears inland and becomes an inviting tree-shaded lane. In about half a mile there will be seen on the left **Dark Lane.** This leads down to the shore, but is a private road. When the tide is low one can walk along the sands to Bognor Regis from the foot of this lane. Similarly, the shore can be followed westward when the water is below half-ebb. At other times a high groyne has to be negotiated and it is better to turn out of Dark Lane into the road leading to *Craigweil*. This leads past several choice residences through Kingsway and into Barrack Lane.

Beyond Dark Lane the road becomes the main street of **Aldwick.** Here are the well-known "Ship Inn", the post office and a few picturesque thatched cottages – almost lost in luxuriant gardens – which are among the few remains of ancient Aldwick. In Gossamer Lane, about a quarter of a mile west of the post office, stands a beautiful Gothic church, one of the finest modern churches in West Sussex. Turn off left at the end of Aldwick Street by Barrack Lane, and after passing the old coastguard cottages, find ourselves on the shore at another point much favoured for a bathe or picnic.

Tide permitting, the return to central Bognor is best made along the sands.

Felpham

Felpham, now a part of Bognor Regis, is delightfully unconventional and one can spend lazy days on the splendid sands, fish, bathe, sail or play golf or tennis. It is a favourite spot for motorists from London. Eastward of Felpham many bungalows and attractive residences have been built. Perhaps the principal charm of Felpham arises from the broad stretch of golden sands beyond the sea-wall. Between Felpham and Bognor is a large holiday camp.

The **Church,** dedicated to St. Mary, is a venerable stone building dating from the early twelfth century. The nave walls or part of them, are very thick and lean from the perpendicular. Twice last century the building was restored. The font is Norman. There is a peal of six bells, one dating from the fifteenth century.

Middleton-on-Sea

Building first took place during the first World War when a seaplane base was established at Middleton and has proceeded at such a rate on the eastern side of Bognor Regis that the coast as far as Elmer Sands is now thickly dotted with bungalows and houses. Praiseworthy efforts have been made to develop on "Garden City" lines. Having the sea only a few yards distant, and bus communications with Bognor ‹Regis, the houses and bungalows are in steady demand as summer quarters, and the congenial climate renders this a very pleasant spot for all-the-year-round residence. The estate is private and public access to the sands is restricted to certain defined paths.

Angling, boating and sailing may be enjoyed and the sands are firm and safe. Temporary membership of the *Middleton Sports Club* is available (application may be made to the Secretary) where there are facilities for tennis, squash, cricket, bowls and hockey.

Walks and Excursions from Bognor Regis

From Pagham to the Arun and between the Downs and the sea is a stretch of comparatively flat country dotted with villages, hamlets and farmsteads of much interest to the observant rambler. The Downs keep watch on the north, and the spire of St. John's Church sentinels Bognor Regis, so that with two such landmarks it is difficult to get lost.

An exhilarating walk is along the sands at low tide towards Littlehampton. In the opposite direction the hard sands give place to shingle just beyond Aldwick, and though a rough path skirts the shore thence to Pagham, the walk onward to Selsey has to be made by the embankment behind Pagham Harbour, and so *via* Sidlesham and Church Norton to Selsey village.

To South and North Bersted. Bognor Regis and South Bersted are so linked by houses that the village appears to be a part of the town. As a matter of fact, the reverse is the case, for such portions of Bognor as are not in the ecclesiastical parish of St. John are still in the parish of Bersted, which formerly included the whole of the town.

Bersted Church is three-quarters of a mile from Bognor Railway Station by way of Longford Road and Chichester Road, turning to the left on reaching the latter thoroughfare.

The Church, dedicated to St. Mary Magdalene, was consecrated in 1405, but the building is of much earlier date. There are traces of Norman and even of Saxon work, and the nave is certainly of the thirteenth-century. The arches in the nave are supported by pillars, alternatively round and octagonal. On one of the pillars are traces of a fresco, probably of the time of Henry VII. Part of a Norman arch of an earlier church was built into the north wall, and is still preserved. There is also some Norman work in the belfry arch. The tower is surmounted by a dwarf shingled spire, which leans slightly to one side through a carelessly constructed joint in the central timber. In the choir vestry the remains of the village stocks are fixed high on the west wall; a fourteenth-century chest stands in a bay to the north of the Sanctuary.

North Bersted is a mile or so from its southern neighbour, but has little of interest to the holiday visitor.

To Nyetimber. Nyetimber is a growing residential area, some two miles west of Aldwick, containing a large holiday club, several picturesque half-timbered cottages and remains (at Barton Farm) of a Manor-House pronounced to be a "very early example" of its kind. Here, a few years ago, was found a primitive "aula" thought to date from before the Conquest, and there is also a little thirteenth-century chapel. The name of the village was originally "New-Timber," and probably referred to that "Main Wood" perpetuated in the neighbouring Hundred of "Manhood".

Nyetimber can be made the objective of a pleasant walk of about six miles. Follow the shore from Bognor past the end of Barrack Lane and at the new Kings Beach Estate turn inland and continue north-westerly coming out on to Pagham Road by Church Way. The return to Bognor can be made by turning right along Nyetimber Lane opposite the *Bear Inn*. Where the road turns abruptly to the left follow the new road running straight ahead – it is continued by a foot-path terminating in Barrack Lane, Aldwick.

An alternative return route from Nyetimber is to continue northwards along Pagham Road and take Hook Lane nearly opposite Mill Farm Caravan Site and follow it into Rose Green Road and Grosvenor Gardens to the main crossroad junction and on through Aldwick.

To Pagham. The most direct way from Bognor is along the sands to Aldwick and thence by the path skirting the shingly beach. The road route is as to Nyetimber (*see* above), thence by the road leaving the *Lamb Inn* on the left. An enjoyable circular excursion can be made by proceeding or returning through Nyetimber and using the shore for the other portions of the journey.

The shore at Pagham consists of a wide bank of shingle sloping on one side to the sea and on the other to what is left of Pagham Harbour and to the low-lying lands that were inundated when the sea broke through in 1910. There was a harbour at Pagham as long ago as 1345, but it had become so choked with mud that in 1870 the land was reclaimed. But in December 1910, the sea burst the retaining walls and now, at high tide, a great inland lake is formed. Pagham Harbour is a noted resort of rare birds, and is now a nature reserve. (Caravan sites at Church Farm and Mill Farm).

YOUR HELP IS REQUESTED

A GREAT part of the success of this series is due, as we gratefully acknowledge, to the enthusiastic co-operation of readers. Changes take place, both in town and country, with such rapidity that it is difficult, even for the most alert and painstaking staff, to keep pace with them all, and the correspondents who so kindly take the trouble to inform us of alterations that come under their notice in using the books, render a real service not only to us but to their fellow-readers. We confidently appeal for further help of this kind.

THE EDITOR

WARD LOCK LIMITED
116, BAKER STREET,
LONDON, W.1

FLANSHAM, BARNHAM, YAPTON

Pagham Church, dedicated to Thomas à Becket, unexpectedly spacious, is an Early English building. The west front was built in 1837 in Norman style, though weathering of the storm causes it to look older than the original building. One of the lights of the east window contains the Royal Arms, with "V.R. 1837". Some of the foundations of a former rectory and a moat are visible a little to the south-east of the Church.

To Flansham, Barnham and Yapton. The hamlet of Flansham can be included with Felpham in a circular walk of six miles. Proceed to Felpham either by road from Upper Bognor or by Ivy Lane, starting from the railway footbridge at the end of the lane, where a pathway across the fields leads to Felpham Church. From the church follow the main road to the village school. Turn north and then a short distance along the eastward road brings one to a footpath on the left leading to **Flansham.** Return to main road. There turn to the right. Buses pass this point. At the *South Downs Hotel*, at the corner of the Felpham Road, turn to the right again, and proceed through Felpham to Bognor.

From Flansham the ramble may be continued to Barnham and Yapton. The path starts opposite the end of that described above, and leads across a couple of fields to a grassy lane. Follow this straight ahead for a hundred yards or more and then cross a stile on the right and take a footpath leading towards the Downs, Barnham windmill shortly coming in sight ahead. Crossing a stream, the path soon joins a lane which runs into Yapton.

Those who would like to visit **Barnham** *(the church is about a mile south of the station)* should turn to the left by a lane running in front of some buildings on the outskirts of Yapton (a path cuts off a corner). The continuing path passes some concrete outbuildings and crosses several fields to the disused Chichester and Arundel Canal, the bank of which should be followed to the lane leading up to Barnham Church.

There was a church at "Berneham" at the time of the Domesday survey, and in the south wall are still two Norman windows, while the font is also of that period. The chancel and porch date from the thirteenth-century. The church contains a pre-Reformation statue of St. Genevieve. The graveyard is well worth a visit by those interested in curious inscriptions.

Near the church is a fine *Manor House* dating from 1640. Barnham village is famous for its nurseries. Here the Bognor branch line joins the main Portsmouth–Brighton railway route.

From the east end of the graveyard a lane (ignore two lanes running southwards) leads to the main road a mile from the Windmill. Here turn to the right, in about a mile reaching **Yapton.**

The return to Bognor may be made by following the southward lane from Yapton to the footpath to **Bilsham,** near which the buses pass on their way between Bognor and Littlehampton via Flansham and Felpham. One of the roads from Bilsham to Felpham runs through Middleton, whence it is four miles to Bognor.

To Bailiffscourt, Climping and Ford. The Bognor-Littlehampton buses pass within a few hundred yards of Climping Church, but a pleasant circular excursion can be made by walking at low tide along the sands from Bognor or Felpham to Climping Beach. With the exception of two cottages, the former village at Atherington lies buried by the sea. A short distance from the beach is **Bailiffscourt,** a unique building resembling a mediaeval castle yet built only in 1928. In 1947 it was converted to a licenced residential hotel *(Birers)*. From the beach a walk up Climping Street of about 1½ miles leads to Climping Church, a total distance from Bognor of six miles.

For a description of **Climping** and its church, *see* p. 221.

Instead of at once returning to Bognor the visitor can go northward from Climping Church to Ford Junction, about 1¼ miles, and make the return by rail.

Bognor Regis to Selsey. As the crow flies, only five miles separate Bognor and Selsey. The road route, however, measures nearly fifteen miles, since it is necessary to travel *via* North Mundham. The walker can reduce this latter distance considerably by going to **Pagham** and following to its termination the lane past the church. It leads to a field in which a footpath runs along the hedge on the left to a gate giving access to the embankment forming the inner wall of Pagham Harbour. Along the top of the bank runs a path. Follow the embankment as far as possible, then take to the field-path on the right; this soon passes through some farm buildings and out into the road. Turn left and follow the lane past the old *Crab and Lobster Inn*, round the head of the Harbour, and so to the main Chichester-Selsey road at *The Jolly Fisherman,* where the buses may be joined. **Selsey** is then about 3½ miles to the south.

Bognor Regis to Chichester. This is a run of seven miles. Bognor Regis may be left by Upper Bognor Road, London Road or Victoria Drive. South Bersted church is soon passed on the right, and passing the cross-roads at North Bersted church, we enter open country, with good views on the right of the South Downs. Away to the north-east, the clump of trees marking Chanctonbury Ring, above Worthing, may be seen. Almost facing Bersted is the disused windmill on Halnaker Down, while the slender spire of Chichester Cathedral can be seen from time to time in the north-west.

Past Elbridge is the *Nelson Arms*, by which is a road to Oving, Tangmere and Boxgrove.

The *Nelson Arms* stands approximately midway between Bognor and Chichester. Continuing, we reach in a mile or so the turning (on the left) for **Merston,** a small village with a church hidden among trees.

A short way farther is a right-hand turning to Drayton and **Goodwood.**

Crossing the Chichester by-pass at Bognor Bridge, we are at once in Chichester, the city being entered by way of the Hornet and East Street.

Oving is of no special interest, but the little church at **Tangmere** is worth a visit. Rather more than a mile east of Oving is **Aldingbourne,** with a church occupying the site of a building that stood here when Domesday Book was compiled. The original altar slab remains, there are traces of frescoes ascribed to the eleventh–fifteenth centuries, and a very fine arch, dividing the nave from a former chantry at the end of the south aisle.

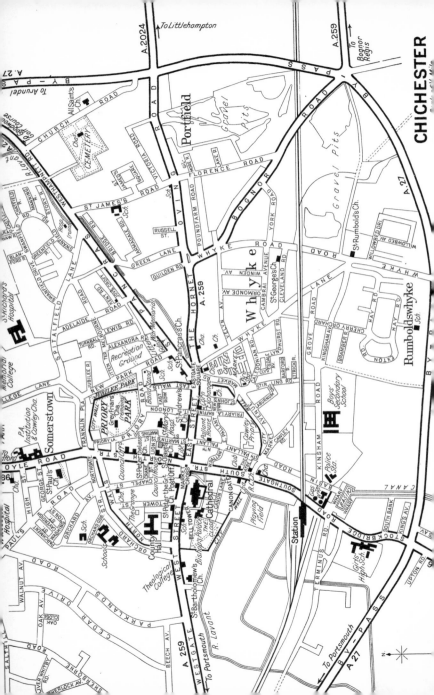

CHICHESTER

Chichester

Chichester is pleasantly placed about equi-distant from the western boundary of Sussex, the South Downs on the north, and the English Channel towards the south. The city is nearly surrounded by an intermittent stream, the *Lavant*. On the south side is a branch of the Arundel and Chichester Canal, and a mile and a half to the south is its port at **Dell Quay,** accessible for small vessels at high tide.

Chichester was one of the earliest of the military cities which the Roman conquerors of the Britons founded in our land. To the Romans the city was **Regnum,** and not till after they had left the country did it receive its present appellation.

In A.D. 445, a Saxon chieftain named Ella landed at West Wittering, midway between what are now Selsey Bill and Portsmouth Harbour and, after many sanguinary encounters with the natives, established the South Saxon kingdom. Ella was succeeded by his son Cissa, who made Regnum his headquarters, and renamed it, in honour of himself, *Cissa's Ceaster* – Cissa's Camp – a designation changed, as the years rolled on, into Chichester.

For holidays or for permanent or temporary residence, Chichester has many attractions. It is clean, healthy and quiet. Sheltered by the Downs on the north, it is open on the south to the invigorating breezes from the not distant sea. Its main streets are wide, and the principal thoroughfares are lined with good shops and substantial red-brick houses.

As in other cities founded by the Romans, the four principal streets of Chichester lie in the direction of the cardinal points. The wall by which the Romans surrounded it had a circumference of nearly a mile and a half and an average height of 20 feet. The greater part is still standing, but its four gates have been swept away, and of the sixteen towers that helped to guard it, several remain, one being at the back of the Corporation yard, and another on the portion of the wall facing the Westgate Fields. A fragment of the wall on the south encloses the private grounds of the episcopal Palace and other clerical residences. On the east there exists a portion which has been planted with limes and converted into a public promenade. Between the ends of North and West Streets there is a much larger piece, which has also been made into a pleasant public walk.

Four feet below the surface of West Street there was found, during excavations, the paved road – Stane Street – which the Romans constructed between their camp here and London. Coins, pottery and other relics of the occupation of this part of Britain are unearthed from time to time, and in a wall of the Council House is embedded a stone which, as its inscription testifies, had been the foundation-stone of a Roman temple.

When the site for the Post Office in West Street was being cleared there came to light parts of a base of a statue to Jupiter including some lines of the inscription on one face and bas-relief sculpture on the other three faces. This is now in the Guildhall, with finds from other recently explored sites. In addition to Roman remains, relics of later periods have been found: Saxon pottery and loom weights; interesting pottery from Norman to Elizabethan times, and foundations of buildings of various dates throughout the Middle Ages.

The chief trade of the city is in agricultural produce, livestock and timber. There are two industrial estates in the city catering for light industry.

The countryside around the city is both varied and beautiful, the extensive plain to the south and east and the wooded Downs to the north having their full share of picturesque and historic spots that may be made the objective of pleasant excursions.

In and About Chichester

Taking the **Railway Station,** on the south side of the city, as our starting-point, we turn leftward along Southgate to **South Street.** The fine modern buildings on the right are the **Courts of Justice,** completed in 1939.

As we approach the city some charming Regency houses (Nos. 37 and 38) are seen and another, a little farther on, has coursed flints and a bow window over the doorway. The most important house (No. 55) has been replaced by a supermarket. The turning on the right is Market Avenue some 300 yards along which is the new **Roman Catholic Church** (opened 1958).

On the left-hand side of South Street is the **Congregational Church,** and just beyond it is –

The Canon Gate, dating from the reign of Richard III. It was thoroughly restored in the last decade of the nineteenth century. In the upper chamber, now used an an office, was formerly held the Court of Pie Powder, during the annual Sloe Fair, to compel pedlars and hawkers and those with whom they dealt to fulfil their contracts. The curious name of the court is, of course, a corruption of the French "pieds poudreux", or "dusty foot". Such courts were common at wakes and fairs. An interesting reference is made to them in Ben Jonson's comedy *Bartholomew Fair.* Sloe Fair is still held each October.

Adjoining the Canon Gate is **Vicars' Close,** built in the fifteenth century. The north end contains a hall with fine timber roof and a fourteenth-century lavabo in the north wall. Below is a twelfth-century vaulted undercroft.

The lane from the gateway leads to the Deanery, the Bishop's Palace, the Cloisters and the South Porch of the Cathedral, but we continue northward to –

The Market Cross, which is next to the Cathedral in general interest. It stands at the junction of the four principal streets, on a site given by the Mayor and Corporation to Bishop Storey, by whom the cross was erected in 1500 for the accommodation of the country folk who brought the produce of their dairies, their gardens and their poultry yards, and it was so used until, in 1808, the present Market House was built in North Street.

The cross is octagonal in shape and 50 feet high. Over the centre of each arch is a niche for a statue. On the east side is a bronze bust of Charles I. The lantern, an unsightly addition, supplanted a beautiful finial in order to accommodate the two bells of a clock in 1746. But in spite of this, the Cross remains the most beautiful specimen of its type in England. It was thoroughly restored a few years ago, and is now scheduled as an ancient monument.

The Cathedral

Admission. – Open free.

Services. – On week-days: Holy Communion, 8 a.m.; Matins, 9.30; Evensong, 5.30. Sunday Services, 8, 10.30, 11.30 and 4.

The year 1108 is given as the date of the consecration of the original building. The first cathedral was partially destroyed by fire half a dozen years after it was built. A restoration was immediately effected, only to be attended by the same fate in 1187. Again the building was restored, and from that time to the period of the Commonwealth it enjoyed prosperity. Many additions were made to the original structure, notably the upper portion of the central tower and spire, and the side chapels to the nave.

In 1861 the spire fell. It had been found to be unstable, and the strengthening of the foundations of the piers from which it rose was in progress. As the spire telescoped, no great damage was done to the rest of the building. In 1866, the old weathercock was restored to its former position, and beneath it an almost exact copy of the spire which, for long years it had previously surmounted.

The Campanile, or Bell Tower. The Bell Tower stands in the north-west corner of the churchyard, detached from the main building, and in this respect Chichester Cathedral is unique in Britain. The tower, which was erected in the first half of the fifteenth century, has a height of 120 feet, and contains a peal of eight bells, as well as a bell known as *Big Walter,* weighing 74 cwt., on which the hours are struck. The oldest is the third, cast in 1583, and is inscribed, "Geve thanks to God, S.W". The faceless clock in the tower was erected to the memory of Dean Hook (1859–1875).

CHICHESTER

The Exterior

At a first glance the Cathedral looks small, but it is not really so. In length it is 411 feet, and the breadth of the nave is 91 feet, a greater breadth than is possessed by any other English cathedral, except York Minster and St. Paul's.

The **West Front** presents much of its original appearance. A good Norman doorway (now closed) may be seen on the exterior south side of the South Tower. The two **Towers** are similar, the upper stage of that on the north being an imitation of its companion, which was erected in the thirteenth century. Instead of one **West Window,** there are two. The upper is a modern copy of fourteenth-century examples; the lower is original Early English work. The most interesting features of the **Porch** are the buttresses at the north and south angles, and the arcading on the north and south walls.

The Interior

The Nave. On entering by the West Door attention is at once arrested by the massive Norman architecture of the piers and arches of the ground storey and triforium of the Nave. The later vaulted roof and the Purbeck marble columns in the facing of the lower wall and clerestory mark the restoration after the fire of 1187. The *Arundel Screen*, first erected in 1450 and removed in 1859, was re-erected, in memory of Bishop Bell at the entrance of the choir in 1961.

Under the south-west tower is the **Font,** a copy of an ancient one in Shoreham Church.

The outer South Aisle originally formed two chapels, the western-most being dedicated to St. George, and the other to St. Clement. The former has been restored as the Memorial of both world wars to the Sussex Regiment.

Then comes the **Sacristy,** and at its north-eastern angle is a door opening to a staircase giving access to the **Chapter House,** formerly the Bishop's Consistory Court. Connected with it is a small chamber above the south porch, popularly known as the **Lollards' Prison.**

The South Transept. Here is the beautiful tracery of the "great sumptuous" South Window, 47 feet high and 27 feet wide, possibly one of the best examples of Decorated work in the country. It was erected by Bishop Langton (1305–1337), whose tomb is beneath it. The glass is nineteenth century. On the west wall are two large Pictures, executed in the early years of the sixteenth century by a Chichester man, Lambert Barnard.

Under the pictures in the transept are portraits of some of the Kings of England, by Barnard and his son. Some of the series have been damaged and replaced by plain wood.

The **South Choir Aisle** is notable for two magnificent stone carvings, probably dating from about 1130 A.D. They are generally regarded as the finest mediaeval stone carvings to be found in Britain.

Between these two sculptures is the tomb of **Bishop Sherburne.** It is entirely of alabaster, and was erected during the lifetime of the Bishop. Opposite Bishop Sherburne's tomb is the cenotaph of **Dean Hook.**

Close to where we are standing, is the quaintest of the interesting bosses at the intersection of the vaulting of the Cathedral. It has six human faces, each apparently with two eyes, yet there are only the same number of eyes as of faces.

Beyond the ancient sculptures is the doorway at the end of the east walk of the Cloisters. In the spandrels of the arches are the arms of New College, founded by William of Wykeham, the great architect-bishop of the latter half of the fourteenth century.

The east end of the aisle forms **St. Mary Magdalene Chapel,** with a painting by Graham Sutherland. The east window was designed by C. E. Kempe. On the north is the **Lady Chapel,** one of the gems of the Cathedral. It was mainly erected by Bishop Gilbert de Sancto Leophardo, about 1290, but the first three bays are older. The Chapel was restored in 1871.

On the north side of the Chapel is a coped tomb, probably that of **Bishop Ralph,** the founder of the original Norman church. He died in 1123. Under an arch, on the south side, are the reputed tombs of **Bishop Hillary** (1147–1169) and **Seffrid II,** who restored the Cathedral after the fire of 1187.

The **Reredos** is part of the memorial of the modern **Bishop Gilbert.** Other objects of interest are a triple sedilia, a double piscina and the lectern, which is in the form of a pelican instead of the customary eagle.

The **Retro-Choir,** or **Ambulatory,** from which the Lady Chapel opens, is in architectural details the most elaborate part of the Cathedral. In it, immediately behind the high altar, stood the shrine of St. Richard, until it was destroyed at the Reformation by order of the King. On the south side is the tomb of **Bishop Daye,** who occupied the see during some of the most troubled years of the sixteenth century.

At the east end of the North Choir Aisle is **St. John the Baptist's Chapel.**

Next may be noticed the bust of **Bishop Otter** (1836–1840), who founded the Diocesan Association as an aid to the clergy and laity in the provision of new or better schools and the enlargement of churches. The Bishop also, in conjunction with Dean Chandler, established the Theological College, which is one of the important institutions in the city.

Near Bishop Otter's bust is the beautiful alabaster tablet with effigy of **Bishop Wilberforce,** who was translated to the see from Newcastle in 1895.

The Choir occupies the space under the central tower and three bays to the eastward. The **Stalls,** with the exception of those for the Dean and Precentor, which are modern, have been in use since the fourteenth century, and exhibit good examples of the quaint conceits of monkish carvers. The **Bishop's Throne** and the beautiful iron grilles between the eastern part of the choir and the aisles are modern. The **Screen,** originally erected by Bishop Sherburne, was restored as a memorial of Archdeacon Mount in 1904.

On the north side of the Sacrarium is the tomb of Bishop Storey (1478–1503), to whom the city is indebted for the Market Cross and refounding of the Prebendal or Free Grammar School.

The **Treasury** originally formed the Chapel of the Four Virgins, and later the chancel of the Parish Church of St. Peter the Great, the North Transept being used as the nave of the Church. Many curious relics are to be seen here.

The North Transept. Under the great window are the supposed portraits of the pre-Reformation bishops from St. Wilfrid to Robert Sherburne, 1536. In the west wall of the transept are the two round-arched windows of the twelfth century. Near the south springing of the arch leading to the **Library** is a fine sculptured head, one of the few pieces of figure-carving in the Cathedral. This transept contains memorials of musicians and the ashes of Gustav Holst.

Having completed the circuit of the interior of the Cathedral we may pass to the south door and enter –

The Cloisters, built probably in the fifteenth century and occupying three sides of an enclosure called the **Paradise.** In a niche in the south porch is an effigy of St. Richard de la Wych in the act of giving his episcopal blessing. He held the see from 1245 to 1253. No other Bishop of Chichester has been canonized, and additional interest attaches to St. Richard from the fact that he was the last Englishman to receive that honour until the canonization of Sir Thomas More. The Cloisters contain several monuments of interest.

At the east end of the South Walk of the Cloisters is the door, surmounted by a mutilated late mediaeval sculpture, of the house in which the poet Collins died.

Hard-by is the entrance to a walled passage, known as **St. Richard's Walk,** and connecting the Cloister with Canon Lane. Opposite the Walk is the **Deanery,** built in 1725.

Westward of the Deanery is a modern house; to the east are two fine ancient houses, the Residentiary and the Chantry. A large gateway in Canon Lane gives entry to the **Episcopal Palace,** which was rebuilt in the time of Bishop Waddington (1724–1731). Although the south front has Georgian windows much of the mediaeval building remains, including a thirteenth-century kitchen and a fifteenth-century hall. The dining-room has a splendid panelled ceiling painted by Barnard. In the Chapel, an Early English structure, is a small thirteenth-century roundel of the Virgin and Child.

We step from the churchyard into **West Street.** Near the Market Cross is the old coaching inn, the *Dolphin and Anchor*, with a cobbled courtyard, and near-by is the Post Office and Telephone Exchange.

Opposite the gates of the Cathedral precincts is the modern stone **Church of St. Peter the Great.** In the south aisle is a noteworthy carved chest, dated 1602.

Going down West Street, we soon have on the left a flint building, the **Prebendal School** founded in 1497 by Bishop Storey, and placed under the superintendence of the Prebendary of Highleigh. It has been enlarged by adding the Georgian house next to it and the former Vicarage of St. Peter the Great (also Georgian).

Near-by are more excellent Georgian houses. A little below the Prebendal School and on the opposite side of the road is a fine mansion bearing on its pediment the date 1696. Tradition says it was designed by Sir Christopher Wren.

Farther down West Street on the left is the **Theological College** and on the left **St. Bartholomew's Church,** the latter an uninteresting building on the site of an earlier one dedicated to St. Sepulchre and thought – from its circular shape – to have been erected by a returning Crusader after the pattern of the Church of the Holy Sepulchre, Jerusalem.

A turning past the **County Hall** (the offices of the West Sussex County Council) leads to the **North Wall,** one of the defences originally erected by the Romans.

By following the North Wall we reach **North Street,** which should be crossed and the lane opposite followed round to the gateway of Priory Park (*see* below). North Street is continued beyond the boundary of the ancient city by **Broyle Road,** the site of interesting structures. The modern **Church of St. Paul** is soon reached, and a short distance beyond it are the former *Cawley Almshouses*, under the chapel of which lies the body of William Cawley, sometime the parliamentary representative of Chichester in the seventeenth-century, and one of those who signed the death-warrant of Charles I. His interment here is explained by the fact that the land around was occupied by almshouses erected by him in 1625.

Farther along the road, on the left, is the old **Royal West Sussex Hospital,** built in 1825 and extensively renovated in 1913 as a memorial to King Edward. Beyond this building are the Barracks, on the site of the Roman military camp called the **Broyle,** and at a mile from the city is the pretty suburb of **Summersdale.** Mid-Lavant is a short distance farther along the same road.

Eastward of Broyle Road, and parallel to it, is **College Lane,** where is the **Bishop Otter Memorial College,** a training college for teachers. It can be reached from Northgate by way of Franklin Place, on the north side of which is **Oaklands Park** with its **Festival Theatre.** Opposite is –

Priory Park, an enclosed area of about ten acres. A wall tablet records that in 1918 the Duke of Richmond and Gordon presented it to the citizens of Chichester for purposes of recreation and as "a perpetual memorial of the Great War". It is supposed to have been the site of a Castle built by Roger Montgomery. Later, it became the site of a monastery of Grey Friars. At the dissolution nearly the whole of the buildings were destroyed. The only remains are some fragments of the cloisters, and a portion of the Church, which for a long period served as a Guildhall and Shire Court. This beautiful building is known to few outside architectural experts. It was used for the Sussex Assizes alternately with the Shire Hall of Lewes up to 1748 and for the nomination of knights of the Shire up to 1888. It now houses a most interesting collection of Chichester's historical relics and is *open to the public June–September on Tuesdays and Fridays.*

Adjoining Priory Park is the shady little **Jubilee Park.**

The road opposite the gateway by which we entered Priory Park leads back to **North Street,** in which we turn left towards the City Cross. This street has many attractive Georgian houses. One built about 1790 is now the *Ship Hotel,* and contains a very fine staircase. The Council Offices are housed in an old house with an eighteenth-century front and bow window.

The **Council House,** built in 1731, is carried over the pavement on stout pillars. It replaced a timber market-house. It contains a fine Assembly Room in addition to the Council Chamber, in which are portraits of local and general interest.

Upon a block of grey Purbeck marble now set in the wall near the main entrance was discovered an interesting inscription during excavation for the foundations of the building. The inscription, with conjectural restoration, records the dedication of a temple to Neptune and Minerva in the year 14 of our era, the ground being given by Pudens, son of Pudentius.

On the north side of the Council House is **Lion Street,** giving access to St. Martin's Square, a beautiful little close of Georgian houses, in which lies –

St. Mary's Hospital. *Open, except Sunday,* 11 *to* 5 *in summer,* 11 *to* 4 *in winter (closed between* 12 *and* 2*). Visitors* must *apply at the Porter's Lodge for permission to view.* Owing to its retired position, the hospital is far less visited than it deserves but it is one of the most interesting places of its kind in the country. The plan resembles that of a church and follows the earliest types of hospital plan. The entrance from the street is through a narrow archway, which admits to a small courtyard. The building consists of a hall reminiscent of a mediaeval barn and originally 100 feet long now curtailed to 79 feet, with rooms on each side, and a chapel at the eastern end. The Chapel, built of stone, has a length of nearly 50 feet, contains fine oak stalls with grotesquely carved misereres, beautiful window tracery, carved piscina and canopied sedilia, and is divided from the hall by a rich oak screen. The apartments, which are accessible only from the hall, provide living accommodation for eight women. The inmates attend service in their Chapel at 10.00 every morning, except on Saturdays and Sundays.

The Hospital is believed to have been originally erected as a nunnery, and to date from about 1158, although for the first hundred years of its existence it probably stood on a site near the Market Cross. The first record of it is in a document of 1229 when the Church of St. Peter, at the corner of South Street, was pulled down and the site handed over to the Hospital of St. Mary. In 1269 the hospital was transferred to the present site, formerly occupied by the Grey Friars.

Returning to North Street and continuing our former route, we come to **St. Olave's Church** which was originally erected in the eleventh century. The building is not now used for regular services, and is maintained as a religious bookshop.

Near the Church is the **Buttermarket,** designed by T. Nash and opened in 1808. An upper storey added later houses the **Art School.**

At the Cross we turn to the left for a survey of –

East Street, in which are two houses that were formerly the mansions of the Earls of Scarborough. The inn known as the *Old Punch House* has now been renamed the *Royal Arms*. Originally it had an elaborately carved overhanging front. This was replaced by an eighteenth-century plaster front, but much of the original building remains, including decorated ceilings portraying the Tudor rose and fleur-de-lys. Farther eastward we have access to four ancient thoroughfares called the **Pallants,** and having the same general direction as the four principal streets of the city.

A little farther down East Street is the **Corn Exchange,** which in addition to its original purpose also serves as a cinema. Opposite the Exchange is **Little London,** a spot so named by Queen Elizabeth because it seemed to her to be the busiest part of the city. Farther down the street are the **East Walls.** Just beyond are the **Cattle Market,** on the right (here is a public **Car Parking Place**), and **St. Pancras's Church,** on the left.

Farther along St. Pancras Road are the remains of the **Leprosy Hospital,** the **Cemetery,** and **All Saints' Church.** St. Pancras churchyard occupies the site of the Roman cemetery and is now a War Memorial garden. St. Pancras Road covers the site of the opening stages of **Stane Street,** that remarkable Roman military road between Chichester and London. For the first few miles it is still used and leads to the capital by way of Petworth.

The Stane Street was designed by the Romans about A.D. 70 with the object of reaching, by the shortest route, the southern end of London Bridge. The point-to-point distance is a little over 55 miles, and such was the ability of the Roman engineers that, although natural obstacles precluded the formation of the road along a single straight line, they were able to find a route consisting of four long straight sections, the total length of which exceeded the shortest possible distance by only a mile and a half. The first section lay between Chichester East Gate and Pulborough Bridge, on a line considerably eastward of the direct route, which lies over Goodwood Hill and by Petworth. The reasons for this divergence were the necessity for negotiating the steep northern slopes of the South Downs and the desirability of crossing the Arun below its junction with the Rother, so that only one stream had to be crossed.

Excursions from Chichester

To the Roman Palace and Bosham. The city is left by West Street. To the north of the road, just past its junction with the Chichester by-pass, and reached by Salthill Road is the –

Roman Palace and Museum *(daily, May–October, fee)*. The palace is the longest Roman residence found in Britain, and was probably the headquarters of a local king, Tiberius Claudis Cogidubnas. The buildings formed three wings, around a colonnaded great court, and covered $5\frac{1}{2}$ acres. Recent excavations of the northern wing are now under cover and show remarkable mosaic flooring. The adjoining Museum illustrates the history of the site from the initial military base in A.D. 43 until the final destruction by fire about A.D. 280. In Roman times Chichester Channel was navigable right to the Palace boundary.

Bosham lies about 3 miles from the city at the head of a creek of Chichester Harbour. The place might be called *Bozam* by those who would wish to please the inhabitants. It is a favourite place with both yachting people and artists and full of charm. The historic *Quay Meadows* are in the care of the National Trust. They are best seen when the tide is full. Roman relics have been found, and the first church in Sussex was built here in the seventh century. Traditionally Canute had a palace here and it is said his young daughter was buried in the church. It was from Quay Meadow that Harold embarked for Normandy, and the famous Bayeux Tapestry begins with a pictorial representation of Harold journeying to Bosham, and attending Mass in the church.
The village now caters for a large influx of yachting enthusiasts for first-class sailing in the Chichester Channel. The church, which still retains Saxon and Norman work, exalts its dumpy spire above a clump of trees at the head of an inlet, the haven of small coasting craft and hardy fishers' boats. The recessed tomb by the south door is thought to be that of Herbert of Bosham.

To Goodwood, Halnaker and Boxgrove. Rather more than a mile out along the ancient Stane Street is **Westhampnett,** with a church of Saxon origin containing Roman brickwork in the south wall of the chancel. The base of the tower probably at one time formed a small chapel: the niche for a statue remains. In the church-yard lie three bishops who have monuments in Chichester Cathedral: A. T. Gilbert, R. Durnford and E. R. Wilberforce.
At **Maudlin** bear left (the right-hand road is that to Slindon and Arundel). To the left of the road is **Goodwood Park,** with the Downs rising beyond.

Goodwood

Admission. – Goodwood House is open to the public on certain days of the week from May until the end of September from 2–6 p.m., except during Goodwood Race Week and the week preceding. The Park is always open except on one day in the year. Dogs must be kept on a lead. Car park free.

Goodwood House and Park, the magnificent ancestral home of the Duke of Richmond and Gordon, is $3\frac{1}{2}$ miles by road from Chichester.

GOODWOOD

Goodwood House. The house stands in a park which has a circumference of about six miles, and contains over 1,200 acres. The building is a good example of Sussex flint work and was designed by James Wyatt. It consists of a principal front, 166 feet in length, and two recessed wings, each 160 feet long. The front has a portico of six Doric columns, which support another of the same number of Ionic pillars, surmounted by a balustrade. At the extremity of each of the wings is a circular tower. The entrance hall, 38 feet long, 35 feet wide, and 18 feet high, has six columns of Guernsey marble. The Ballroom, Circular Ante-room adjoining and the Supper Room have now been restored and house some of the splendid picture collection.

The pictures and sculpture include works by Vandyck, Lely, Kneller, Reynolds, Lawrence, Romney, Nollekens, Battoni and many others. Among the paintings are the world-famous views of the Thames from Whitehall and Richmond House by Canaletto and there are many interesting portraits including that of Charles I with his queen and two of their children, and another of the children alone which is said to have hung in the king's room in Whitehall prior to his execution. Also in the Collection are the well-known sporting paintings by Stubbs who stayed at Goodwood for the purpose; they are said to be the finest examples of his work.

The collection of Sevres china given to the Third Duke by Louis XV is unique and there are some fine pieces of Chinese porcelain.

The very fine tapestries depicting scenes from the life of Don Quixote were made at the Gobelin factory and purchased by the Third Duke in 1763 when Ambassador to the Court of Louis XV.

Midway between Goodwood House and the Racecourse stands the **Shell House** *(not open to the public)*, a grotto chiefly by Sarah, Duchess of Richmond, and her daughters. From the doorway is obtained a view embracing the whole of the country from Littlehampton on the east to Portsmouth on the west, and giving a glimpse of the Isle of Wight in the distance. Facing the doorway is a small circular mirror, in which may be seen the reflection of the spire of Chichester Cathedral.

The **Park** may be visited at all times except upon one day of the year. Dogs must be kept on a lead, and cars must not stop in the Park.

Its most magnificent trees are some lordly cedars of Lebanon. In the upper part of the Park, just half a mile from the Hall, is a small Palladian temple, named **Carne's Seat**, which is adjacent to the Shell House.

A little to the north of Carne's Seat is –

The Goodwood Race-course, which, for beauty of situation, is probably without a rival in Europe. The **Goodwood Races** were established in 1802, during the life of the third Duke of Richmond. The traditional July meeting commences on the last Tuesday in July and two-day fixtures are held in August and September.

Overlooking the course at the west end is the camp-crowned **St. Roche's Hill,** or **The Trundle** (677 feet), one of the principal summits of the Downs. It affords views, in clear weather, of Leith Hill, near Dorking, thirty miles away; of Beachy Head; and of the Isle of Wight. The Trundle was probably the site of a village from which Chichester originated. The ancient earthworks are clearly marked.

Halnaker, which is part of the Goodwood Estate, is reached by the road which runs straight on from Waterbeach Lodge. After passing the whole length of the wall of the **Home Farm** there is a turning to the left leading to **Halnaker Park** and the ruins of the **Hall,** which was built by Lord de la Warr in the reign of Henry VIII.

In front of the Hall are the remains of a fine avenue of Spanish chestnuts, and behind the Hall is the beautiful **Halnaker Gallop,** which puts many in mind of Ascot. It extends for a mile and threequarters, and the upper part is a lovely avenue between Red Copse and the Winkins, both good covers for foxes. **Halnaker**

Hill (400 feet), with its windmill on the summit, is half a mile east of Halnaker Park.

The name of Halnaker was often jocularly written by mediaeval scribes as "half-naked", a term which persisted until comparatively recent times. In Domesday it is given as Helnache.

South of Halnaker is –

Boxgrove

The **Church** is commonly designated "the Cathedral of Parish Churches in Sussex." It is one of the finest group of monastic remains in the country.

It is the church of a Priory which was founded in the first half of the twelfth century. The monastery was originally for only three monks, a number that was gradually increased to nineteen, but at the Dissolution, after an existence of just over 400 years, the number of monks had fallen to eight.

The Priory Church was not the first church at Boxgrove, for mention is made of one in the deed endowing the house, and the edifice now standing is only half the building that formerly existed. It is 132 feet long by 46 feet wide, but at the western end there once was a nave 90 feet in length, which served as the Parish Church. The similarity between portions of Boxgrove Church and Chichester Cathedral suggests some common influence on the builders. The tower was built *c.* 1110. The timbers of the bell chamber show signs of fire, believed to have occurred when the tower was struck by lightning in 1674.

On entering the edifice, attention is at once attracted by the large and elaborate chantry chapel of *Lord de la Warr*. It was erected in 1532 as an oratory for a chantry priest.

Over the arches of the transepts are curious galleries which are believed to be unique in England, although similar structures are not uncommon in monastic buildings on the Continent.

The vaulting of the nave is decorated with painted coats of arms and floral and other devices, and there are some curious carved bosses. In two of these chapels the altar stones are of thirteenth-century date.

Among the mortuary monuments is one to the memory of the *Countess of Derby* who, having survived her husband for many years, died in 1752, in her eighty-fifth year. She was remarkable for her charity, and is represented sitting under an oak tree assisting poor travellers. The almshouses she endowed in the parish can still be seen.

In the churchyard, and on ground adjacent to it, are some remains of the ancient nave, the cloisters and the splendid guest-house. In the churchyard also is the grave of the first American serviceman to fall in the Battle of Britain.

The Selsey Peninsula

The tongue of land providing the southernmost point in Sussex lies directly south of Chichester, the distance from the city to Selsey Bill being nine miles. In its widest part it measures eight miles from east to west. Actually, it is more peninsular than a glance at the map would suggest, for from Pagham up to North Mundham runs a region of low-lying pasture land crossed by no intersecting road and by very few tracks. The inland scenery of the peninsula is not striking; but many a pleasant day can be spent awheel or afoot exploring the winding lanes between the main thoroughfare and "farthest west" at Wittering.

In other aspects, too, the peninsula is interesting and attractive. Its historical and antiquarian associations are remarkable, and as a field for geological exploration the **Bracklesham Beds** have made it famous. They lie off the coast, but at certain seasons are entirely uncovered, and are then visited by geologists from all parts.

The Chichester-Selsey Road, along which a good bus service is maintained, leaves the city by South Street and **Rumboldswhyke.** Approaching **Hunston** the disused Chichester-Arundel Canal is crossed, and the canal running up to the city is passed on the right. Soon we run across Sidlesham Common and through **Sidlesham.**

Sidlesham Church is an Early English structure tucked away. An examination of the surrounding tombstones should not be omitted if interest is felt in deciphering curious names, striking examples being Warwicker, Glue, Bravy and Boniface.

Sidlesham consists of a number of hamlets, the three chief of which are that around the church; Highleigh by the old stone pound; and that around the head of Pagham Harbour (reached by a turning opposite *The Jolly Fisherman*, a mile south of the church).

Some three miles southward from *The Jolly Fisherman* we reach the heart of the village of –

Selsey

Selsey (population 5,780) is at once the capital of the peninsula and a popular quiet holiday resort. There are modern hotels, restaurants, and apartment and guest-houses. There is a large and popular holiday camp, and many caravan sites.

From the Bill the fine sands of **Bracklesham Bay** stretch round towards Wittering. At high tide there is good bathing; at low tide cricket and other games are enjoyed on the firm sands. In the other direction the shore is shingly to Pagham: sloping rather more steeply, it provides deep water for bathing and boating at nearly all states of the tide.

For many years Selsey Peninsula suffered very seriously from the effects of coast erosion and extensive sea-defence works have recently been constructed.

Selsey **Church** is as nearly as possible a facsimile of an older building, the chancel of which still stands at **Church Norton**, about two miles north of the village. There is an ancient Norman font, two grotesque heads on one of the pillars, and a wooden eagle lectern.

The imposing War Memorial at the entrance to the churchyard incorporates four carved stones which probably formed part of a cross erected by St. Wilfrid in the old graveyard at –

Church Norton. Here is the chancel of the old church. Its most interesting feature is an elaborately carved monument to "Jhon Lews, and Agas his wife"

Adjoining the old churchyard is a **Mound** dating from Roman times, when it served as a defence for Pagham Harbour. At the head of the lane is *Norton Priory*, a former rectory, a fine mediaeval and Tudor building, incorporating fragments of Saxon masonry.

From the churchyard wall meadows run down to the edge of Pagham Harbour – at low tide rather muddy, but at high tide, when the water swirls in through the breach in the shingle, a great inland lake across which sailing-boats skim gaily.

Selsey Bill was once a great headland running far beyond the present peninsula. The Selsey of to-day is but the representative of an older Selsey the site of which is now a great shoal, a few hundred yards from the shore. At the southern end a **Beacon** warns shipping of the dangers of the spot. Between the shoal and the shore is a narrow stretch of deep water, and here the tide comes and goes like a mill-race.

Selsey Villages

Though the scenery of Selsey is not striking, it charms the rambler who quits the main road and explores some of the tracks and lanes that wind amid the villages and hamlets dotted over the peninsula.

Sidlesham has been described on p. 250. The rambler who would visit Pagham should turn down opposite *The Jolly Fisherman*, past the site of the tide mill to Halsey's Farm, on right, whence a footpath leads across two fields and then along the embankment to a lane near Pagham Church.

Hunston has a fine modern Gothic church set in beautiful surroundings. Next to it is the old Manor House mentioned in Domesday. East of Hunston is the pleasant village of **North Mundham.** In the porch of the church are two Elizabethan carvings that have puzzled antiquaries. The Sussex marble font is reputed to be the largest in the county.

Donnington is close to a pretty reach of the Canal, which is here crossed by a culvert. The Church, rebuilt in 1942, stands at the end of a shady avenue.

Appledram, two miles south-west of Chichester and a mile north-west of Donnington, has a quaint little church with interesting features, and may have been built by the monks of Bosham. Note the remarkable manner in which a "squint" has been pierced through the jamb of one of the chancel windows (the true form of hagioscope).

Birdham is situated on an arm of Chichester Harbour and is a well-known yachting centre with a new Marina giving round-the-clock access to its fine basin and including

SELSEY VILLAGES

such facilities as car parking, chandlery, boat repairs, shops, a fuel jetty and all amenities necessary for carefree boating. The Church has been considerably restored but retains a good 16th-century tower. Nearby is the attractive Court Barn Estate with its old cottages. Two miles to the west is the small village of **West Itchenor,** another boating centre, pleasantly situated opposite the mouth of Bosham Creek. It has a simple Early English Church.

Close to the westernmost point of the peninsula is **West Wittering,** a peaceful little village with inns and a 12th-century late Norman church with a Saxon font. West Wittering has a little peninsula of its own with long stretches of fine sands.

East Wittering lies two miles eastwards along the coast and includes the popular resort of Bracklesham. Safe bathing and beach sports may be enjoyed along fine stretches of firm, tide-washed sand. The sea views extend to the Nab and the Isle of Wight with considerable interest added by passing shipping. The modern resort that has developed at East Wittering has good shops, cafes, clubs, hotels, etc. There are permanent holiday camps and numerous caravan sites at The Witterings and Bracklesham.

Chichester Cathedral

Index

253

INDEX

INDEX